THE ETHICAL ECONOMY

THE ETHICAL ECONOMY

REBUILDING VALUE
AFTER THE CRISIS

Adam Arvidsson
Nicolai Peitersen

COLUMBIA UNIVERSITY PRESS   NEW YORK

COLUMBIA UNIVERSITY PRESS
Publishers Since 1893
NEW YORK   CHICHESTER, WEST SUSSEX
cup.columbia.edu

Library of Congress Cataloging-in-Publication Data
Arvidsson, Adam.
The ethical economy : rebuilding value after the crisis /
Adam Arvidsson and Nicolai Peitersen.
pages   cm.
Includes bibliographical references and index.
ISBN 978-0-231-15264-8 (cloth : alk. paper) — ISBN 978-0-231-52643-2 (ebook)
1. Economics—Moral and ethical aspects. 2. Capitalism—Moral and ethical aspects.
3. Economic development—Moral and ethical aspects. 4. Value. 5. Social
responsibility of business. I. Peitersen, Nicolai. II. Title.
HB72.A768   2013
174'.4—dc23
201300945

*Columbia University Press books are printed on permanent and
durable acid-free paper.*
This book is printed on paper with recycled content.
Printed in the United States of America

c 10 9 8 7 6 5 4 3 2 1

Jacket design: Thomas Stvan

CONTENTS

Almost a decade ago we were invited to a seminar with the top management from one of the world's largest consumer goods companies. The event was held in an informal setting, a converted brewery, consciously designed to promote "creativity" and "thinking outside the box" (read: cushions to sit on and plenty of toys and Post-it Notes). And the theme was "ethical challenges to business" or some such. We set out to plow through our PowerPoints, only to be interrupted, at about the third slide, by a stern businesswoman who declared, "Listen, we all know this. We know that we cannot go on being a capitalist company!" At the time, we thought her comment was quite startling (this was in 2006), but as we have talked to more and more executives and businesspeople, similar statements have become commonplace—particularly since the crisis of 2007. In fact, businesses, big and small, are investing heavily in alternative values. In the Anglo-Saxon world it is difficult to find a large self-respecting company that does not have a corporate responsibility policy (in fact, spending on such issues has skyrocketed in the last five years), and many companies partner with NGOs and support social entrepreneurs (with the abundance of new corporate money, this sector is growing rapidly). Many companies now publicly declare that their purpose is not primarily to make money but to save the world, contribute to a more sustainable society, or, more concretely, address the social context in which their key product is deployed by, for example, "helping people make informed food choices to improve their nutrition and health," instead of "selling yogurt."[1]

At the same time, activists are more amenable to working with corporations. The social movements that we remember from Seattle and Genua are becoming social enterprises with which large corporations can function as partners rather than enemies. The Naomi Klein era is over, replaced by the likes of Umair Hacque and John Grant, who preach a reformed capitalism ready to address wider social concerns.[2]

Although a lot of this is green-washing, a lot of it is sincere as well. Companies and managers have a wide range of reasons to trash Milton Friedman and his recommendation to focus on profits alone, and to try to become a "Force for Good" (as one successful UK-based initiative is called).[3] These reasons range from the obvious—we are all in the same boat on a sinking planet (if such an expression can be allowed); public opinion is demanding a social conscience; most people who work in large corporations are conscious moral agents who want to feel that they are doing something meaningful or at least something that is not downright destructive; "green" and "ethics" are great marketing opportunities that can open up new areas of business—to less obvious motivations that we will describe in this book and that we actually believe are more important. (The ability to create cohesion around a common cause is, for example, very useful as a motivation for creative knowledge workers.) The question that we want to pose in this book is not about the sincerity of it all (we leave that to Naomi Klein). What we want to find out is whether it can work. Or rather, can the ethical turn that we are presently witnessing among corporations, consumers, investors, employees, activists, and other stakeholders—their desire to address a number of concerns that go beyond the profit motive—become a basis for a new "social contract" in which the interests of business and the interests of society can coincide? In other words, *can there be such a thing as an ethical economy?*

We believe that there can be, but it is more complicated than the usual story about corporations acquiring a conscience out of the blue. In the main argument of this book, we suggest that the movement toward an ethical economy is driven by deep structural tendencies that are firmly related to the ways in which value is produced in the information society. And we suggest that corporate investments in responsibility and sustainability, however sincere, are just a surface manifestation of this. That is, the possibility of an ethical economy is inherent in the development of the means and relations of production, as Marx would have said. But its realization is contingent on active engagement and political agency by interested actors. In particular, we suggest that a necessary precondition for realizing a (more) ethical economy is the construction of a new public sphere, in which diverse value concerns can have a more direct impact on the processes by which economic values are set, and make these processes public in new ways.

But before we set out to tell that story, let's spend some more time on the concept of a "social contract" and why we think a new one is needed.

SOCIAL CONTRACT

Industrial society—that old textbook example of how economics and social systems are supposed to work—was built around connecting economic value creation to overall social values—an imaginary social contract. Business was supposed to contribute to the well-being of society by furthering economic development and a growing prosperity that could trickle down the social pyramid, or be redistributed by the welfare state. Although this "contract" was not always respected in practice and quite intense conflicts arose as to how it should apply, virtually everybody argued that it should apply, at least in theory, and most people agreed on the basic common values: economic growth and increasing prosperity. From this perspective, even the raw profit seeking of business could be understood to be functional for the overall social good; to make a profit could be said to be an important, or even, as Milton Friedman argued, the only social responsibility of business.

Today that social contract has been shattered. Globalization and the socialization of production have undermined the national arenas in which the redistribution of wealth used to play out, and have radically diminished the power of the industrial working class, who used to be an important party to that process. Three decades of neoliberal policies have separated the market from larger social concerns and relegated the latter to the private sphere, creating a situation where there is no society, only individuals and their families, as Margaret Thatcher famously put it, and no values, only prices. Most importantly, perhaps, a growing awareness of the planetary consequences of industrial capitalism has led to questioning the very desirability of continuous economic growth, at least in its consumerist, materialist version.

Yet the new values that are emerging in our society—a growing popular demand for a more sustainable economy and a more just and equal global society—have only weak and unreliable ways of influencing the actual conduct of corporations and other important economic actors. True, a lot of companies now claim to be socially responsible and to behave in a sustainable way, but we have no way of reliably or "objectively" evaluating the social efficacy of their efforts. Quite paradoxically, though we are in the midst of an explosion of ethics, with more and more people routinely evaluating their everyday actions in terms of the planetary consequences of those actions (what foods to buy, where to work, how to live), there are few ways in which such ethical values can really influence the processes through which crucial decisions are made. We need a system that can create and strengthen such a link, allowing for new ways to decide the overall social value of economic value creation, and for those decisions to have tangible effects on economic value creation.

We are of course not alone in suggesting that radical economic reform is needed. After the relative complacency that marked the "end of history" and the ensuing belle epoque of the 1990s, the first decade of the new century brought a wealth of ideas about reforming business practices and economic systems, many of them from writers close to the business community. Similarly, the financial crisis of 2008 spurred ideas for reforming and better regulating financial markets.[4]

This book is part of that literature, but it goes beyond that purview in an important way: we not only suggest what we think needs to be done— we also point to what is actually possible. In other words, we claim that the solution we are proposing is a *realistic* solution, firmly anchored in the forces and contradictions currently operating in the global economy. We describe what those forces are, how they operate, and how they might develop. In doing so, we argue that the foundations for such a new system are emerging around us, in the form of three crucial developments, and that the solution to our quandary is perhaps much closer than we realize.

FOUNDATIONS

The first development is the transformation of how wealth is created and the emergence of what we call "productive publics" as an important way of organizing immaterial, and increasingly also material, production. Productive publics are collaborative networks of strangers who interact in highly mediatized ways and who coordinate their interaction through adherence to a common set of values. One example is the networks of peer production that are today responsible for the lion's share of software production globally and that are making inroads into new kinds of collaborative material production through Open Design and Open Biotech via urban creative scenes and online participatory culture, thus generating value for the media and creative industries. Another is the kinds of collaborative knowledge work that have been identified in organizations as being crucial to maintaining a climate of innovation and flexibility. Indeed, in chapter 2 we argue that organizational models similar to what we describe as publics have become crucial also to the global value networks where mundane material goods like mobile phones and washing machines are produced today. In other words, publics are an organizational form that is well established in the contemporary economy. As ways of coordinating production, publics are different from markets and bureaucracies in that they allow a wider range of concerns to serve as motivations. Knowledge workers are motivated by the prospect of economic gain, but also, particularly as we move up the value chain, by possibilities for self-realization, for having a meaningful impact, and for garnering peer recognition. In other words, publics introduce a wide range of orders of worth in economic life (and in chapter 4 we argue that these diverse orders of worth converge, at the individual level, in reputation and what we call "ethical capital"). To accommodate this development, managerial thought has begun to emphasize the crucial role of values. Indeed, the recent emphasis on ethics and social responsibility among corporations can be understood as an attempt to accommodate the more diverse orders of worth that productive publics bring forth. But publics also tend to be highly autonomous in conferring value on the productive contribution of their members. As we will argue, the value thus conferred tends to depend on how other members of those productive publics evaluate the ways in which they conduct themselves *as* members of such publics. Thus publics offer the possibility of a new kind of ethical economy, in which the value of individuals, organizations, and brands is determined by collaborative evaluations of their virtue and excellence.

The increasing significance of financial markets and the spread of social media constitute the second and third developments in this process, both of which have sparked controversy. The spectacular growth and importance of financial markets over the last three decades have been accompanied by their heightened self-referentiality and detachment from overall social concerns. This has not only encouraged unethical practices but also has radically increased both social inequality and economic irrationality, as an isolated group of disproportionately wealthy individuals and institutions (like investment banks) have acquired excessive influence over key economic decisions. At the same time, financial markets have institutionalized a new way of making economic value decisions. Ever more often the value of assets traded on these markets is set through processes of deliberation that weigh diverse value concerns against each other, as traders, market analysts, financial journalists, and other asset valuators struggle to interpret an abundance of complex information. In this book we suggest that the social inequality and economic irrationality that financial markets generate today to a large extent results from the lack of a common standard for making such value judgments. If we had such a common standard, financial markets *could* become an arena where the ethical diversity of value concerns that marks the information economy could be integrated into tangible economic valuations. We suggest that such a common standard is already emerging and that this process is linked to the spread of social media.

In recent years social media have been depicted in a similarly negative light. Since the enthusiasm of the Web 2.0 boom in the early 2000s, a number of critics now argue that the proliferation of social media creates new conditions of collective loneliness (of being "alone together," as Sherry Turkle puts it),[5] that they foster attention-deficit disorder and excessive preoccupation with surface and image (with personal brands), while threatening traditional conceptions of privacy. Furthermore, the social media industry is dominated by a few powerful actors, and their control over personal data is, as yet, unregulated. Social media might, or might not, do all of these things. Our argument is that whatever else they do, they also provide a new and interesting foundation in which collective value decisions can be grounded. Social media grant a new objectivity to word of mouth and reputation. What people like and do not like, and how much they like it, becomes visible through objective indicators like number of blogposts, activity on profiles, "likes," "re-tweets," and other "social buttons," ratings of various kinds, Klout scores, and the kinds of sentiment that can be automatically mined from text. We call this new factor "general sentiment," and we suggest that it might play an important role as a measuring rod for determining the overall social desirability of the particular value concerns that emerge as part of the contemporary ethical explosion. Indeed, in our view this is already happening, as general sentiment is now being incorporated into diverse valuation processes ranging from evaluating the return on investment in online marketing campaigns to influencing the market value of stocks and other financial assets.

We argue that a new system for making value decisions can be built by fostering tighter connections among these three developments. It is desirable to have value decisions about financial markets be more sensitive to online reputation, or general sentiment, and to create ways for the articulation of such sentiment to better reflect the diversity of ethical horizons that have resulted from the proliferation of productive publics. Indeed, once again we argue that stronger connections are already being built, potentially creating a situation in which economic valuations would be more sensitive to ethical values, and the ability to maximize one's overall ethical impact, or virtue, would be a direct factor in economic profits. These developments have the potential to culminate in an ethical economy, in the sense that the creation of economic value and the contribution to ethical values would coincide. Such an ethical economy would supply a new way of anchoring economic wealth creation to greater social concerns, but not through a static social contract consisting of rigidly defined values. Rather it would allow for continuous and widespread processes of deliberation that would be more responsive to the demands of our complex and highly flexible economic system. It would also allow us to move beyond the present condition of moral relativism without attempting to impose any new universal values, since ethical value as general sentiment depends only upon the strength of the positive or negative sentiment that a particular actor or venture is able to accumulate, and not on the content of the particular ideas or values that it expresses.

Evidence that these connections are already becoming stronger can be noted. As corporations adapt to the demands of productive publics, thus broadening their value horizons and investing in social responsibility concerns, as members of productive publics as well as large corporations depend ever more on collaborative peer judgments mediated via social media to construct a valuable reputational score or brand, and as financial operators become ever more sensitive to online sentiment in their operations such a concept as an "ethical economy" becomes more clearly visible on the horizon. That said, however, we do not advocate sitting back and relaxing in the expectation that social media and the reputation economy will somehow miraculously save the world.

Even though we can point to some movement in the right direction, the infrastructure of the ethical economy still needs to be built. The actual positive developments to date already depend, to no small extent, on people's active engagement—for example, forcing companies to be more sensitive to social-media-based reputation. In addition, the concrete workings of the ethical economy depend significantly on the technological infrastructure on which it is based, on what many call the "protocol" that is put in place. The design of that protocol will affect how individual value judgments online are translated into general sentiment, who is allowed to mediate and shape that process, and how these factors translate into data that affect concrete value decisions. The difference between participation in a society-wide process of deliberation and subjection to a totalitarian, Big Brother type of information regime similarly depends on the levels of power and influence that a particular protocol gives individuals over the kinds of information that they want to "emit" as they move through an ever more "wired" lifeworld. And such decisions are legion. In historical terms, our situation today is similar to the construction of the modern public sphere during the development of modern capitalism in the seventeenth and eighteenth centuries. At that time, too, a multitude of actors— who launched journals and debating societies, founded social movements, banks, and insurance companies, invented new ways of trading wealth on the stock exchange, and wrote and circulated political pamphlets—determined through their multitude of minute actions, and without any central coordination, what sorts of protocol would govern the economic and political processes of industrial society. We must set ourselves a similar task: to construct the technical infrastructure that will be able to support a new and more rational and democratic way of reconnecting the economy to social concerns. And we are well equipped to do so, since the ability to program and the ease within which software and online appliances can be deployed and combined has already created an explosion of innovation to drive the technological evolution of the Internet.

We believe that the construction of such a new public sphere can lead to a better connection between economy and society, a stronger coherence between what is socially desirable and economically valuable, and higher levels of economic rationality and stability. We also think that higher levels of economic democracy would result. In view of present projections for the spread of Internet connectivity and social media use—particularly through expansion of cell phones with Internet connection in the poorer parts of the world—such an infrastructure, if built in the right way, might allow a much wider share of the productive multitude to have an influence on how economic value decisions are made. It might create the basis for a new kind of global public sphere that can accompany the global value chains in which wealth is already being created in the contemporary economy.

THE ARGUMENT

Chapter 1, "Value Crisis," further discusses why we need such a thing as an ethical economy. Industrial society was endowed with what we call a "value regime," a common understanding of both how to measure eco-nomic values and what the most important societal values were. This value regime was institutionalized in a wide range of devices, from accounting to commercial law via welfare systems. It functioned as common ground on which conflict and consensus around value, both economic and ethical, could be played out. In the postwar years, in a process that has acceler-ated over the last three decades, the value regime has been shattered, as a combination of the financialization of value and the socialization of pro-duction has rendered it obsolete. The result is what we call a value crisis, which manifests in two ways. First, there is no common way to measure the value of economic assets. This is particularly true for the intangible assets that are ever more important as components of financial valuations. Second, there is no common language by means of which value conflicts can be settled, or even articulated. Thus ethics degenerates into relativism and virtue becomes a matter of private conduct. Ethics as a way of making value decisions at the societal level becomes impossible.

Chapter 2, "Intangibles," looks at the roots of this value crisis as it plays out at the economic level. It starts with an analysis of the processes of networking of production that, empowered by the diffusion of networked digital technologies, have accompanied the shift away from an industrial mode of production. We show how the "old" factory paradigm has given way to socialized networks of productive collaboration that rely more and more on common resources. The concept of intangible assets represents an attempt to come to terms with these new processes of wealth creation. And even though at present no common established standard exists for measuring the value of intangible assets, the use of the term "intangibles" in management theory and, above all, in corporate practice indicates that "from the point of view of production" intangible assets build on excellence in the use of common resources. We go on to analyze how the socializa-tion of production has contributed to the financialization of the economy and suggest that a more rational and transparent link between productive excellence and the financial valuation of intangible assets might constitute a stepping-stone for a new value regime.

The remaining chapters lay the groundwork for such a regime. Chapter 3, "Publics," provides a first definition of this new way of organizing wealth creation. Although publics are no new phenomenon, they have been sub-stantially empowered by the spread of information and communication technologies, since these technologies facilitate both the actual creation of useful things and the practice of association whereby individuals can come together to participate in that creation. We provide a brief history of the emergence and significance of productive publics as a way of organizing wealth creation—from the amateur countercultural economies of the 1970s to today's managerial attempts to constitute corporations as collaborative publics. We conclude by suggesting that the popularity of publics as ways of organizing economic wealth creation is deeply tied to the transformations in the relations of production that have marked the industrial economy since the first impact of information and communication technologies in the 1970s and the subsequent abundance of skills and capital necessary to engage in material production.

Chapter 4, "Value," analyzes how value is created and circulates in productive publics. Contrary to contemporary theories of collaborative production as a "gift economy" and to attempts to reduce new kinds of wealth creation to the dynamics of industrial labor, we argue that publics are endowed with highly compelling reputation economies. A person's reputation is set by other members of a public on the basis of her excellence in the use of common resources—either her excellent work, in the form of technical brilliance in adding to the common product or her excellent action in contributing to the social coherence of the public and the strength of its values. In turn, reputation functions as a kind of capital—we call it ethical capital—that can be realized in a variety of ways: as social capital that enhances a person's ability to lead and motivate others; as personal enjoyment; or as conventions that underlie monetary evaluations of that person's skills (as in personal brands). The same thing goes for organizations for which ethical capital is a valuable resource in cultivating flexibility, nurturing a culture of innovation, or building an attractive brand. This theory of value is able to explain individual participation in productive publics in terms that render it compatible with established models of economic rationality, and it provides a mechanism with which to connect the valuation of intangibles to a rational substance: the ethical capital that organizations accumulate by their excellence and virtue.

Chapter 5, "Measure," argues that even though reputation economies are growing in importance, we do not yet have a common standard whereby a transparent measure of the relative values of excellence in one public can be compared to those of excellence in another. Present developments of social media and of data mining technologies are pointing toward the emergence of such a new standard, what we call general sentiment, whereby different values can be evaluated. In contrast to the general equivalent of labor time around which the social contract of industrial society was built, general sentiment is a bottom-up, peer-based measurement, and it is dynamic as it consists in aggregation of the affective investments that a multitude of actors would have in a particular asset at a particular point in time. Furthermore, general sentiment enables us to connect the minute ethical decisions that actors routinely make as they participate in publics to the processes through which the economic value of assets is set. At the abstract level, this definition of value as general sentiment could constitute the foundation for the institutional architecture of an ethical economy (much like the institutions of industrial capitalism were based on the idea that value derived from labor time). But this abstract possibility is not enough.

In chapter 6, "Ethical Economy," we go on to call for a politics of standards that, building on this new abstract measure, makes the formation of value public and opens it up to processes of deliberation in a wide variety of ways. Finally we suggest that the present financialization of the economy should be read as a sign of the decline of the industrial model of development, and we propose that the ensuing crisis can be solved only by the institutionalization of a new value regime that can guide development in a new direction. We then elaborate what the institutionalization of such an ethical economy would mean, including the democratization and rationalization of finance, the strengthening of publics and their ability to have stronger impact on individual economic action, and how a reputation economy would function. Finally we examine what kind of ethics can be understood to stand at the basis of this new value regime, and what kind of value that regime creates.

ACKNOWLEDGMENTS

This relatively short book, long in the making, builds on advice, input, and criticism from a wide range of people from many different walks of life. It would be impossible to list all of them, but some come to mind with particular clarity. In the early 2000s, we coined the term "the ethical economy" and in 2006 we published our first working paper on the topic through the cross-disciplinary think tank Kesera, which Nicolai Jens Martin founded in 1999. We would like to thank all the members of Kesera who provided initial feedback from a variety of disciplines. In particular, we would like to acknowledge the development of the initial thinking on ethics with Jens Martin Skibsted, which was substantiated by Janus Friis and elucidated by Frank van Hasselt in the management book *Actics*, which Nicolai coauthored. Frank has been a constant sense-making companion for Nicolai throughout the years. Adam would like to thank the University of Milano, which has provided an excellent environment in which to think and write, along with all the wonderful people who work there—colleagues, students, and collaborators. In particular, he is grateful to Tiziano Bonini, Alessandro Calliandro, Elanor Colleoni, Alessandro Delfanti, Alessandro Gandini, Luisa Leonini, Bertram Niessen, Zoe Romano, Roberta Sassatelli, and the staff at the Centro Studi di Etnografia Digitale. Other people in Italy who have made significant contributions are Francesca Bria, Giampaolo Capisani, Andrea Fumagalli, Elisa Giomi, Giannino Malossi, Cristian Marrazzi, Gianfranco Poggi, and, crucially, Alex

Giordano and the participants of the Societing Summer Schools. Outside of Italy, Carolina Bandinelli, Celia Lury, and Angela McRobbie at Goldsmiths College, Mette Morsing and Pierre Guillet de Monthoux at the Copenhagen Business School, Craig Prichard at Massey University (who also graciously hosted Adam for a month in 2009), Thomas Bay at the Stockholm School of Business along with the Critical Finance Network, and Hasan Bakshi at NESTA and Nicolas Guilhot in New York have all made valuable contributions. Nicolai would further like to acknowledge all investors and colleagues in his early attempt in 2005 to launch an online tool for ethical rating and improvement for businesses that provided learning and insights into the limitations and opportunities of an ethical economy. Numerous people from the financial industry in London have been subjected to our thinking over the years and have provided guidance, particularly Tareck Safi and Ralph Sueppels. Daniel Beunza and Morgan Gabereau taught us about the sociology of finance and impact investing, and Tia Kansara and John Grant showed us the world of social entrepreneurship. Michel Bauwens has been a constant source of inspiration and support, and George Por proved to be encouraging and optimistic every time that we met.

The ideas in this book have been presented in many different contexts. We especially want to thank the participants at the following events: the Reboot meet-ups in Copenhagen and their host, Thomas Madsen-Mygdal; the Internet as Playground and Factory Conference at the New School of Social Research in New York in 2009; the events organized by SPACE and Tomorrow's Company in London; the Institute for Network Cultures in Amsterdam; the Heinrich Böll Foundation in Berlin; the British Institute in Rome and CRASSH at the University of Cambridge; the 2011 conferences by the Beijing Sustainable Development Committee; the Hanwang Forum; and the China NBA Development Forum. We have gained a great deal from discussing our ideas with the students and faculty of the London School of Economics, the University of Sussex, the Essex Business School and the School of Business at Lund University Sweden, and Goldsmith's College London. We also thank the anonymous reviewers of *Ephemera, Organization, The Information Society*, and last but not least, Columbia University Press. Their zeal and professionalism did a lot to improve the manuscript and sharpen the ideas therein.

Finally, we owe Lauren Pearson at Regal Literary Agency thanks for taking this unusual project on, and we appreciate the support that both she and Markus Hoffman have provided in bringing the book to market.

THE ETHICAL ECONOMY

I

Value Crisis

In the most dramatic moments of Italy's debt crisis, the newly installed "technical" government, led by Mario Monti, appealed to trade unions to accept salary cuts in the name of national solidarity. Monti urged them to participate in a collective effort to increase the competitiveness of the Italian economy (or at least to show that efforts were being made in that direction) in order to calm international investors and "the market" and, hopefully, reduce the spread between the interest rates of Italian and German bonds (at the time around 500 points, meaning that the Italian government had to refinance its ten-year debt at the excruciating rate of 7.3 percent). Commenting on this appeal in an editorial in the left-leaning journal *Il Manifesto*, the journalist Loris Campetti wondered how it could be at all possible to demand solidarity from a Fiat worker when the CEO of his company earned about 500 times what the worker did.[1] And such figures are not unique to Italy. In the United States, the average CEO earned about 30 times what the average worker earned in the mid-1970s (1973 being the year in which income inequality in the United States was at its historically lowest point). Today the multiplier lies around 400. Similarly, the income of the top 1 percent (or even more striking, the top 0.1 percent) of the U.S. population has skyrocketed in relation to that of the remaining 99 percent, bringing income inequality back to levels not seen since the Roaring Twenties.[2]

The problem is not, or at least not only, that such income discrepancies exist, but that there is no way to legitimate them. At present there is no way to rationally explain why a corporate CEO (or a top-level investment banker or any other member of the 1 percent) should be worth 400 times as much as the rest of us. And consequently there is no way to legitimately appeal to solidarity or to rationally argue that a factory worker (or any of us in the 99 percent) should take a pay cut in the name of a system that permits such discrepancies in wealth. What we have is a value crisis. There are huge differentials in the monetary rewards that individuals receive, but there is no way in which those differentials can be explained and legitimated in terms of any common understanding of how such monetary rewards should be determined. There is no common understanding of value to back up the prices that markets assign, to put it in simple terms. (We will discuss the thorny relation between the concepts of "value" and "price" along with the role of markets farther on in this chapter.)

This value crisis concerns more than the distribution of income and private wealth. It is also difficult to rationalize how asset prices are set. In the wake of the 2008 financial crisis a steady stream of books, articles, and documentaries has highlighted the irrational practices, sometimes bordering on the fraudulent, by means of which mortgage-backed securities were revalued from junk to investment grade, credit default swaps were emitted without adequate underlying assets, and the big actors of Wall Street colluded with each other and with political actors to protect against transparency and rational scrutiny and in the end to have the taxpayers foot the bill.[3] Neither was this irrationality just a temporary expression of a period of exceptional "irrational exuberance"; rather, irrationality has become a systemic feature of the financial system.[4] As Amar Bidhé argues, the reliance on mathematical formulas embodied in computerized calculating devices at all levels of the financial system has meant that the setting of values on financial markets has been rendered ever more disconnected from judgments that can be rationally reconstructed and argued through.[5] Instead, decisions that range from whether to grant a mortgage to an individual, to how to make split-second investment decisions on stock and currency markets, to how to grade or rate the performance of a company or even a nation have been automated, relegated to the discretion of computers and algorithms. While there is nothing wrong with computers and algorithms per se, the problem is that the complexity of these devices has rendered the underlying methods of calculation and their assumptions incomprehensible and opaque even to the people who use them on a daily basis (and imagine the rest of us!). To

cite Richard Sennett's interviews with the back-office Wall Street technicians who actually develop such algorithms:

"I asked him to outline the algo [algorithm] for me," one junior ac-
countant remarked about her derivatives-trading Porsche driving superior, "and he couldn't, he just took it on faith." "Most kids have computer skills in their genes . . . but just up to a point . . . when you try
to show them how to generate the numbers they see on screen, they
get impatient, they just want the numbers and leave where these came
from to the main-frame."[6]

The problem here is not ignorance alone, but that the makeup of
the algorithms and automated trading devices that execute the majority of trades on financial markets today (about 70 percent are executed
by "bots," or automatic trading agents),[7] is considered a purely technical
question, beyond rational discussion, judgment, and scrutiny. Actors tend
to take the numbers on faith without knowing, or perhaps even bothering
about, where they came from. Consequently these devices can often contain flawed assumptions that, never scrutinized, remain accepted as almost
natural "facts." During the dot-com boom, for example, Internet analysts
valued dot-coms by looking at a multiplier of visitors to the dot-com's
Web site without considering how these numbers translated into monetary revenues; during the pre-2008 boom investors assigned the same
default risks to subprime mortgages, or mortgages taken out by people
who were highly likely to default, as they did to ordinary mortgages.[8] And
there are few ways in which the nature of such assumptions, flawed or
not, can be discussed, scrutinized, or even questioned. Worse, there are
few ways of even knowing what those assumptions are. The assumptions
that stand behind the important practice of brand valuation are generally
secret. Consequently, there is no way of explaining how or discussing why
valuations of the same brand by different brand-valuation companies can
differ as much as 450 percent. A similar argument can be applied to Fitch,
Moody's, Standard & Poor, and other ratings agencies that are acquiring
political importance in determining the economic prospects of nations
like Italy and France.

This irrationality goes even deeper than financial markets. Investments
in corporate social responsibility are increasing massively, both in the West
and in Asia, as companies claim to want to go beyond profits to make a
genuine contribution to society. But even though there is a growing body
of academic literature indicating that a good reputation for social respon-

sibility is beneficial for corporate performance in a wide variety of ways—from financial outcomes to ease in generating customer loyalty and attracting talented employees—there is no way of determining exactly how beneficial these investments are and, consequently, how many resources should be allocated to them.[9] Indeed, perhaps it would be better to simply tax corporations and let the state or some other actor distribute the resources to some "responsible" causes. The fact that we have no way of knowing leads to a number of irrationalities. Sometimes companies invest more money in communicating their efforts at "being good" than they do in actually promoting socially responsible causes. (In 2001, for example, the tobacco company Philip Morris spent $75 million on what it defined as "good deeds" and then spent $100 million telling the public about those good deeds.)[10] At other times such efforts can be downright contradictory, for example when tobacco companies sponsor antismoking campaigns aimed at young people in countries like Malaysia while at the same time targeting most of their ad spending to the very same segment.[11] Other companies make genuine efforts to behave responsibly, but those efforts reflect poorly on their reputation. Apple, for example, has done close to nothing in promoting corporate responsibility, and has a consistently poor record when it comes to labor conditions among its Chinese subcontractors (like Foxconn).[12] Yet the company benefits from a powerful brand that is to no small degree premised on the fact that consumers perceive it to be somehow more benign than Microsoft, which actually does devote considerable resources to good causes (or at least the Bill and Melinda Gates Foundation does so).

Similar irrationalities exist throughout the contemporary economy, ranging from how to measure productivity and determine rewards for knowledge workers to how to arrive at a realistic estimate of value for a number of "intangible" assets, from creativity and capacity for innovation to brand. (We will come back to these questions below as well as in the chapters that follow.) Throughout the contemporary economy, from the heights of finance down to the concrete realities of everyday work, particularly in knowledge work, great insecurities arise with regard to what things are actually worth and the extent to which the prices assigned to them actually reflect their value. (Indeed, in academic managerial thought, the very concept of "value" is presently without any clear definition; it means widely different things in different contexts.)[13]

But this is not merely an accounting problem. The very question of how you determine worth, and consequently what value *is*, has been rendered problematic by the proliferation of a number of value criteria (or "orders of worth," to use sociologist David Stark's term) that are poorly reflected in established economic models.[14] A growing number of people value the ethical impact of consumer goods. But there are no clear ways of determining the relative value of different forms of "ethical impact," nor even a clear definition of what "ethical impact" means. Therefore there is no way of determining whether it is actually more socially useful or desirable for a company to invest in these pursuits than to concentrate on getting basic goods to consumers as cheaply and conveniently as possible. Consequently, ethical consumerism, while a growing reality, tends to be more efficient at addressing the existential concerns of wealthy consumers than at systematically addressing issues like poverty or empowerment. Similarly, more and more people understand the necessity for more sustainable forms of development. And while the definition of "sustainability" is clearer than that of "ethics," there are no coherent ways of making concerns for sustainability count in practices of asset valuation (although some efforts have been made in that direction, which we will discuss) or of rationally determining the trade-off between efforts toward sustainability and standard economic pursuits. Thus the new values that are acquiring a stronger presence in our society—popular demand for a more sustainable economy and a more just and equal global society—have only very weak and unreliable ways of influencing the actual conduct of corporations and other important economic actors, and can affect economic decisions in only a tenuous way. More generally, we have no way of arriving at what orders of worth "count" in general and how much, and even if we were able to make such decisions, we have no channels by means of which to effect the setting of economic values. So the value crisis is not only economic; it is also ethical and political.

It is ethical in the sense that the relative value of the different orders of worth that are emerging in contemporary society (economic prosperity, "ethical conduct," "social responsibility," sustainability, global justice and empowerment) is simply indeterminable. As a consequence, ethics becomes a matter of personal choice and "standpoint" and the ethical perspectives of different individuals become incommensurate with one another. Ethics degenerates into "postmodern" relativism.[15]

It is political because since we have no way of rationally arriving at what orders of worth we should privilege and how much, we have no common cause in the name of which we could legitimately appeal to people or companies (or force them) to do what they otherwise might not want to do. (The emphasis here is on *legitimately*; of course people are asked and forced to do things all the time, but if they inquire as to why, it becomes very difficult to say what should motivate them.) In the absence of legitimacy, politics is reduced to either more or less corrupt bargaining between particular interest groups or the naked exercise of raw power. In either case there can be no *raison d'état*. In such a context, appeals to solidarity, like that of the Monti government in Italy, remain impossible.

There have of course always been debates and conflicts, often violent, around what the common good should be. The point is that today we do not even have a language, or less metaphorically, a method for conducting such debates. (Modern ethical debates are interminable, as philosopher Alasdair MacIntyre wrote in the late 1970s.)[16] This is what we mean by a value crisis. Not that there might be disagreement on how to value social responsibility or sustainability in relation to economic growth, or how much a CEO should be paid in relation to a worker, but that there is no common method to resolve such issues, or even to define specifically what they are about. We have no common "value regime," no common understanding of what the values are and how to make evaluative decisions, even contested and conflict-ridden ones.

This has not always been the case. Industrial society—that old model that we still remember as the textbook example of how economics and social systems are supposed to work—was built around a common way of connecting economic value creation to overall social values, an imaginary social contract. In this arrangement, business would generate economic growth, which would be distributed by the welfare state in such a way that it contributed to the well-being of everyone. And even though there were intense conflicts about how this contract should apply, everyone agreed on its basic values. More importantly, these basic values were institutionalized in a wide range of practices and devices, from accounting methods to procedures of policy decisions to methods for calculating the financial value of companies and assets. Again, this did not mean that there was no conflict or discussion, but it did mean that there was a common ground on which such conflict and discussion could be acted out. There was a common value regime.

We are not arguing for a comeback of the value regime of industrial society. That would be impossible, and probably undesirable even if it were possible. However, neither do we accept the "postmodernist" argument (less popular now, perhaps, than it was two decades go) that the end of values (and of ethics or even politics) would be somehow liberating and emancipatory. Instead we argue that the foundations for a different kind of value regime—an ethical economy—are actually emerging as we speak.

The present irrationality of economic value judgments not only is manifest in the arcane mechanics of speculative finance, but also is deeply ingrained in the everyday workings of the corporate economy. This is most clear in the notion of "intangibles." In fact, these mysterious assets have become key to the market value of companies and constitute about 70 percent of the market value of the S&P 500 average today, up from around 20 percent in the 1950s.[17]

The concept of intangibles is an excellent point of entry for understanding the value crisis of the contemporary economy—not because of what it says, but because of what it does not say, because of what it hides. As chapter 2 explains in more detail, the rise of intangibles as a way of conceptualizing the value of companies is directly linked to the parallel tendencies toward networking production and a financialization of value that have been central to the transition from an industrial economy to an information economy. These are complex developments that have a wide range of causes and effects, which we will discuss in more detail later. Here we touch on some basic points to provide a better understanding of what we mean by the value crisis, as it manifests with regard to the important issue of intangibles.

The size and importance of financial markets have consistently increased during the postwar years. In the United States, the dollar value of trading on financial markets had risen to fifty times GDP by 2000, after being roughly equal to GDP in the 1950s. But the growth of finance has not been only a matter of creating an additional speculative or casino-style layer on top of the real economy of goods and services. Rather, the financial and the commodity economies have become deeply intertwined. In fact, in the same period the share of corporate profits attributable to financial rent has risen from 15 percent in 1970 to 40 percent in 2005. And figures are similar in other advanced "postindustrial" countries, like France and the UK.[18]

This rise of financial rent vis-à-vis the manufacture and sale of commodities as a source of profits has been accompanied by a rise in the market value of companies in relation to their book value. Since "book value" signifies "value that can be measured by established accounting techniques," this means that the market value of companies often now exceeds such "clearly measurable value" by a factor of 8–9 (for the S&P 500 average), as opposed to 2 in the 1950s. And for some companies the factors may be even higher. For Google it was 29, and for Facebook, 143 in 2011.[19]

This large share of immeasurable value in the composition of corporate equity could be a matter of speculation and irrational exuberance. Who knows? However, the concept of intangibles has arisen as an attempt to make sense of the discrepancy by attributing the divergence between market value and book value to a new class of assets that have emerged along with the intense networking of production.

The production of goods once took place in large factories that tried to concentrate as many aspects of the production process as possible within a single building (or at least institution). Today the production of most goods—cars, television sets, computers, washing machines—takes place in complex, and sometimes global, value networks that may comprise thousands of factories. This means that the source of profits and any competitive edge no longer lies with the material production of goods per se. As management scholars Paul Adler and Charles Heckscher sum up the matter: "The 'mysteries' of effective commodity production have become common knowledge; they are now merely tickets for entry rather than keys to winning the competition."[20] Rather, profits and competitive advantage derive mainly from other factors, such as the ability to innovate continuously, to ensure integration and flexibility of complex value chains, and to create a perception of one product as somehow different from a wide variety of functionally and aesthetically similar ones.

These assets—"flexibility," "innovation," and "brand" (to use simple terms)—are what are commonly referred to as "intangibles." (The terminology is complex and imprecise, with a number of terms like "social capital," "knowledge capital," creative capital," "image capital," and so on circulating, but the content of most definitions can be roughly summarized in these three terms.) The concept of "intangible assets" has developed as a way of rendering measurable what emerged as an immeasurable value discrepancy (between market value and book value), by attributing that discrepancy to a new class of "real" assets: flexibility, innovation, and brand. The problem, however, is that this discussion remains mere rhetoric, as there is no coherent or commonly accepted way of measuring the value of intangible assets. (Rather, there are as many measurement methods and approaches as there are consulting companies in this field. Each company generally launches its own definition and method as a way of acquiring a competitive edge.)

Take brands, for example. Brands are arguably the most important intangible asset today, accounting for about 30 percent of the market capitalization of the S&P 500, up from about 5 percent thirty years ago.[21] Some companies, like Apple or luxury goods companies, rely on brands for more than half of their market value. In 2011, the Apple brand alone was estimated to be worth between $153 and $33 billion, depending on the measurement used.[22] And that's just the point. A recent survey of the brand valuation industry shows that there are fifty-two key operators globally and that they use seventeen different methods. These methods range from the simple estimation of differences between market value and book value to more-complex approaches like the "royalty relief method"—accepted in some countries for fiscal purposes—which estimates the alternative costs of leasing the brand for an organization that does not own it. Some of the more sophisticated methods, like that of Interbrand (the market leader), take into account a number of indicators, some of them, like status in trend indexes or response to customer surveys, quite distant from traditional economic indicators.[23] These techniques also have widely different outcomes. Salinas and Ambler, for example, show how the valuations of Apple, Toyota, and Samsung by the market-leading valuation firms Interbrand, MBO, and Vivaldi differ by as much as 300 percent.[24]

So what are brands, and intangible assets? Two interpretations are possible. One is that the notion of intangible assets is simply a fiction that has been invented to legitimate and cover up the increasingly speculative valuations of companies and other assets that have resulted from the financialization of the economy. In this sense the concept of intangibles is part of the mythology of a period of economic irrationality that signifies the end of corporate capitalism as we know it (and maybe the end of capitalism itself). This is a plausible interpretation and we will come back to it later. The other hypothesis is that however irrational and incoherent the measurements, the concept of intangible assets actually refers to some sort of real productive assets—like flexibility, innovation, and brand—that should play a part in the valuation of companies because they actually contribute to creating value by creating new knowledge, making the production of commodities and services more efficient, or rendering the goods produced more agreeable. In chapter 2 we present a number of arguments for this second, "realist" interpretation of the concept of intangibles.

But even if we accept that concepts like "brand" might not be entirely mythological, but actually refer to *something*—that there is, in effect, some sort of real basis for the values that they represent—we still have no way of knowing exactly what brand value means and how it can be measured. And consequently we have no way of criticizing existing methodologies for brand measurement. Or rather, we can dismiss all of them, but we have no way of determining that, say, Interbrand's valuation of Apple at

$33 billion is more adequate than BrandZ's valuation at $153 billion. Who is right? Is Apple worth $33 billion or $153 billion? We do not even know how to begin that discussion. First, we have no idea of how these measurements have been arrived at (since the methodologies are trade secrets). But even if we did know that, we have no way of comparing or criticizing them, since there is no common agreement on what brand value really *is*. Does it build on market strength? On consumer loyalty? On reputation? On social responsibility? On distribution channels? On some combination of these factors? In that case, *what* combination? This is a value crisis: there is no common definition of value that can enable us to make these kinds of decisions.

But does this even matter? After all, the economist would say, market prices are a rational estimate of value. Or better, the concept of "value" is a form of metaphysical speculation that economics did away with in the nineteenth century.[25] And the notion that things could be worth something other than their market prices is just absurd. Somewhat caricatured, this is the position of orthodox neoliberal economists, like Eugene Fama, the founder of the rational market hypothesis in its modern form. In a 2010 *New Yorker* interview, Fama denied the very possibility of understanding the pre-2008 housing boom as a speculative credit bubble: "I don't know what a credit bubble means. I don't even know what a bubble means. These words have become popular. I don't think they have any meaning." Of course such terms would be meaningless from his point of view: if market prices by definition reflect all available information, then how could there be any notion of value that is different from price? How could the market ever misprice anything?[26]

The subsumption of "value" under "price" and the negation of any independent reality of the former concept has been a key premise of both neoclassical economics and neoliberal ideology. In the former, this operation has served as a fundamental simplification that has permitted the development of mathematical economics with its often advanced and sophisticated (albeit consciously abstract and often unreal) models. As part of neoliberal ideology the subsumption of value under price has served to reinforce the notion of the market as the supreme arbiter of all values, and has worked as a powerful defense against the critique of the high differentials in wealth distribution discussed earlier. (Why should a CEO be paid 400 times as much as a worker? Well, that's the going market price for a competent CEO.) The basis for this supremacy of price over value, both as a purely technical device in economics and as an ideological construct, has been the hypothesis of market rationality.

The hypothesis of market rationality is based on the assumption that markets constitute the best possible way to process information about the value of assets. This way the outcome of markets, where a multitude of rational actors seek to maximize their profits, will constitute the best possible synthesis of available information about an asset, and the "wisdom of market crowds" is bound to outperform any other actor, like state bureaucracies or even public opinion, in estimating the real value of the asset. From a normative point of view this also means that market competition, insofar as it remains free and unconstrained, will be an ethically sound way of distributing wealth.[27] We can raise three critiques of the market rationality hypothesis, two of them empirical and one normative. (In fact they tend to intersect.)

From an empirical point of view, the first objection would be to argue that market rationality could perhaps apply ceteris paribus—everything else being equal—a phrase that economists use to isolate their models from reality. That is, this could work if markets were actually free, barriers to entry virtually nonexistent, and information flowing freely. Even neoclassical economists concede that such is not the case. Most markets are blatantly oligopolistic (financial markets in particular), barriers to entry are high, and information is costly (just subscribing to the Bloomberg information terminal is too costly for most individuals).[28] The neoclassical economists' answer is generally to point to what they regard as excessive regulation—that is, not enough markets. Consequently the solution is deregulation, providing more space for markets. While appeals to deregulation have been a standard feature of neoliberal politics for several decades, and while these appeals have often been used to argue for what in practice has been re-regulation (using "deregulation" to enable private monopolies to take over railway transport or water provision from public monopolies, for example), the appeal for "really free markets" does merit serious consideration. As the French historian Fernand Braudel argued, though, its realization would give capitalism-as-we-know-it serious problems.[29]

A second empirical critique of the free market hypothesis employs the quite simple insight, which has been building up in economic sociology over recent years, that markets are actually not free arenas where individual actors meet to pursue their own rational goals independently of others. Rather, markets are institutions that build on a complex web of devices—computer programs, accounting systems, communication channels, currencies, trading strategies, and so on—that process information about assets and transform that information into prices. These "calculative devices" are generally taken for granted by market operators (as indicated by the quotes above, to a Wall Street trader the colorful figures that jump up and down on his computer screen *are* the market) as a "natural" rendering of the underlying reality of the market. But as a broad stream of research has shown, these devices are selective, in the sense that they employ a set of implicit and seldom discussed values that determine how information should be interpreted and visualized and how prices should be calculated. Thus, however purposely "value free" the markets may be, they actually build on particular sets of values that have been naturalized—"turned into furniture," to use sociologist Bruno Latour's fortunate expression—and that as furniture, as hidden assumptions that are seldom reflected upon, those values actually do affect the way information is processed into prices.[30]

From this point of view, the rational market hypothesis can hold only if there is some form of agreement on what values should be incorporated into the "furniture" of the market. In other words, there must be an implicit law of value that structures the formation of market prices. This is so because the idea that market prices are the best possible interpretation of available information about the future holds only when there is *one* correct interpretation of that available information. In a situation where multiple orders of worth prevail, and when there is no established hierarchy that determines which of them should be the most important or, to put it in less complex terms, when there is no overall agreement on value, many correct interpretations of available information can exist. (Should the fact that BP is launching a new deepwater drilling project off the coast of Sicily be interpreted as something that contributes to its value as an energy company or as something that detracts from its value as an environmentally responsible company, or both? In the last case how should these two, equally correct, interpretations be balanced in determining its market value?) This means that the transformation of uncertainty into calculable risk, on which present methods of valuation relies, is increasingly ambiguous, and that we ever more approach a situation of what economists call Knightian uncertainty.[31]

And that is precisely what is happening today, as markets are more and more often "asked" to price a wide range of different "orders of worth." Manifestations of such different orders of worth range from calls for new ways of measuring GDP that take into account factors like happiness and environmental impact, to the rising economic values of brands, to the popularity of social responsibility as a standard of corporate performance and of ethics or fairness as a determinant of the price of/demand for consumer goods. The salience of such diverse orders of worth increases as a wider diversity of actors (consumers, NGOs, other members of the public) become directly involved in processes of wealth creation. To date there is no common rationality to these orders of worth. Though standards and evaluation tools have proliferated, there is no common definition of what, exactly, constitutes corporate social responsibility and how the relative performance of one company in this field can be evaluated in relation to that of another. Similarly, though tools that claim to measure brand value have emerged, no common definitions exist as to what the substance of brand value is (does it build on the experience that brands can give consumers, on their ability to contribute to consumer identity, on mere attention, or even just on the strength of a brand's distributional channels?) nor how it should be measured. Indeed, the proliferation of measurement systems and consultancy businesses in these fields can be viewed as an indication of the absence of common standards. For example, the McDonald's brand is said to represent 54 percent of the market value of the company. But this figure is arrived at mainly by subtracting the book value of the McDonald's company from its market value; there is no precise way of determining how much of the difference represents mere speculation and how much represents the social utility of the McDonald's company above and beyond its ability to make and sell hamburgers.[32] Similarly, the mortgage-backed securities around which the last financial bubble was constructed were built on the securitization of the life conduct of borrowers, and as such they proved to be very poorly representative indeed. So while the market does set prices, those prices are not tied to any common definition of value; they cannot be said to be representative of anything other than the dynamics of the market itself.

If the present value crisis creates problems even for the rational market hypothesis, which on an ideological level has been an efficient way to avoid the question of value, then an opportunity for a normative critique becomes available. Although supposedly value free, the rational market hypothesis actually presupposes certain values. These values are generally not explicit, but rather are invisible: they have been made into "furniture," inscribed in the mechanisms used by market actors to set prices (like Capital Asset Pricing Models, which financial operators use to price assets or methods for brand valuation or accounting principles). It might have been possible to defend the rational market hypothesis and its implication, the subsumption of value under price, so long as these implicit values more or less mirrored the values—economic growth and increasing prosperity—that were shared by most people. But in a period when alternative orders of worth—sustainability, responsibility—are proliferating, it becomes obvious that the values by which markets set prices no longer represent any common values. Obviously, then, the legitimacy of markets as a mechanism for the distribution of wealth is eroded.

The only solution to this legitimacy crisis, this value crisis, is to find a way to enable markets to price in a wider range of value concerns. So, paradoxically, the way to save the rational market hypothesis may be to do away with its basic premise, the value-neutrality of markets. We might then be able to arrive at a more extended market rationality that incorporates weighing different value concerns against each other, or, in other words, an ethical economy.

After Ethics?

The idea that there are implicit values that support and guide the calculations of supposedly value-neutral markets creates a direct connection between the question of economic value and the question of ethics, the question of the value of the values that we live by. And maybe it is the case that we do not have any notion of economic value, any idea of how to value, say, sustainability in relation to profit, because we no longer have any values in the ethical sense of that term. Just as our markets are irrational, our outlook on life is nihilistic. Or at least that is what many contemporary moral philosophers have argued. But the reality might be more complex.

On the one hand, we seem to be in the midst of an explosion of ethics. For several decades now, numerous surveys have pointed toward the emergence of a new value structure, at least among the educated middle classes. There is a consistent turn to what is known as "post-materialist values," whereby qualities like self-realization and, lately, sustainability and global justice are valued over economic growth and material prosperity.[33] And these new values have been expressed in forms of collective action, from the so-called new social movements of the 1970s and 1980s to today's ethical consumerism, social entrepreneurship, and calls for corporate social responsibility and socially responsible investments. But there is also evidence that the approach to values is changing. To put it bluntly, the question of values is now a question of ethics rather than of morality.

In industrial society most people belonged to larger collectives, classes, ethnic groups, or religious groups that had their own fairly stable value structures, their own moral rules that counted when individuals had to make decisions. The question of values was already solved for most people, and what remained was a question of morals, or how to apply existing values to one's own life conduct. Today these larger collective identities (being Swedish, working class, Jewish, and so on) remain important for many people. But overall they are less important for people's values, or rather they face competition from a pluralization of different kinds of lifestyles in which each lifestyle has its own particular concerns. This decline of the modern value structure and the ideologies and movements in which it was reflected, together with a growing exposure through the media to the sufferings of others means that we are forced to make value decisions on a daily basis. In the absence of universal rules, we must choose what values to adopt. In other words, we are forced to be ethical. But contemporary ethics is different from the ethics of modernity. Simply put, modern ethics was a Kantian ethics, which (like its Christian predecessor) sought to elaborate on universal rules for moral conduct. And it presupposed that those rules could be arrived at through learned intellectual debate, or even, as in the case of the utilitarians, a quasi-scientific procedure. Contemporary ethics takes a more "postmodern" view, confronting the specificities of each situation without much in terms of universal guidelines.[34] Thus the diversity and complexity of the ethical demands on economic actors are increasing.

Combining these arguments, sociologists and moral philosophers have suggested that the present diffusion of an ethical outlook on life is the consequence of an implosion of the moral systems that were inherent in the modern, Fordist order. Zygmunt Bauman, in *Postmodern Ethics*, makes the point succinctly. He argues that in modern times most people had most of their ethical decisions made for them. Their allegiance to larger, collective identities, as embodied in the institutions of nation, family, or party, came with a particular worldview that featured strong and universal moral codes. A socialist and an American each operated according to a particular definition of right and wrong. This consistency saved people from having to continuously make decisions in these matters themselves. Today, however, such collective identities, along with the grand narratives that supported them, are no longer as powerful, and people tend to live without an established moral framework to shelter them from daily exposure to ethical decisions. While this argument is perhaps overly simplistic, it does point toward a general thesis:[35] Just as the rise in intangibles and the increasing importance of financial value signify that economic values are less and less determined by an established and institutionalized societal law of value, so the proliferation of ethics signifies that the determination of moral values has been similarly delinked from large-scale social structures and from an institutionalized common morality. The question of values is, in a sense, up for grabs, or at least for discussion.

There is nothing wrong with this tendency toward a de-traditionalization of ethics. After all, it is good if people decide for themselves what they want rather than blindly accepting tradition. According to Bauman and his fellow sociologists, though, the problem is that this approach leads to the individualization and fragmentation of ethical horizons. While ethics seems to be more present than ever before as part of the contemporary existential condition, ethics in the sense of a procedure for determining what is socially useful or desirable has become an impossible venture. Bauman summarizes this perspective well in his lecture "Does Ethics Have a Chance in a World of Consumers?" His answer is no, since as a consequence of the expansion of consumerism and "the market," the grand social vision has been fragmented into a multitude of individual and personal, strikingly similar but decidedly not complementary portmanteaus. Each one is made to the measure of consumers' bliss—intended, like all consumer joys, for utterly individual, lonely enjoyment even when relished in company.[36]

The transition to a consumer society, and the resulting expansion of the economy into all spheres of life, has created individualization and social fragmentation that make almost impossible the experience of having something in common—of community—which is the foundation for fruitful ethical debate. In arguing that consumerism has destroyed the possibility of a true ethics, Bauman builds on a long philosophical tradition that has constituted a persistent tragic vein in modern social thought. This narrative has stressed alienation and social fragmentation as the consequences of the spread of modern technology and a market society, and argued that this transformation has destroyed the very possibility of a true humanity. The case has perhaps been best argued by Alasdair MacIntyre. In his 1981 work *After Virtue*, MacIntyre begins by arguing that today we are unable to even talk about ethics in a meaningful way: we lack any kind of conceptual scheme that would allow us to make ethical judgments (and as a consequence, "modern moral debates are interminable"). As French philosopher Alain Badiou observes, we are caught between impossible universalism and relativist multiculturalism. The fragmented life of contemporary "postmodern" individuals, trapped in the vortex of global consumer culture, makes it rare to encounter any standards that will stand up to the test of everyday existence.[37]

While this argument might be a tad exaggerated, and probably is highly affected by the romantic/tragic mood of the strand of critical social thought from which it derives, it does make a point. The problem is not primarily a lack of values or ethical concerns. Contemporary phenomena like ethical consumerism, engagement in sustainability, and popular pressure on corporations to behave in responsible ways seem to indicate the contrary. The problem is rather that there are few ways in which such ethical concerns can develop into something more than sources of personal anxiety or guilt. There are few arenas in which individual ethical worries can be elaborated into the types of common values that can influence how important decisions are made.

In short, the paradox is that while contemporary life seems to be saturated with ethics on the existential level, it affords no space for ethics as a method for the deliberation of overall societal values. This has to do with what sociologists and historians call the "decline of the public sphere." The idea is that in the past there were spaces where people could quite naturally come together—the pub, the café, the neighborhood square, the workplace, the union night school, and so on—to engage in critical debates and transform their individual concerns into common values. (And then there were institutions like political parties, trade unions, and social movements that were able to act on these common values and imbue them with an overall social influence.) Today we have seen the commercialization of public spaces, the spread of consumer culture, the speed-up of work, higher levels of surveillance and control in the workspace, and smoking bans in pubs and cafés. These developments have combined to make such venues less social and less convivial, less permissive of unstructured social relations and of the kinds of diversity and conflict that can lead to constructive discussion. (For example, a 2002 Canadian survey of the users of Internet dating services showed that they were predominantly college graduate knowledge workers. One of the reasons they used online dating services was that new forms of workplace surveillance—principally sexual harassment policies—had made the traditional way to meet a partner, through an office romance, far too risky.)[38] The result is that instead of the kinds of strong solidarity that develop around common values that have grown out of conflict and contestation, we have what Richard Sennett calls "weak cooperation," forms of cooperation built on loose commitments to lofty principles, acted out without deeper commitments and shattered by the first real conflict that comes along. Such weak cooperation arguably also prevails among consumers of the same ethical brand, residents of the same themed, gated community, and customers at the same shopping mall.[39]

Once again, the issue here is not that people are not concerned about ethics or do not want to have common values. On the contrary, and as we will argue later, contemporary transformations in the relations of production, making the production of wealth more cooperative and more communicative, tend to foster an "ethical mentality," whereby people are open to and interested in communicating with others and arriving at a shared understanding of a given situation. Management scholar Paul Adler argues that contemporary highly networked forms of knowledge work tend to be conducive to a more "interdependent self," a sense of self more conscious of the importance of others, as well as "collaborative community," a new way of jointly arriving at the values that should guide cooperation. The problem is that the push toward a mentality of interdependence and collaboration is counteracted by the logic of corporate institutions that, through bureaucratic command structures, clumsy performance metrics, and rapid turnover of teams and tasks, constantly threaten to fragment any emerging reality of genuine collaboration.

The ethics of consumers can be described in similar terms. Never before have people in general been so aware of the plight of others located far away along the value chains that make up today's networks of commodity production, and never before have they had such a concrete experience of being connected to those "suffering others" through the production and consumption of commodities. People have probably never been as aware as they are today of the global consequences of their lifestyles, nor have so many let those concerns guide their everyday choices. The problem, however, is that this new ethical awareness is developing within an institutional framework, that of corporate consumer society, that does not allow it to generate the kinds of new common values that count. Instead, concerns for sustainability and global justice are incorporated into existing product lines and transformed into consumable lifestyle choices (like "ecological cars") that have little or no impact on the overall orientation of the productive economy.

Political parties, too, have virtually ceased to listen to the demands of the electorate or even to its own activists, and have instead developed powerful techniques to manipulate those demands through communication and spin.

Clearly the problem is not that we do not have any ethical awareness. The problem is that we do not have the kinds of institutions whereby a widespread ethical awareness can generate powerful common values that actually make a difference.

VALUE REGIMES

So what is value, really? While modern economics has done away with the question of value, viewing it as "unscientific," modern social theory has tended to understand value as a natural fact, as something anchored in the realities of the physical world. The only serious modern theory that might be pertinent here is the labor theory of value. Developed by "political economists" like Adam Smith and David Ricardo, who wrote during the industrial revolution in the eighteenth and nineteenth centuries (in Smith's case actually a bit before that "revolution"), the labor theory of value became the bulwark of Marxist economics and political thought. Simply put, it states that all values in the economy can be derived from the average labor time necessary for their production. And consequently, profits represent a "theft" of such labor time. As a theory of how prices are formed, the labor theory of value might have functioned in the simpler realities of early nineteenth-century factory production. But as Marx himself already realized in the 1850s, movement toward a higher complexity of cooperation and extended value chains made it increasingly difficult to isolate the contribution made by labor time to price. Nevertheless, the labor theory of value became highly influential as a way of thinking about value and making value decisions in industrial society. Wages were set in relation to labor productivity, pensions depended on time spent in productive activity; activity outside of the factory, like (mostly) female household work, was considered unproductive and hence not given monetary remuneration; definitions of corporate wealth that built on accounting for the resources that a company used in production—or book value—accounted for market valuations pretty accurately; and so on. This overall relevance of the labor theory of value was political, reflecting the role and influence of the workers' movement in the construction of the Fordist welfare state.[40]

So the truth is that value is a convention; it is not a natural fact. To be effective, a value regime needs to encompass several kinds of standards: for how to set economic values, for how to make ethical decisions, for how to arrive at decisions about what values are most important from an overall "human" point of view, and for how to make these values count in political and economic decisions. The standards that are developed need to be coherent and mutually reinforcing. They also need to "make sense" to the multitude of actors involved, given the varied experiences of these actors. So standards cannot be entirely arbitrary but must correspond to subjective experience in some way. A certain definition of value becomes real and effective as it is institutionalized as a value regime and becomes accepted as the basis for making value decisions on a multitude of occasions across economy and society.

2

Intangibles

During his first year at Sweden's Lund University, one of the authors of this book was exposed to a classic of Swedish managerial science, Albert Danielsson's *Företagsekonomi.*[1] A basic book in business administration, it depicted companies as closed-off and secluded boxes that process neatly defined inputs (raw materials, labor time) into equally neatly defined outputs (cars, furniture) and thereby create value. The book was written in the 1970s, when Danielsson was professor of industrial organization at the Royal College of Technology (KTH) in Stockholm, and its outlook was clearly marked by the Swedish model of postwar industrial development, centered on heavy industry and an engineering mentality. But the overall picture reflected what was at the time common sense in international managerial science. Since then, the nature of industrial production and value creation has changed. Production has been outsourced, and now happens in globalized value chains or "value networks." Value has come to be conceptualized in mysterious terms like "intangibles," which have a very unclear relationship to the concrete business of processing tangible inputs into equally tangible outputs. In this chapter we will delve deeper into these transformations, into the depths of production, as Marx said, to understand what the concept "intangibles" really means.

Intangible assets are important in postindustrial economies. They make up around 70 percent of the market value of companies and attract some 7 percent of total investments in the United States (similar figures apply for other advanced postindustrial economies as well).[2] But these figures remain tentative, as there is no common agreement on how to measure the value of intangibles. Just defining the value of a brand, for example, remains thorny, with widely varying methods being used, as was noted in chapter 1.[3]

In this chapter we will suggest that the very concept of "intangibles" has emerged as a way to make sense of the discrepancy between the market value and the book value of companies, which has resulted from the declining relevance of an earlier industrial, or "Fordist," value regime. This declining relevance is in turn the effect of two important and interconnected tendencies, what we call the networking of production and the financialization of value.

Two perhaps controversial points should be mentioned here. First, the combination of the networking of value and the financialization of production might point toward a new mode of production, one founded on an economy of commons. Second, the concept of "intangibles," however mysterious and irrational it is *right now*, might harbor the seeds of a new way of rationally determining and measuring value in such an economy of commons: a new value regime.

First, we need a better understanding of what the previous value regime, Fordism, looked like. Given the complexity of these matters, such a description will necessarily be something of a straw man, providing no more than a poor reflection of historical reality (a reality that is in continual flux, partly in reaction to the very tendencies that we seek to describe). Rather, we intend this picture as a Weberian ideal type: a model that does not so much describe reality as it is, but allows us to say something about that reality, if only by providing a contrasting backdrop for the emergence of what we consider to be really new and interesting.[4]

FORDISM

Ever since the 1960s there has been a debate within the social sciences about the possible emergence of a new, postindustrial economic paradigm, and, as a consequence, a number of attempts to delineate the main characteristics of the older, "industrial" model that was supposed to be left behind. The most influential of these efforts—ideas about a "knowledge economy," an "information economy," or the salience of new kinds of "immaterial labor"—have all implied that the core of the transformation under way would be some kind of shift from material production to immaterial production as the strategically most important source of value and profits.[5] While this is true in part, the issue at hand is also more complex. First, although the productive importance of immaterial factors like knowledge and information has increased in recent decades, the early-nineteenth-century industrial economy was also a "knowledge economy," in the sense that it built on the systematic cultivation of innovation and technological change. Indeed, along with Italian sociologist Enzo Rullani (as well as many economic historians), we can argue that the standardization and new ease of knowledge circulation has been the main driver of economic development for the whole of the modern era.[6] Second, although the relative weight of manufacturing has declined in developed economies since the 1970s, industrial production has by no means disappeared from the world economy. What is more, the present integration of material and immaterial production—of products and brand image, for example—makes it very difficult to separate the two. Who produces the materiality of the McDonald's hamburger? Is it only the person who actually fries it up in the kitchen, or is it also the person who brings it to the counter, smiles, and produces the customer experience? Such questions, while possible, become futile and academic in a world where branding and design are ever more integrated into productive processes.[7]

We argue that the transformation under way can be better understood by focusing on how the production process—including the relation between material and immaterial production—is organized. From this perspective we offer an ideal-typical description of the industrial economy that builds on four central divisions: between the factory and society, between "intellectual" and "manual" labor, between production and consumption, and between discrete and neatly separated tasks. In the interest of having a simple term, we follow what is now an established tradition in social science parlance and describe this way of organizing value creation as "Fordism."[8] We will then explain how the changes in productive relations that have been under way since the 1970s have produced a blurring of these divisions.

Factory and Society

The industrial model that we are used to taking for granted developed in the second half of the nineteenth century as a result of the new kinds of productive relations that became possible through new technologies like electricity, the internal combustion engine, railroad transport, and mass communications. Together these advances allowed for new economies of scale to be realized by concentrating production in a central process. Mass-production technologies, like the assembly line, that required massive capital investment could now produce standardized consumer goods for expanding national markets. This model of large-scale, complex productive processes that were spatially concentrated in a single factory soon began to replace earlier, more diffuse networks of small workshops or putting-out systems that depended on domestic labor. The advantages of standardization (themselves given by the relative predictability of demand in mass markets) drove strategies of vertical integration such that ever larger corporations could control an ever larger share of the value chain by buying up suppliers and retailers. (In the 1920s, for example, the Ford Motor Company ran coal and iron mines, a rubber plantation, freighters, sawmills, blast furnaces, and glass works. All of these products were assembled into cars in the giant Ford factory at River Rouge, Michigan.) The ideal for the better part of the twentieth century was a large, integrated corporation that could own and manage most of its assets, while minimizing its reliance on market transactions.[9] The industrial model was thus not open, but closed: production took place in a private space to which access was regulated.

Intellectual Labor and Manual Labor

The rise of large industrial corporations and the implementation of the assembly line favored the popularity of "Taylorist" principles of scientific management. While Frederick W. Taylor himself did not invent these ideas (rather similar practices had been developing since the mid-1800s), his 1911 work *Principles of Scientific Management* popularized them. Taylorism built on the principle that gains in efficiency could be made if production could be reorganized according to standardized, scientific principles. This resulted in the development of a number of disciplines devoted to the study of work, like time-motion studies, ergonomics, psychotechnics, and so on, that created detailed "scientific" instructions for executing each moment in the production process. Workers were supposed to simply follow these instructions. While Taylorism was implemented to varying degrees in different industries, its persistence as an ideal created a general drift toward the separation of the intellectual labor of planning and improving on the work process from the manual labor of actually executing an existing work description. While this separation was never total—many companies continued to rely on worker input as a source of innovation and improvement—it did drive a general tendency toward the "de-skilling of work," particularly in relation to the higher levels of craftsmanship required by pre-Fordist, nineteenth-century capitalism.[10] (It can also be argued that the implementation of the assembly line and of Taylorist scientific management in the United States was to some extent a response to the political militancy of highly skilled workers. These new techniques allowed them to be replaced by less-skilled, and less politically aware, recent immigrants.)[11]

Production and Consumption

Through the development of the industrial corporation, productive processes were ever more separated from everyday life, and productive "work" tended to happen in the "factory," a place distinct from the "home." This obviously had consequences for consumption as well. While people in preindustrial societies mostly used goods that they themselves or people in their immediate vicinity had produced, the development of industrial mass production was paralleled by the growth of consumer markets and the consumption of commodities as a way of satisfying needs and desires.[12] While production and consumption had formerly unfolded within the same social unit, the household, they were now spatially and socially separated. Production took place in large, enclosed factories, the insides of which were hidden from public view, while consumption took place in the equally private sphere of the home.[13] Consequently, consumption was conceived of as a purely wasteful activity that simply uses up the value added in production.

Value and the Separation of Tasks

The large-scale industrial corporations that now governed production required more-advanced forms of managerial control, spurring a "managerial revolution" in which new technologies like scientific management, marketing, and new accounting systems developed, along with the rise of a culturally influential "managerial class."[14] The managerial systems that developed were all bureaucratic, in the Weberian sense of the term: they built on the separation of the production process into discrete, well-defined tasks. This approach was reflected in organizational structures that separated corporations into specific functional departments, like production, marketing, personnel, and so on, and in the practice of providing managers as well as workers with specific "job descriptions" that detailed their tasks and responsibilities, in keeping with the "Taylorist" philosophies of scientific management that increasingly governed the organization of factory production.[15]

Most important was the development of cost accounting as the main source of both financial and operational information. Following the principles of scientific management, engineers developed "scientific" cost standards for each procedure, which could subsequently be used to determine the productivity of each moment in the production process and discover where improvements could be made. Thus cost accounting became an important measure of efficiency and productivity.[16] Along with general bureaucratic principles of management, cost accounting subdivided the complex interactions that now marked productive processes into discrete units that could be measured and evaluated in relation to overall standards, allowing corporations to attribute value creation to singular processes or even to individuals. What eventually developed was a notion of productivity that could be invoked as a common standard for the determination of wages, as Frederick Taylor himself had recommended. (Such a procedure was facilitated by the fact that, in most industries, labor costs were much larger relative to overhead in early-twentieth-century industrial production than today. In the 1890s labor costs amounted to about 90 percent of value creation in U.S. industry; today the figure is closer to 10 percent.)[17]

To summarize: Fordism emerged as a way of organizing production in response to the more complex forms of productive cooperation that became possible with the advent of new technologies like electricity, railroads, and mass communications. It tended to concentrate the production process in closed proprietary spaces (like factories), where it could be subdivided into neat and easily measurable tasks. This supported a value regime built on the convention that economic value could reasonably be understood as related to the precise measures of time spent in productive activity that were now available. Consequently, the value of companies corresponded rather well to the value of their proprietary productive assets that were "put to work" in such measurable forms of productive activity (their book value), and economic performance overall could quite neatly be explained by the productivity of such "tangible assets." But that value convention no longer makes much sense. The productivity of "tangible assets" has been in accelerating decline throughout the postwar years, and the market values of companies, as well as their profits, are more frequently attributed to a different and more mysterious class of assets, intangibles.[18] How can we explain this change?

POST-FORDISM

At the most obvious level, the transformation of the old, industrial economy is clearly indicated by data that show a continuous decline in the share of employment and value added attributed to the manufacturing sector in what used to be called "core" countries, like the United States, Canada, Australia, and Western Europe. Instead, the service sector, in particular finance, retail, transport, and management, has grown in importance.

However, at the same time that the economic weight of industrial production has declined in "core" countries, it has risen in formerly "peripheral" countries, like Korea, Mexico, and Thailand, as well as, importantly, in countries that were formerly more or less isolated from the capitalist economy, like Russia, India, and China.[19] To some extent this process of what used to be called peripheral (or "semi-peripheral") industrialization represents a new competitive challenge to the former core industries, resulting from technology and capital transfer, as in the rise of the Korean auto and ship industries.[20] But it also reflects a different economic organization, a radical transformation within the organization of production itself that has led to the emergence of global value chains where material production is disproportionally located to low-wage former "peripheral" countries, while corporate services like marketing, management, and finance are located to former "core" countries like the United States. However, this description is, once again, too simplistic—first, because the division of labor in "core" cities, like New York or London, is much more complicated, involving a fair amount of material production, sometimes in the kinds of sweatshop conditions that one would expect to find only in low-wage countries, and second, because corporate services and "creative industries" are a growing component of the economy of many formerly peripheral cities, like Shanghai or Mumbai.[21] Most important, however, a perspective that focuses simply on the relocation of industrial production fails to understand the basic reorganization of industrial production, which stands behind these changes—and which might very well drive relocation in the reverse direction in the future. (In fact, multinationals like IKEA are now relocating material production to the U.S. South, where, given higher levels of productivity, labor costs are now approaching Chinese levels.)[22] In order to understand those basic structural changes, we need to delve more deeply into the complex transformations of productive relations that have marked the world economy since the 1970s.

The Italian economist Andrea Fumagalli suggests that the "new paradigm" can be fruitfully understood as a combination of three overlapping yet distinct models: (1) the Japanese, or "Toyotist," model developed at Toyota in the late 1960s and early 1970s, which combines flexible production, self-organized teams, and just-in-time flows with "Taylorist" subdivision of tasks and the organization of production around the large factory, typical of the industrial model; (2) the "Italian" model of "industrial districts," which deploys networks of small, specialized firms; and (3) global value chains, combining a diverse typology of firms, from small component manufacturers to large assembly plants, which are often organized in clear hierarchies (as between first-, second-, and third-tier suppliers).[23] These models share a number of common characteristics.

The Networking of Production

One of the most important features of the debates on industrial restructuring that have raged since the 1980s has been the focus on the "networking" of the production process beyond the factory walls. This notion became popular in the 1980s, as a consequence of the success of Japanese "Toyotist" production systems and of the new forms of "flexible specialization" that economists like MIT's Michael Piore and Charles Sabel identified in Italian industrial districts. In their view, these districts constituted extended production networks, in which flexible adaptation to demand was guaranteed by small producers that could easily enter into cooperation with one another, vary their output, and shift from one product to another. The Toyotist philosophy, developed by Taiichi Ohno at Toyota in the 1960s and 1970s, built on an extended supply chain that involved a large number of small suppliers, located mainly in Taiwan and the Philippines. Both in the case of the Italian industrial district and in the case of the Toyotist factory, a significant part of the production process unfolded within such networks, operating outside the direct control of the central corporation, whether that be Toyota, Armani, or some other company. In other words, the central tenet of the industrial model to concentrate as much of the production process as possible in the factory was inverted, replaced by locating an ever-larger share of production in productive networks that could unfold outside of factory walls. Such increased outsourcing of production continued in the 1980s with the development of ever more global supply chains, principally in the areas of automobiles, computers, clothing, and consumer electronics. Between 1985 and 2000, for example, the share of vehicle value derived from outsourcing increased from 50 to 80 percent for Renault, and between 1997 and 2004 the share of (outsourced) imports to the U.S. auto parts market grew from 40 percent to 65 percent. Today the supply chain of a car maker like Hyundai involves 400 first-tier suppliers and 2,500 second-tier suppliers.[24]

The replacement of large factories and vertically integrated corporations with diffuse networks of small producers, numbering in the thousands and sometimes extended across the globe, clearly suggests a socialization of production. Production no longer only, or even mainly, takes place within the secluded and controlled space of the factory; it happens in a network that extends into the web of social relations that surrounds the factory. This development is even more pronounced in the Italian industrial districts, where, as Piore and Sabel reported, productive relations tended to more or less coincide with social relations. The secret to the success of these districts was high levels of what sociologists call "social capital," which enabled high levels of trust and informational transparency to be derived from normal forms of social interaction.

The Impact of Information Technology

In many ways the new networked model of production resembles a return to earlier forms of craft production, employing small factories that perform highly particular tasks. But there are also substantial differences. The success of the Toyotist model in the 1970s and 1980s was a result of new levels of integration of information and communication technology within the production process itself: the availability of new kinds of programmable and highly versatile computer numerically controlled (CNC) machinery; the development of platforms for collaborative, computer-aided design (CAD); and new technologies, like intranets, that allowed the management of the complex logistics necessary for such extended supply chains. This new technological platform (or "relatively new platform"—both CNC machinery and CAD go back to the 1960s, but the technology had its real breakthrough in the early 1980s) had two principal consequences.[25] First, the integration of CAD and CNC machinery allowed a merger of the standardization of design typical of industrial production with the flexibility and "economies of scope" typical of craft production.

As a result, productive networks became much more flexible and able to produce smaller batches of each product or component. This in turn made possible both the just-in-time philosophy of reduced inventories and the higher degrees of customization and flexible market response that have become central to the post-Fordist production paradigm in sectors ranging from automobiles to clothing. (Such flexibility and ability to "breathe with the market" is now the main driver of the success of "fast-fashion" retailers like Zara.) Second, this new technology allowed more-advanced forms of automation, and thus production costs declined. In particular, the share of value attributable to direct labor costs has declined significantly in highly automated industries, like electronics, machine tools, and automobiles. In the case of the iPod, for example, material production costs (including patents and raw materials) make up about $35 of a retail price of $199, and the labor spent in assembly accounts for $3 or $4. This development has made material production, particularly production of the standardized components that go into mass products like computers and television sets, increasingly "commoditized," with profit margins that approach zero.[26] The spread of technology and the accompanying decline in production costs means that the share of overall value added attributable to material production declines, and the strategic focus on value creation shifts toward other aspects of the process, principally innovation, brand, and flexibility.

In this context "innovation" refers to improvements in the product, in the process, or (perhaps most important for extended networks of production) in the procedures available to implement and guarantee quality levels. This can be a matter of patents and other forms of legally recognized immaterial property, but often it is a matter of "tacit" knowledge, informal know-how of competences that are embodied in singular individuals or particular processes or "communities of practice."[27] "Brand" stands for the significant affective relations that a company is able to inspire in its stakeholders, consumers, employees, subcontractors, and the public at large. Aspects of branding would include reputation, goodwill, and perceptions of social responsibility. "Flexibility" refers to the ability of a company to respond quickly to market changes, to "breathe with the market."

Cooperation

The ways in which these three "immaterial" or "intangible" assets are produced have changed significantly from the industrial model. The production of such immaterial values is no longer the privilege of specially designated forms of "intellectual" labor; rather the production of innovation, brand, and flexibility is increasingly integrated with the labor process itself. Take the case of innovation: while the Enlightenment idea of the "lonely genius" was to a large extent a myth, and while the production of both technical and scientific innovation has unfolded within large-scale collaborative networks for at least the last fifty years, the industrial model did build on a distinct separation between the production of innovation and the production of material goods. Innovation was to take place in R&D departments and employ personnel with particular skills, and it was rare that systematic attention was paid to the ability of ordinary workers or consumers to contribute to that process.[28] In recent decades this model has changed significantly. First, the combination of CAD and CNC creates a platform for standardization of design and technical specifications (in the form of a CAD file). Thus is becomes easier for participants in the productive network, like the factories to which material production has been subcontracted, to contribute their experience toward the elaboration of product designs. The Toyotist system made use of this possibility from the start, favoring communication and knowledge sharing among suppliers and integrating them in co-innovation systems around quality improvement and process innovation. Today this is standard practice in the automobile industry, where globalization strategies have led to the proliferation of strategic partnerships in which suppliers are integrated in co-innovation networks around common platforms, and where assemblers might often require suppliers to achieve certain results in terms of continuous quality improvement or cost reduction.[29] Similar strategies are used in the electronics and pharmaceutical industries, where customers, suppliers, and sometimes even competitors are integrated into innovation commons. Some companies, like Procter & Gamble, have successfully launched open innovation platforms that involve consumers and members of the public at large as well. Its "connect and develop" initiative is said to have increased the productivity of R&D by 30 percent since its introduction in 2002, by directly capitalizing on the knowledge and "creativity" of external actors.[30] The fact that the name of this program replaces the R in "research" with the C in "connect," testifies to a new view of knowledge production: value can be accumulated simply by connecting and linking knowledgeable individuals, organizations, or networks that are located inside as well as outside the "factory walls," to enable them to communicate and exchange experiences. Similar strategies of "knowledge management" or the furthering of collective intelligence have applied to workers as well.

In the original Toyotist model, worker teams were required to participate in quality circles and encouraged to contribute their hands-on knowledge of the production process to product and process innovation. Similarly, contemporary strategies of knowledge management seek to render the individual's tacit knowledge explicit and to constitute new kinds of inter- or intra-firm publics that facilitate knowledge sharing and collective innovation processes among employees. This is particularly pronounced in the case of managerial work, where, as the new discipline of "knowledge management" teaches, the key to gaining competitive advantage is seen as facilitating the flow of knowledge within organizations.[31]

The Toyotist model utilized similar strategies for the maximization of flexibility. In its earlier, pre-computer version, the system required that workers send notes to one another with information on the quantity of materials consumed "upstream" in the production process, thus generating continuous information on the actual quantity of input required. In today's factories, the paper system has been replaced with computerized information systems. But the principle is the same: the high levels of flexibility and adaptability required by just-in-time production systems are themselves produced not by designated "experts," like the engineers that elaborated the "correct" standards for the industrial production system, but by the ability to build on the communication and interaction among workers themselves. Already in the Toyotist system worker teams were encouraged to organize the concrete details of their share of the production process and rendered collectively responsible for its correct, high-quality execution.[32] This philosophy of teamwork has since spread to many sectors of shop floor work, as well as to "knowledge work" proper, where "the project team," responsible for the organization and execution of a particular task, has become the default organizational form. Finally, the production of brand has been equally socialized. Today a brand is much more than a mere symbol of a product, created by the designated marketing division. Rather, brands are better understood as something akin to a common "ethos" that is able to cohere consumers, employees, and other stakeholders around a common "enterprise," be this the reproduction of the particular "feel" associated with a consumer brand or the co-construction of the common sense of purpose that defines a corporate brand. While such operations can be directed and supervised by brand managers, the recent literature on both consumer and corporate branding stresses the necessity to involve consumers, coworkers, and other stakeholders as active participants to the process.[33]

To summarize: the "disorganization" of Fordism has many complex causes. One important structural factor has been the arrival of new information and communication technologies that have permitted more advanced forms of productive cooperation, principally through the networking of productive processes "outside of the factory walls," metaphorically speaking. This new networking of production has had the important effect of reducing the added value that derives from the actual production of goods. In part this has happened as automation has reduced the overall contribution of labor. Mostly, however, it has occurred as the networking of production has transformed the skills and competences needed to undertake advanced forms of material production from exclusive secrets to which only a few factories had access to something close to common knowledge. This shift has relocated the strategic source of profits and competitive advantage from material production per se (and consequently from the productivity of tangible assets) to other assets that are more difficult to measure, chiefly the capacity for innovation, flexibility, and brand. Moreover, it has changed the ways in which these assets are produced. No longer the product of particularly skilled knowledge workers, the creation of innovation, flexibility, and brand is premised on extended forms of cooperation that traverse the whole value network and that put to work common resources, like the common knowledge of workers and consumers that goes into innovation or the common communicative capacity that is put to work in organizing flexibility of response. As Peter Drucker saw in the early 1990s, automation and the impact of information technologies mean that true competitive advantage ever more often comes from the ability to put *universally available knowledge* to work in new and innovative ways.[34]

General Intellect

Put in perspective, this development can be seen as one step in a continuous trend on the part of the capitalist economy to both increase the scope of the cooperative processes on which it depends and deepen its reliance on common resources. Indeed, early thinkers like Adam Smith and Karl Marx already understood this tendency as central to their analysis of the emerging industrial economy.

It is true that Adam Smith stressed the wonders of competition and the market, but that is only part of the story. He also showed how the development of new and more complex forms of production required unprecedented levels of cooperation. Indeed, Smith's *other* famous example (apart from that of him "getting his bacon from the self-interest of the butcher"), that of the pin factory, which begins his *Inquiry into the Nature and Causes of the Wealth of Nations*, is about showing how the productivity of labor increases enormously through such new forms of cooperation. Before the advent of industrial capitalism, pins—and other items like chairs, knives, cheese, and sausages—were made by individual craftsmen who generally finished the product by themselves, mastering every step in its production. In the pin factory, on the other hand,

> one man draws out the wire, another straights it, a third cuts it, a fourth points it, a fifth grinds it at the top for receiving the head; to make the head requires two or three distinct operations; to put it on is a peculiar business, to whiten the pins is another; it is even a trade by itself to put them in paper; and the important business of making a pin is, in this manner, divided into about eighteen distinct operations, which in some manufacture, are all performed by distinct hands, though in others the same man will sometimes perform two or three of them.

By thus involving more people who act in a more coordinated way, the capitalist production process is socialized, and new, higher levels of co-operation can materialize. By thus increasing the levels of cooperation among pin-makers, productivity can be increased:

> Those ten people could, therefore, make among them upwards of 48,000 pins in a day. Each person, therefore, making a tenth part of 48,000 pins, might be considered to be making 4,800 pins a day. But if they had all wrought separately and independently, and without any of them having been educated to this peculiar business, they certainly could not each of them have made twenty, perhaps not one pin, a day.[35]

So there are two sides to the capitalist mode of production—private pursuit of self-interest on the one hand and social cooperation on the other.

Marx develops this argument even further, in particular in the *Grundrisse*—his working notes toward *Capital*, which he never intended to publish (but which were published anyway, in Moscow in 1939, long after his death)—in a dense and somewhat contorted passage that has been retroactively titled the "Passage on Machinery."[36] Here Marx stresses how the capitalist economy creates ever more complex networks of production, from large factories, where workers were connected to steam engines by means of transmission belts and where each department manufactured one piece of the final product, to the world market, where many factories were connected to a great multitude of consumers. As the economy grows it comes to involve ever more people and machines, and they are connected in ever more complex ways. Marx argues that as this complexity and interconnectedness increase, the relative importance of labor as a source of wealth will decline in favor of what he calls General Intellect, or publicly available knowledge and skills. It is not "labor time" itself as much as it is the "forces set in motion during labor time"—the complex network of machinery, competences, and social networks that the worker operates during labor time—that becomes the main source of wealth. Indeed, with the increasing importance of General Intellect, the worker

> steps to the side of the production process instead of being its chief actor. In this transformation, it is neither the direct human labour he himself performs, nor the time during which he works, but rather the appropriation of his own general productive power . . . which appears as the great foundation-stone of production and of wealth.[37]

Where does this "general productive power" come from? From intensified and remediated processes of social communication: complex forms of social cooperation not only render the division of labor more efficient, they also tend to intensify social communication, exchange, and the sharing of knowledge, experiences, and practices. Workers begin to talk to each other and learn from each other. They move from one factory to another and spread new practices and insights. Engineers and managers talk to subcontractors, clients, and even competitors. Overall, the new social formation that arises around a complex system of production, mediated by machinery, transport, and new forms of personal encounters creates a new network of intensified and focused social interaction. This in turn generates a common resource in the form of a stock of knowledge, experiences, and "best practices" that can be drawn upon as a source for further innovation and improvement.

Today, management scholars call this process "collective intelligence," but it is no new thing. Rather, recent historical writings on the industrial revolution stress the fundamental importance of what Marx already called General Intellect. If the scientific Enlightenment, the new discoveries in physics, chemistry, botany, and medicine that took place during the eighteenth century, was generally far too abstract to translate into concrete industrial technologies, at least before the 1830s, the early decades of the nineteenth century were marked by what economic historians now call an "industrial enlightenment." This consisted in a number of more mundane interventions that tended to facilitate and intensify the collective production of knowledge. First, artisan practices began to be surveyed and catalogued, and the superior ones were promoted and diffused. What used to be private knowledge, available only to a particular master and his apprentices, now became generally available as part of the public domain. Second, a common language developed in which to talk about industrial technology, like common forms of drawing and mechanical illustration, common ideas and notions of mechanical principles, common measurements and the emergence of standardization. Third, there was a growing circulation of knowledge. More-efficient transports enabled workers and engineers to move between factories, a new postal system enabled books and journals to spread more efficiently, local scientific societies encouraged the interaction between technicians and scientists. And finally, as a result of these new forms of mediation, a new "scientific mentality" emerged, "which imbued engineers and inventors with a faith in the orderliness, rationality and predictability of natural phenomena—even if the actual laws underlying physics and chemistry were not yet fully understood. . . . In other words, the view that nature was intelligible slowly gained ground."[38]

Seen this way, the increasing socialization of knowledge production, its ability to circulate and be promiscuous in new ways, was one important factor that drove the industrial revolution. It did so by radically increasing the stock of common knowledge, the General Intellect that resulted from these new forms of cooperation. The important thing about General Intellect is that it arises not from individual genius but from communication and interaction. It builds on the generic qualities of the human mind and body, which are made productive in a new sense by being mediated and connected in a different fashion through information and communication technologies. Indeed, Marx defines this "general productive power" as the worker's "understanding of nature and his mastery over it by virtue of his presence as a social body—it is, in a word, the development of the social individual which appears as the great foundation stone of production and of wealth." It is by being part of a social context, through one's development as a social individual, that one comes to have "access" to General Intellect. From this point of view we can argue that the real contribution of information and communication technologies (ICTs) first in the industrial production process, and later, with the diffusion of the Internet, in social relations more generally, has been that of increasing the level and intensity of productive cooperation. This in turn has generated a much greater reservoir of common resources, of General Intellect and publicly available skills and competences that can be employed by a wide variety of actors across a diversity of situations. Thus many forms of knowledge that were previously private and tacit have become public, explicit, and *common*.

VALUE CRISIS

The new levels of productive cooperation that have become possible with the impact of ICTs have posed a serious challenge to the Fordist value regime. That regime was built around an industrial paradigm that was developed at the end of the nineteenth century to accommodate the new and more complex forms of productive collaboration that had evolved in the "second industrial revolution" of the late 1800s. Electricity, the internal combustion engine, and particularly the assembly line and the new mass communication and transport technologies that made possible the formation of national markets had radically increased the levels of productive cooperation within the economy. The modern corporation, with its bureaucratic organization and its specific managerial disciplines, developed during the managerial revolution of the last decades of the nineteenth century as a way to meet this challenge. The development of modern cost accounting was part of this response. As we hinted above, cost accounting systems, along with scientific management, allowed the production process to be subdivided into distinct tasks, with the productivity and value added of each task easily measured by relating the amount of productive time spent (labor time and other variable costs, essentially) to output. This approach was feasible for two reasons. First, since labor time accounted for the lion's share of production costs, measuring the productivity of labor time provided a good source of information on the efficacy of the production process. Second, the Taylorist organization of production itself allowed a "natural" subdivision into discrete tasks, the productivity of which could be related to set standards. Today these factors no longer apply. First, labor costs are now a small share of total production costs, while overheads, in terms of machinery, logistics, patents, and intangibles, have gained in relevance. Second, the types of communicative processes standing behind the production of innovation, brand, and flexibility cut across discrete tasks and functions, thus making them less easy to divide according to the principles of cost accounting. Finally, the production of innovation, brand, or flexibility does not exhibit a linear relation to the amount of time invested. (This assumption of non-linearity is also central to the two economic paradigms that have risen to meet this challenge: learning economies and network economies.)[39] Rather it is a matter of what Italian philosopher Paolo Virno calls "virtuosity," an inspiring leadership, a functioning project team, a brilliant idea.[40] Thus the principle around which established accounting systems have been built—measuring and comparing the productivity of the time spent in production by a discrete unit—no longer makes much sense.

This does not mean that there are no methods that can account for the new productivity. Accounting has advanced since the 1930s when today's systems and standards were stabilized. Even though official standards are slow to change, practical accounting systems used for the provision of managerial information have progressed significantly. The most important development is perhaps "lean accounting" or "value stream analysis," which uses a multiplicity of indicators to arrive at information about the efficiency of each value stream (defined as a business process that delivers a product or service to a customer). This philosophy focuses on the efficiency of the entire production flow rather than just a singular unit. Total Quality Management (or TQM) constitutes an earlier approach that relies on a number of quantitative indicators to measure or provide benchmarks for quality performance. And TQM as well as value stream analysis can easily be extended to include both the supply chain and the distribution network. Within the tradition of knowledge management a number of other indicators have developed, from scorecards and benchmarks to social network analysis (to identify the real communication hubs in an organization).

Two points are important to stress here. First, value stream analysis takes as its object cooperation along an entire value chain rather than the performance of a single unit. This approach effectively severs the link between value and time (since what determines value is not only or even chiefly the time spent by individual units, but also the level of synergy among them). Instead, what is measured is the productivity of cooperation, assessed by a wide variety of diverse indicators. Second, these systems mainly aim at providing information to managers. They have little impact on the financial information that companies provide to their external stakeholders. Rather, a new kind of productivity, defined as the capacity to generate innovation, brand, and flexibility, is reported as intangible assets. From "the point of view of production," intangible assets thus measure and represent excellence in the deployment of common resources.

At the same time, the development of the concept of intangibles has been a reaction to the financialization of the economy, and to rising discrepancies between the market value and the book value of companies in particular. Can there be any rational connection between these two phenomena? Is there a way in which the financial valuation of companies can be understood to rationally reflect their "excellence" in the utilization of common resources? In order to begin to ponder that question we need to take a deeper look at the dynamics behind the financialization of the economy.

The reasons for the spectacular rise in the importance of finance are complex and intertwined. First, the computerization, networking, and technological refinement of financial markets have vastly increased their speed and scope. Financial markets have always been at the forefront in the use of electronic media as market information systems, starting with the introduction of the stock market ticker in the 1870s.[41] In the 1980s, traders and investment banks were connected in a network of computer terminals, and with the rise of quantitative finance in the 1970s automatic trading algorithms became possible. Finally, finance went through something of a technological revolution in the 1990s as the classic "trading pits" were replaced with computer terminals and computerized trading systems allowing the high-speed execution of automatic trading "bots."[42]

Second, deregulation and other policy decisions have further accelerated the process. The financialization of the U.S. economy took off in earnest in the 1980s, as a result of the turn to monetarism and the strong dollar. These were conscious policy choices driven by the goal of substituting finance for a manufacturing sector that had shown strong signs of decline for over a decade. In the 1990s the Clinton administration continued deregulating the banking system, opening the way for "one-stop financial supermarkets" that could combine the previously separate activities of commercial banking, investment banking, and insurance. This tendency continued in the Bush administration, which was instrumental in creating the regulatory environments that made possible the subprime boom of the 2000s, as well as internationally, where the World Trade Organization (WTO) has pushed strongly for the deregulation and opening up of national financial markets. Such policy initiatives were also important at the local level. In the 1980s, Margaret Thatcher was already following an elaborate strategy of substituting financial services for a declining industrial sector as the basis of the British economy. By loosening regulation and introducing favorable treatment, she managed to attract a massive inflow of banks and other financial service companies to London, enabling the capital to regain its former position as a world center of finance. The city of New York pursued a similar strategy after its fiscal collapse in 1975.[43]

There is also a strong connection between the geopolitics of economic globalization and the expanded importance of financial markets. The event that triggered the emergence of the contemporary financial economy was the collapse of the Bretton Woods system in 1971, which put an end to the stable currency regime that had guided the steady economic development of the postwar "golden age."[44] This created higher levels of volatility, which generated a greater scope for financial speculation and fueled the activity on currency markets in particular. The collapse of Bretton Woods had itself been, in part, a result of the growth of offshore "Eurodollar" markets, mainly U.S. corporate profits deposited in the European banking system and thus multiplying outside of the control of the U.S. Federal Reserve. At a certain point, in 1971, the U.S. Federal Reserve had lost its control over the money supply to the point of no longer being able to guarantee the (by now largely symbolic) convertibility of the dollar into gold. Hence the end of Bretton Woods. The OPEC maneuver in 1973 gave an additional injection of liquidity to these markets as the new oil revenues were invested in the U.S. and European banking systems.[45]

Underneath these developments, however, lies an important structural connection between the financialization of value and the processes of networking and socialization of production discussed earlier in this chapter.

In the United States, the finance, insurance, and real estate (FIRE) sector itself has grown to account for the largest share of overall corporate profits (45 percent in 2001), far surpassing both manufacturing (10 percent) and other services (3 percent). In part this development has resulted from the growing turnover of financial markets overall and by the increasing financial orientation of companies, driven to no small degree by the importance of "shareholder-oriented corporate governance."[46] But the growth of financial rent as part of corporate profits has also been an effect of the expansion of the scope of financial instruments themselves, and their integration into the ordinary dynamics of both production and consumption.

The global networking of production has put a premium on flexibility and just-in-time response. But to guarantee just-in-time response seriously strains cash flow and liquidity. In addition, low inventories, intensive use of logistics, and flexible and often short-term inter-firm relations have combined to greatly increase the levels of risk inherent in the system. This has expanded the financialization of inter-firm relations, as individual actors now have greater needs for advance liquidity or insurance against client default. Indeed, large multinationals often exercise control over their value networks through the financial level, anticipating liquidity to their suppliers and consumers and thriving on differentials in terms of payment. Hence companies like General Motors or Fiat, as well as many other producers of consumer durables, make more money from financing suppliers and consumer purchases than from the direct sale of commodities. From this perspective, General Motors makes automobiles as an excuse for being able to make money as a bank. Combined with the reduced contribution of direct commodity production to value added, the implications of the spread of the financialization of inter-firm relations are quite radical. In the industrial economy, the production of wealth and the appropriation of value tended to coincide. Simply put, a capitalist bought a plant, hired some workers, and skimmed off the surplus value through his ability to control the production process. Today, the production process is financialized at a multitude of points (supplier relations, consumer credit, insurance, etc.), and value is skimmed off to financial markets, where it circulates globally.[47]

A similar point can be made about households. The most important aspect here has been the transformation of welfare systems. This field has seen a general shift from state financing to financial markets as the main vehicle of distribution. The change has been most often expressed in the field of pensions, where in the 1980s the introduction of 401(k) plans in the United States (and of similar systems in other countries, like Sweden, in the following decades) directly channeled parts of pension savings into financial markets. This move constituted a major injection of liquidity that further boosted the growth of these markets and made the future wealth, and even livelihood, of a large share of the population directly dependent on their dynamics.[48] Similarly, the neoliberal policies that have been implemented in most of the West since the 1980s have promoted private home ownership. Thus a growing number of people have become dependent on mortgage financing, and hence on the level of interest rates set on bond markets. Since the 2000s, the introduction of new financial instruments that have allowed for the securitization of mortgage debt has further expanded the access to mortgage-financed private housing, and hence has further strengthened the link between access to housing and the dynamics of financial markets.

The second most important source of rising household debt has been the financialization of consumption. This is primarily visible in the rise of credit card and other kinds of consumer debt, such as the forms of "captive" financing that accompany the sales of automobiles and other durable consumer goods. While debt-financed consumption has a long history in the United States, it has boomed in the 2000s, along with the proliferation of new forms of "subprime" securities by means of which risks can be passed on and absorbed by the market. In February 2008, total U.S. home mortgage debt was $11 trillion, credit card debt around $1 trillion, and automobile debt around $700 billion. This rise in debt related to consumption and housing has not only created a negative savings rate in the United States (and the tendency, if not the numbers, is similar in Western Europe), but also points to a new centrality of financial markets as mechanisms of both wealth creation and wealth distribution.[49] Simply put, in the industrial model wealth would primarily be accumulated through private savings, and once one had saved enough, one would go out and buy an automobile or a washing machine. (This is, of course, a gross oversimplification, but the steady fall of the household saving rate gives some substance to the caricature.) In the present model, financial markets anticipate the resources needed to purchase a house or a car, or whatever else one might need, in exchange for a share of one's future earning capacity.

We can add two other developments to this picture. First, financial rent as a share of personal income has risen, particularly among the wealthier classes, who have been able to participate in the inflation of asset prices that has marked the last three decades (and for the upper levels of the managerial class who have seen a substantial rise in share of their overall income attributed to bonuses).

Second, the centrality of the salaried male breadwinner as the main provider of household income has declined. Instead, household income tends to derive from a multitude of diverse sources: regular salaried employment, short-term work, consultancy, children's work, unpaid activities that can be monetized in different ways, entrepreneurship, engagements with the informal economy, and importantly, real estate speculation and other forms of financial rent.[50] Conversely, the financialization of everyday life, particularly through the expansion of mortgage and credit card debt, provides a way of capturing value from a wide range of diverse activities that might have little to do with the (mostly male) breadwinner wage that, at least theoretically, was the most important mechanism for wealth distribution in the industrial model. In that model, the employment contract guaranteed the worker a secure long-term access to the means for the reproduction of life. And it provided the capitalist with a secure long-term predictable stream of surplus labor in the form of the productivity of the working day that exceeded the cost of labor. In the present model the financial system anticipates necessities for the reproduction of life (a house, health insurance, etc.) and receives in turn a long-term and (relatively, or at least calculably) secure value stream in the form of interest payments. The interest payments become a direct extraction of surplus from the whole life, from the *bíos* of the population.

This model suggests that financial markets are becoming increasingly influential as factors in determining not only corporate profits but individual wealth and welfare as well. Indeed, for more and more people the tendency is that position vis-à-vis the financial system, and ability to attract rent, grows in importance in relation to revenues from employment as a factor of wealth. In an economy where the production of wealth is ever more socialized, and ever more occurs outside the direct control of the Fordist wage relation, access to wealth is ever less determined by that wage relation and instead is determined by one's position with respect to financial markets.

Maybe what we have here is the basis of a new value regime. In the Fordist regime, value was mainly appropriated and distributed "privately," via the private ownership of the means of production and the concomitant ability to control specific production processes. Now we might claim that wealth is ever more created in socialized networked processes, and the value of that wealth is socialized on financial markets, where it is distributed in some way. But how is it distributed? How are the prices of such "immeasurable" values set?

HOW THE VALUES ARE SET

To a great extent values are determined through automatic algorithms that process complex data and spit out a result that is often acted on as if it were a natural fact. But those algorithms are based on value propositions that are in themselves seldom thematized. And as much recent research on the actual dynamics of financial markets shows, the choice of what values should determine valuation is crucial. Most of this research has been done by sociologists, who are less limited by the often ideological conflict between the "rational markets" and "behavioral finance" perspectives that constrain economists.[51] These sociologists have emphasized the importance of what they call "frames" or "conventions."

What they mean is the day-to-day labor of market analysts to transform the complex flow of market information into what Daniel Beunza and Raghu Garud call "calculative frames" that make possible the rational evaluation of particular assets. In devising "a story that makes sense" about an asset, market analysts create a frame that radically simplifies the everyday elaboration of information on the part of traders, to the point of transforming "Knightian uncertainty, namely, information that is unclear, subject to unforeseeable contingencies or multiple interpretations," into information that can be processed and acted upon.[52] The creation of such "calculative frames" affects the formation of asset prices by providing a "story" within which an asset can be made sense of in a particular way. And these frames can be persistent. Beunza and Garud use the example of Amazon.com during the dot-com boom of the 1990s (admittedly an extreme period):

> In May 1999, Blodget and Abelson [two influential analysts] interpreted the announcement of larger-than-expected annual losses at Amazon in sharply different ways: whereas the former saw them as a signal to sell the stock [because Amazon.com was interpreted as a bookseller, similar to Barnes and Noble], the latter viewed them as a reason to buy [because Amazon.com was framed as an Internet company].

These diverse frames persisted over time, "and the differences in valuation between Blodget and other Amazon analysts presented in the first episode did not narrow by May 1999 despite the presence of more information."[53] The idea that analysts have the ability to create persistent frames that affect market valuations of assets points to something quite profound. While the neoclassical view rests on the assumption that there is a single correct (rational) way to process information, the notion of calculative frames suggests that there are, in fact, many ways to do so: "that several alternative and equally plausible ways of assembling information co-exist"—in particular when that information is complex and abundant. But the decision about how to interpret information is, by definition, not a decision that follows from that information. It is a decision that moves on another level, a decision about what information to value more and what to value less; it is a decision about what values should guide the interpretation of information. Adopting this view, analysts direct market valuation by creating the values that guide the interpretation of information.

Beunza and Garud's analysis of calculative frames makes an interesting suggestion. In situations where there is an abundance of information and where that information is subject to multiple interpretations, what actually determines value is the ability to interpret that information, to render it comprehensible and calculable. (Beunza further elaborates this point in his work with David Stark on arbitrage traders: "After months of field-work we realized that, as increasingly more information is almost instantaneously available to nearly every market actor, the more strategic advantage shifts form economies of information to the sociocognitive process of interpretation.")[54] This is accomplished by the creation of a "frame." But what does it mean to create a frame? It means more than to make a choice, to "create a value" in the Nietzschean sense of that term. It means the ability to create a *shared value*, to enable a common view of the world sustained by a community of interpretation to form. This is not done by applying set rules, but rather by enabling a consensus to form around an idea of what the values are, around a common *ethos*—in the rhetorical sense of that term—that guides the interpretation of data. And such a consensus is formed as different views are weighed against each other and different actors are connected to each other around a common interpretation. So what determines (economic) value in situations of information abundance seems to be the ability to create a value consensus, however transitory, that can give direction and coherence to collective interpretation and action. The question then becomes this: Is there some way in which such a value consensus can be said to have been formed in a rational way?

Seeds of a New Rationality

In this chapter we have advanced two ideas: first, that "from the point of view of production," intangible assets, chiefly innovation, brand, and flexibility, represent excellence in the use of common resources; and second, that "from the point of view of value," the emergence of intangible assets has been driven by a movement toward the financialization of value that has resulted in enhanced importance of financial rent as a component of corporate profits and a concomitant rise in the discrepancies between the market value and the book value of companies. A growing share of value tends to derive from dynamics that lie outside of what traditional forms of accounting and measurement have defined as the production process proper.[55]

This is particularly clear from the story of brands, the most important intangible asset. The notion that brands could have economic value has a long prehistory. It goes back to the marketing revolution of the 1950s that began to shift managerial focus from production to sales and market demand as a source of value creation, and the parallel development of the concept of brand image as something distinct from the product. A more mobile consumer culture that created forms of demand that were more difficult to anticipate, along with the development of a global consumer culture and global brands, put an additional premium on the ability to predict demand that came with brands. Along with these developments there was a growth in practices and devices, such as customer relationship management, that extended the scope of management to the relations that a company could entertain with consumers, and eventually other stakeholders.

While these developments have paved the way for the notion that the value of brands was ultimately set by consumers, the necessity of measuring the value of such relationships became particularly acute with the financial bubble of the 1980s. The wave of mergers and acquisitions that marked the "creative destruction" of the remains of the Fordist industrial economy called for a legitimate way to account for discrepancies between market value and book value. A number of brand valuation companies rose to the challenge, pointing to brands, or the relationships that a company had established with consumers, as a credible source of the difference in value. For example, while today's leading brand valuation company, Interbrand, was founded in 1974 under the name of Novamark, it remained a brand and design consulting company for that decade. It took up brand valuation only in 1987. As its founder, John Murphy, told the trade magazine *Brand Management* in 2001, there was "a huge buying and selling of branded-goods businesses where what was essentially being bought and sold was brands. But nobody knew how to value brands."[56]

We have suggested that this combination of the socialization of production and the financialization of value might become the basis for a new economic model. (Interestingly, Marx noticed these tendencies and claimed that they would lead to what he called "the communism of capital"!) The production of wealth is socialized and deploys common resources, the appropriation of value is socialized thorough a multiplicity of securitization tools and, thus appropriated, value is distributed on financial markets. This new economic model also comes with the fundamentals of a new value regime: a new way of setting prices and distributing value. Or at least the last part, the new way of distributing value, seems to be falling into place. Simply put, in the Fordist value regime financial markets rewarded companies for their ability to extract value from the resources that they owned and directly controlled (their tangible assets). In the new value regime financial markets reward companies for their ability to put resources that they do not own or control, common resources, to excellent use. The concept of intangibles presently represents the two sides of this "equation." But can there be a rational connection between these two aspects of intangibles—their capacity to represent the "excellent" use of common resources and their capacity to legitimate financial valuations in excess of book value? Or to put the question in more synthetic terms: Is there any way for financial markets (or other markets, for that matter) to rationally represent such excellence?

At present this is not the case. Most value decisions on financial markets are not made through rational analysis of the productive powers that underlie the assets that are evaluated (*pace* Warren Buffett!). In part, this is because what the productive power of, for example, a brand *is* remains unclear. In part, it's because even if such a definition could be arrived at, the socialized productive processes that make up, say, the Apple brand might be complex enough to remain essentially incalculable.

The value of the Apple brand is created by about a thousand factories to which the production of the components that make up Apple products and their assemblage are subcontracted. It is created by Apple's in-house designers and by the large community of external developers who create applications for devices like the iPhone. It is further created by a couple of hundred Apple stores with the distributive network and marketing channels to which they are attached. Finally the value of the Apple brand is determined by the fact that millions of consumers take the brand seriously, discuss it in forums online, queue up for hours outside the Apple store when the iPad is launched, and so on. The complexity of this web of co-creation is beyond calculation. Mostly, however, such brand values remain incalculable because a consensus on how to perform such calculations (and thereby reduce the complexity of the task) does not exist.

Instead, values are set by the ability to form a convention that allows interpretation and the reduction of complexity. Today such conventions are set in ways that are fairly arbitrary (for example in the brand valuation "industry"). But perhaps there could be a rational way to arrive at the setting of such conventions. Such a rationality would need to be concerned with the very basic question of what values should ground the interpretation of value. What we need in order to make the new value regime work is a new kind of ethics. In the following chapters we will suggest that a new kind of ethics is actually already emerging as a consequence of the very productive developments described above.

3

Publics

Productive publics, a fundamental building block of the ethical economy, are voluntary associations of strangers who are united by their devotion to a common project or pursuit, like open-source software, urban agriculture, or Ducati motorcycles. In recent years such productive publics have become an important source of value creation, both inside and outside corporate organizations. And they are likely to become even more important in the future. We argue that productive publics present a modality of wealth creation that is particularly apt for an economy of commons. They have also developed a particular way of setting the values of that wealth, a way that is different from that of the Fordist value regime.

The importance of productive publics has been a consequence of what we call the socialization of value creation in general. By "socialization," we mean that, in parallel with the extension and networking of corporate value chains, a general blurring of productive and non-productive activities has occurred, to the point that value-creating activities are ever more difficult to identify as "productive labor"—or labor that is phenomenologically distinct from other kinds of human activity. Instead, the creation of economic value tends ever more often to coincide with the ordinary human actions that sustain the webs of relationships and meanings that constitute everyday life. This does not mean, of course, that any kind of human action immediately becomes "labor" that creates value. But it does mean that it becomes difficult to identify and describe beforehand the difference between the kinds of action that do so and the kinds that do not. A couple of examples: Re-tweeting a message that derives from a corporate viral advertising campaign is phenomenologically not very different from re-tweeting a message that originates with a friend. Mothers who contribute to an online discussion about motherhood might be studied and surveyed by manufacturers of child care products, or they might not. In the first case, their communication and interaction clearly creates value; in the second, it does not.

While its origins are more distant and complex, the trend toward the socialization of production has been greatly empowered by the diffusion of digital media. (In fact, from a phenomenological point of view, the omnipresence of computers tends to blur the difference between actions that are economically productive and others that are not. For example, to keep track of our achievements in *World of Warcraft* we use the same Excel spreadsheets that we use at work. At work we use strategic insights from *World of Warcraft* in playing at office politics.)[1] We suggest that, as in the case of the networking of material production described previously, one important impact of digital media has been the socialization of value creation, that is, a tendency for value-creating activities to coincide with and become indistinguishable from ordinary actions. This has occurred both within corporate forms of knowledge work and, importantly, outside the boundaries of corporate organizations, in the "participatory culture" that is becoming a central feature of life itself. Consequently, many corporate institutions, like brands, have evolved into hybrid formats that transverse these boundaries and ever more aim at including ordinary action as elements of the corporate value chain.

This tendency can, of course, be understood as yet another step toward the corporate dominance of every aspect of human life. Many initiatives do point in that direction, for example, the ubiquitous surveillance and mining of user-generated digital data. But we also suggest that the productive publics that emerge as a particular way of organizing such socialized productive activities have the potential to give rise to a new conception of value—in both the economic and the ethical senses of that term—that points to a radically different way of organizing economic activity.

In the first part of this chapter we explain how the double tendency toward the socialization of value creation and the affirmation of productive publics can be identified in corporate as well as non-corporate forms of value creation. In the second part we offer a more robust definition of "productive publics" and show how they contain the foundation for a new way of organizing value creation in an economy that ever more relies on common resources.

THE SOCIALIZATION OF PRODUCTION: THE STORY OF BRANDS

Consumer brands have a long history, starting with the origins of modern consumer culture (and even before that). But their emergence as a significant economic institution coincides with the development of mass production and mass consumption in the late nineteenth century. Branding provided a necessary, recognizable identity for the abundance of standardized and mass-produced goods that consumers encountered, allowing them to make meaningful choices (Lux or Persil detergent for your laundry?) and, importantly, to put their trust into a recognizable product with clear origins. Brands began as symbols of products, giving them a precise cultural identity that they otherwise lacked, and that managed to create an affective tie with consumers that could help them to differentiate one product from the others.

Even in their first incarnation, as symbols of products, consumer brands functioned as a new kind of connecting device. They forged connections between goods, people, and practices that enabled an experience of closeness and identification in a world where consumer goods were ever more anonymous. The second step in the evolution of brands was marked by an even further increase in the fluidity and instability of the things to be connected—of practices, consumer tastes, and indeed, goods themselves—and consequently, an even higher relative value was conferred on the ability to forge such connections. This "fluidity" of the things connected was manifested in three main ways. First, in the 1960s there was already a conviction—among marketers and among the public at large—that consumer habits and tastes were becoming more fluid. Previously it had been thought that consumer motivations and preferences coincided with particular social roles—for example, a middle-class suburban housewife was understood to naturally harbor a particular kind of taste. However, in the 1960s two important developments worked to change this characterization: first, the impact of television and the new, more differentiated media landscape that it fostered, and second, more refined and diversified consumer tastes among the middle classes. These shifts, together with innovations in market research and marketing theory, led to the notion that consumers had relatively fluid "lifestyles" rather than fixed tastes and preferences, and that these lifestyles could to a certain extent be constructed. Consequently, the game of branding became that of constructing a context of consumption around a product that forged connections among values, objects, and practices that might not have existed before. (Pepsi-Cola was successful in connecting its product to a watered-down mainstream version of the youthful counterculture, or the "Pepsi Generation"; Marlboro and *Playboy* both successfully crafted new forms of masculinity around their products).

Later, in the 1980s, the deregulation of media markets created the kind of global media culture that made global brands possible. For the first time the same television programs could be seen around the world, creating a common cultural raw material that allowed products to be advertised in the same way in widely different contexts. This increased the potential synergies from creating a globally coherent context of consumption around a product and increased the value of brands as connecting devices.[2]

Combined with the globalization and networking of material production, these developments sparked a wave of brand extensions, with companies venturing beyond their core product line to sell an increasing array of accessories, like clothes, sunglasses, perfume, bikes, wallpaper, etc. Thus the identification between a brand and a particular product—such as that between Mercedes and a car—became less direct. (The wave of brand extensions was particularly prevalent in fashion. For example, in 1995, 20 percent of the business volume of the Italian fashion company Armani came from accessories. In 2005 the figure was 38 percent.)[3]

Third, the media environment that developed in the postwar years—with the impact of television, the advent of cheaper and more portable new technologies for the reproduction of music, and then the arrival of networked information and communication technologies—progressively destabilized the boundaries between production and consumption. This was visible already in the 1960s as the emergence of street fashions and new forms of grass-roots music production transformed the nature of the fashion and music industries. The onset of networked information and communication technologies sparked a further proliferation of productive consumer practices, as consumers came together online to form "tribes" or "fan communities" or "brand communities" that, to varying degrees, could provide valuable input to brands. And brand management has developed an interest in such "prosumer activities." Today's businesses often rely on user-led innovation projects that directly include consumer creativity in the corporate value chain. These initiatives range from the relatively disorganized, tapping in to or studying the development of a fan culture or a user community, to the highly organized and systematic, like Nokia Beta Labs, where users play a decisive role in finalizing software solutions for mobile phones (or the iPhone, where a partially open-source code has created a proliferation of consumer-generated applications that enhance the value of the iPhone platform). Indeed, many now speak of overcoming the traditional roles of producer and consumer and moving toward new forms of "produsage," a process that involves firms and consumers in collaboratively generating continuous changes and improvements to a product platform, no longer regarding the material objects as final "products," but more as temporary snapshots of an ongoing process or collaborative evolution.[4]

The story of brands tells us three important things. First, brands have come to rely ever more significantly on public processes of value creation. In their first version, the symbolic identities and lifestyles that brands incarnated were mostly crafted and controlled by brand-owning corporations (or by their advertising agencies). Subsequently they came to rely on productive processes that evolved in the public domain, from the new fashions, trends, and lifestyles that consumers themselves created as consumer culture became more creative and less "conformist," to today's dependence on online platforms for user-led innovation, where consumers contribute to the very evolution of brands, and to the development of new products. These processes are public in the sense that they spring up outside of the secluded space of corporate organizations, out where they are, in principle, open for anyone to participate and where their dynamics can generally be reconstructed through the traces that they leave on publicly available discussion forums and mailing lists, as well as on social media platforms like Facebook and Twitter.

Second, the value of brands tends to become less "symbolic" and more "social." That is, brand equity begins to rely less on the ability to construct an attractive identity that can signify status or distinction according to a predefined cultural scheme. Instead it places more emphasis on the ability to create connections between people and things that can cohere consumers to participate in co-creation, or simply to remain loyal to brands, by virtue of their experiencing some form of identification with the brand, or "affective proximity," to use a more technical term. (And the ability to install such "affective proximity" has become one of the most important ways in which brands create value. In his work on customer loyalty, Frederick Reichheld shows that a 5 percent improvement in customer retention rates can today yield up to a 100 percent improvement in profits.)[5]

Third, this story suggests that the ability to create and maintain a web of such relations of affective proximity depends less on factors that corporations can directly control, like advertising, design, pricing, and marketing—although these remain of course important—and more on what they cannot control, that is, the willingness of consumers and other actors to contribute to maintaining and strengthening these connections without being directly pressured to do so or rewarded for doing so. Marketing scholar Bernard Cova calls this process "linking value."[6] Indeed, contemporary brand management literature reveals a broad consensus that "the power over brands is shifting over from managers to consumers." It is thought that consumer-based advocacy now counts for much more than advertising, and that "earned media" (what consumers freely say about brands) counts for more than "owned media" (what companies can say about brands in their advertising). And there have been corresponding suggestions of a new "community based" brand paradigm, in which brand managers are open not only to "conversation" with consumers (that is, to understanding and possibly profiting from their point of view) but also to "debate" (that is, allowing consumers to have a say in the management of the brand and its core values).[7]

Of course consumers are not now sovereign in determining the values that keep brands together simply by virtue of the changes mentioned above. On the contrary, brand management has developed a large repertoire of techniques that aim at manipulating and programming any such potential sovereignty. In the last two decades this has entailed a number of efforts at scripting the consumption experiences through a rising emphasis on retail design, including using smell, sound, touch, and other senses to create a particular experiential space. It has also featured an expansion of call centers and other forms of customer relations work, as well as a substantial expansion of the communication, PR, and brand consultancy sector. It has included a new emphasis on strategies like viral marketing or guerrilla marketing, which actively put to work the spontaneously occurring sociality of consumers, the word of mouth that flows freely and rapidly in a networked communications environment, to ensure such an experience.[8]

What it does mean is that successful brand management more and more becomes a matter of initiating and sustaining a *public* around that brand, a public that is able to contribute to maintaining the strength of the brand's values and contribute to ongoing development by offering input that ranges from market intelligence to direct suggestions for product innovation. A public can be understood as a mediated association among strangers that is directed toward the pursuit of a "common thing," in this case the brand. Publics are thus weaker forms of association than communities, in the sense that they can involve a larger range of actors in weaker ways. (Millions of people contribute to sustaining the value of the Apple brand, but they do not all interact or even know of each other; they can hardly be understood as a community.) At the same time the publics that brands initiate are "stronger" than networks, and the people involved experience themselves as part of a common pursuit and have, however weak, common values. The fact that value creation shifts over to publics also implies a problem of control. Publics are sovereign, at least in theory. That is, ever since their emergence in the nineteenth century, as mass media began to circulate, publics have constituted a source of opinion and buzz that has retained some degree of autonomy in relation to institutions like corporations or the state. And branded publics are similarly difficult to control, even if they might be more "loyal" than others. The difficulty of controlling publics has to do with the fact that they represent an emerging "third" modality of value creation, beyond the direct control of markets and hierarchies. To understand this better, let us look at how contemporary managerial thought has dealt with the affirmation of productive publics.

Beyond Markets and Hierarchies: The Story of Corporate Values

Modern managerial thought has been based on the idea that economic activity is organized and motivated either by markets or by hierarchies. On the market, people are free entrepreneurs who compete with each other and remain motivated by monetary rewards. Sometimes, or so the theory goes, markets are too risky and will be replaced by hierarchies, in which people do what they are told, controlled by the stick of sanctions and motivated by the carrot of career achievement.[9]

Practitioners have long known, however, that even though markets and hierarchies are important, what really makes organizations work, even highly bureaucratic ones, is informal relations. It is the informal networks that enable people to bypass too rigid job descriptions and actually get things done. (Conversely, a popular form of labor protest in bureaucratic organizations follows formal rules and regulations with excessive zeal, thus paralyzing everything.) In modern managerial thought the importance of such informal relations was "discovered" in the 1930s through the now famous Hawthorne studies. These studies also made

another important discovery: the willingness to put such informal relations to work, to cooperate with other workers beyond what was speci-
fied in one's job description, to do things in ways that were different
from what one was supposed to do but that might be more efficient, was
generally motivated not by money nor by the prospect of formal advancement, but by the experience of affective proximity with other workers, or
with the company as such. (Indeed, in the Hawthorne studies, workers'
experience that "management cared about them" was found to increase
productivity in itself.)[10]

Just as in the story of consumer brands, the story of management
thought and practice shows a connection between the growing importance
of informal relations as a source of productivity and a growing reliance on
"values," or more specifically, what we will call ethos—the ability to install
a particular affective climate as a management tool.

Significantly, the systematic reliance on a company's ability to foster
an ethos as a managerial device was first established with the shift away
from Fordist models of industrial organizations to post-Fordist, or post-
bureaucratic, organizational forms. As Japanese "Toyotist" organizations
began to turn to relations between workers to foster their potential for
self-organization, they also developed strong corporate cultures in which
values were inculcated through everything from corporate welfare to slo-
gans, design, and the infamous morning singing of the corporate anthem.
Significantly, Tom Peters's recommendation as a recipe for "excellence" in
his famous management bible from the early 1980s was this: "Autonomy
on the shop floor, and strong centralized values."[11]

The emphasis on values-based leadership became particularly important
in the case of knowledge work, where the capacity for self-organization and
"creativity" was understood to make up the very source of value. Through
concepts like "clans" and "communities of practice" that developed in the
1980s up to today's notions of "collaborative community" or "post-bureau-
cratic organizations," knowledge workers have been understood to be most
productive when empowered to organize their own production processes.
A strong and coherent corporate ethos ensures that this freedom is deployed in desirable ways. As management scholar Paul Adler has stressed,
trust between employees will come to matter more than both bureaucratic
organizations and monetary rewards as an organizational and motivational
factor when wealth creation becomes more knowledge intensive. Organizations with high levels of trust are able to put knowledge in the common
domain, while still ensuring that it is put to adequate and "respectable" use,
and this tends to increase the productivity of knowledge-intensive forms of

wealth creation.[12] Today, knowledge-intensive companies deploy a variety of measures that serve to stimulate and control the self-organization and collective intelligence of their employees. Such techniques seek to work on the ethos of the company to construct a context in which (1) commitment and identification with the organization are not only the norm, or even a condition for further employment, but, ideally, a constituent component of employee identity, and (2) employees are encouraged to use their freedom and take charge of their own situation.[13] (Often such management-by-freedom is paralleled by a proliferation of performance reviews and benchmarking systems that measure not only employees' ability to use their freedom, but also their level of commitment to the company and their own careers.)[14] Indeed, if early approaches to organizational identity stressed the importance of charismatic leadership able to set the values of the organization from above, contemporary approaches advocate a more varied leadership style. Visionaries are still important, but so are "bridge builders," who are able to make connections between formerly disparate parts of the organization, and what Michael Maccoby and Charles Heckscher call "heterarchical team leaders," who are able to *build a sense of community*, to empower a team of diverse individuals and competences to create the values that best support efficient cooperation.[15]

Until quite recently the basic assumption was that such value-based management naturally unfolded in social formations that could be described as communities. In social theory a community is a tight-knit group of people, kept together by a dense web of face-to-face interaction and connected to a common territory, or at least identity. In a community people trust one another because they know one another. (Granted, in U.S. parlance the term has since expanded to comprehend almost anything. The "gay community" is not a community, at least not in the social science sense of that term.) It might once have made sense to speak of self-organized knowledge work as happening in communities insofar as the people who collaborate were physically proximate, located in the same office building, as well as socially proximate, well known to each other because of a long period of frequent face-to-face interactions, or at least sharing the same corporate culture. But today the tendency is in the opposite direction. Knowledge work is becoming ever more precarious, and employment periods are shorter, with higher levels of turnover. Many companies are making more use of freelancers or even platforms for ultra-short-term contracting of standardized tasks, like Amazon.com's Mechanical Turk, where people like Web designers are available by the day, or even by the hour. (By 2017 IBM plans to shrink its workforce by 75 percent through using crowdsourcing platforms like Mechanical Turk.)[16] More generally, the globalization of value chains together with more-efficient use of digital media (like collaborative software tools and videoconferencing) has created a situation where people interacting in collaborative projects do in fact not know each other, either because they have never met or interacted before or because they remain members of a team for too short a time for community to form. This is of course particularly true for cutting-edge organizational forms like open-source software networks or open innovation platforms, in which different corporations cooperate with non-corporate actors (like universities or members of the amateur public) around the development of a common knowledge pool. As management scholars Paul Adler and Clara Chen note in an article from 2011, such networks of what they call "large-scale collaborative creativity" are becoming ever more frequent in the information economy, and it is difficult to subsume them under the concept of community. Instead they should be understood as publics, as looser forms of association that are held together by weaker kinds of affective ties and where attachments are more fluid and less important for members' overall sense of identity.[17] Indeed, given the importance of intangible assets, as described earlier, wealth creation comes to depend on a wide variety of actors, like consumers, that might not be involved in the direct production of either material goods or knowledge, but that are nevertheless important in sustaining the kinds of conventions that are able to support value decisions.

In a sense, a convergence between corporate organizations and brands has occurred, as both have come to rely ever more on their ability to give direction and coherence to loose associations, publics of actors that come from a wide range of positions. In both corporations and brands this has also created a greater need to involve employees, and other stakeholders as well, in the collaborative creation of a common ethos, reflecting the need to provide new forms of coherence to extended value chains. In managerial theory this shift has moved the focus away from corporate values themselves to the notion of a corporate or organizational brand that, like consumer brands, is conceptualized as something co-created by employees and stakeholders. In this sense the organizational brand comes to be understood as a common "enterprise" that emerges from the "interconnected conversations" of an extended network of stakeholders, including consumers, suppliers, and the various publics that surround a company and its efforts, with the social responsibility of a company as a key aspect. As is evident in the accelerating trend toward corporate social responsibility, the wider variety of value horizons that now participate in the elaboration of a corporate ethos has shifted the object of corporate branding from a number of values that reflect the aspirations of a single corporate entity to more generally desirable "social" concerns that are better suited to lending coherence to the complex and extended stakeholder networks that participate in such value-creating enterprises.[18] As companies have had to forge forms of ethos with wider appeal, which are able to motivate and cohere a public of more diverse actors, the emphasis has shifted from centrally elaborated strong values that are specific to a particular organization to more generally embraced appeals to "responsibility."

PARTICIPATORY CULTURE

The general "becoming productive" of social life has often been discussed in terms of "participatory culture." This term might seem a bit strange— as if previous cultures did not contain elements of participation—but its use mainly serves to highlight that whereas previous media and consumer products invited more or less passive forms of consumption, contemporary media and commercial culture actively invite participation and co-creation. Indeed, the traditional modernist concept of culture stressed that cultural participation happened outside of the commercial sphere of consumer culture, and that the exercise of culture was somehow opposed to corporate practices of value creation. The term "participatory culture," on the other hand, highlights the fact that cultural participation occurs within the sphere of commercial mediation, or at least the mediation of the Internet, and through consumer goods, content brands, and other commercial products.

Arguably the roots of a participatory culture in this particular sense of the term go back to the 1960s, when middle-class consumer patterns became more expressive and varied, emphasizing lifestyle and individual self-expression, and when the new counterculture rebelled against the imposed conformity of "mass society" by taking the production of culture and identity into its own hands. But the term has acquired its recent prevalence with the rise of what is known as Web 2.0.

In part Web 2.0 is a technical phenomenon, a matter of new programming languages and applications that allow data migration and mash-ups and that facilitate tasks like the creation of a Web page or the production and sharing of designs. Basically, Web 2.0 makes content production online, whether this be a Web site, a video, a presentation, or a mash-up, simpler. But Web 2.0 is also a matter of a new structure of Web platforms themselves. If the Web used to be a broadcasting medium where users were invited to watch content produced by others, it is now more of a space for participation, where users are invited to upload their own creations, to form and manage social relations, or, importantly, to make judgments (in the form of ratings and "social buttons," like Facebook's "Like" button) on the quality of their experiences of other users or of companies and their services. And Web 2.0 business models, like those of Facebook or Amazon. com, are based on inviting and encouraging such forms of participation.[19]

With the proliferation of and easy access to such tools, participatory content production has become a widespread phenomenon. In 2006, according to the Pew Internet survey, 49 percent of the American population (and in 2007 64 percent of all teenagers) had contributed to creating online content. And since then the use of video-sharing sites (like YouTube) has doubled, and the use of social networking sites like Facebook has increased sixfold. For many people, particularly young people or those with an activist interest, the creation of videos, blogs, or other kinds of online content has become a natural way of making their presence felt publicly.[20]

If the proliferation of the technological backbone of such a widespread participatory culture has already revolutionized how we create and share cultural artifacts, the future looks even more radical, for at least two reasons. First, access to such participatory technologies is bound to become even more widespread. In the 1990s Internet access was predominantly a feature of Western, developed countries. Today this is no longer true. Almost one third of the world's population already has Internet access and countries like China, Brazil, and Korea are becoming important sources of co-created online content. In addition, mobile phones with Internet connections are rapidly proliferating, especially in the poorer South, and will allow new forms of cheap connectivity. (Globally, mobile data traffic is on track to double every year through 2013, increasing 66-fold between 2008 and 2013.)[21]

Second, and of equal importance, the kinds of content created through participatory technologies are also changing. When we think of participatory culture, we are perhaps used to thinking of more ephemeral things like brand communities and social media profiles. But other things are emerging as well. The blogosphere and bottom-up forms of citizen journalism have seen massive growth in the last decade. And regardless of their qualities and civic responsibility, they have radically transformed the ways in which politically relevant information is created and circulated. Even more importantly, there has been an accelerating movement toward the creation of more-tangible and technically useful forms of content. Free or open-source software began as a restricted amateur movement but has become the central component of the software industry. Today Free/Libre Open Source Software directly supports 43 percent of U.S. software development. At the same time the production of "packaged, proprietary software" accounts for only 10 percent of job hiring in the U.S. software industry. These figures suggest that the field of expansion is not the production of software itself, but the production of customization and services around software, which, to a greater extent than ever, can itself be found for free, by virtue of the free or open-source software "movement."[22]

Today we are seeing how similar open or peer-to-peer models are migrating offline, toward the production and diffusion of material goods. Open Design is a rapidly expanding field in which designers, engineers, and artisans come together in publics to co-create the designs and technical specifications for a wide variety of objects that can subsequently be downloaded and realized for free. Such Open Design or open hardware systems are used in social-minded initiatives like OpenFarmTech, a platform devoted to the co-creation of designs for the equipment needed for the construction of an ecologically sustainable farm, complete with solar turbines and machinery for the transformation of garbage into biodiesel. But they are also an emerging business reality. In the fashion industry, for example, a number of Open Design initiatives are under way, like FashionStake, a platform for crowdsourced design of haute couture.[23] In parallel, open manufacturing reflects a movement toward cheaper and more versatile machinery for material production. 3-D printers are already a commercial reality, used by, among others, designers, architects, and dentists (to create dental prostheses). In 2008 a 3-D printer cost about as much as a laser printer did in 1985, but prices are moving downward rapidly, and at the same time these machines are becoming more versatile and multipurposed. There is a lot of experimentation with 3-D printers that are able to work not just with plastic resin but with sand and metals as well.[24] In the next step, projects like fab labs and RepRap suggest various non-commercial ways of distributing such machinery. Fab lab, an MIT-initiated project, aims at projecting neighborhood workshops, at which a few versatile, numerically controlled machines are able to produce a wide range of objects for everyday use. RepRap, a project initiated by Adrian Bowyer at the University of Bath in the UK, aims to develop a cheap 3-D printer that can be assembled from off-the-shelf components. RepRap is an Open Design project, for which designs and specifications can be freely downloaded. And the RepRap machine is designed to be virtually self-replicating, able to "print" out most of its own parts. (At present, 80 percent of the components of a RepRap printer can be printed with a RepRap printer.)[25] On top of this, we can witness an accelerating trend toward open biotechnology, driven by standardized systems of bioengineering (like BioBricks) and the emergence of a number of community labs, like the San Francisco–based Biocurious.[26]

The combination of open hardware and Open Design suggests the possibility of a quite radical reorganization of material production, which, as Eric von Hippel of MIT notes, happened to software in the 2000s (through the rapid rise of free or open-source software projects) and might very well happen to hardware in the 2010s.[27] In short, the scope and reach of new participatory technologies point toward the future movement of participatory culture away from the production of purely "cultural" content (like images, video, or music) and to the manufacture of technological products, whether immaterial, like software, or material, like solar panels or automobile parts, or even genetically modified seeds.[28]

Publics in Participatory Culture

Sometimes Internet use, even participatory use, is viewed as an individual or isolated activity. We create content, social relations, blogposts, comments, and *World of Warcraft* characters alone, in isolation in front of our screens. (Facebook is to socialization what masturbation is to sex, someone said.) But this idea does not seem to square with available research.

Henry Jenkins, in his 2005 work for the MacArthur Foundation on the implications of a participatory culture, stressed the connected, social nature of the new productive activities that he was surveying:

> A participatory culture is a culture with relatively low barriers to artistic expression and civic engagement, strong support for creating and sharing one's creations, and some type of informal mentorship whereby what is known by the most experienced is passed along to novices. A participatory culture is also one in which members believe their contributions matter, and feel some degree of social connection with one another (at the least they care what other people think about what they have created).[29]

Since that time, this social or connected dimension has kept resurfacing, starting with early Internet research. Contrary to initial ideas that the

Internet would increase fragmentation and social isolation, a number of early studies showed that being connected online correlated with an active offline social life, with a high degree of what sociologists call "social capital," and that the Internet also facilitated the durable connections and shared experience of community with strangers. In 2001 a Pew Internet and American Life Project report indicated that 84 percent of Internet users had some sort of contact with others online (whether through "communities" devoted to the exchange of recipes, to the sharing of experiences of particular illness, or to discussions of the habits and intentions of space aliens). And in 2008 the Annenberg Digital Future Project reported that 55 percent of the members of such "communities" feel as strongly about them as they do about their "real world" communities. Robert Kozinets summarizes these impressions in a 2010 book on ethnographic approaches to what he calls "online communities":

> [Research] reports support the idea that what is happening in our society is not just simply a quantitative change in the way that the internet is used, but a qualitative shift. As more people use the Internet, they use it as a highly sophisticated communications device that enables and empowers the formation of communities.[30]

The term "community" is imprecise, however. If by "community" we mean a more or less dense web of social interactions, whether online or face-to-face—like those depicted by Jane Jacobs in her famous idealization of New York's inner-city neighborhoods—then these productive configurations are not communities, because they have as their essential element relations with strangers.[31] This feature emerges quite clearly if we look at the field in which the term "community" has been used perhaps most frequently, when discussing associations of productive consumers, or prosumers, like "brand communities."

It is certainly possible to find collective practices of productive consumption that take the form of communities. And arguably consumer research has come to privilege the study of such practices, as a result of its embrace of ethnography, or "netnography," as a methodological strategy. And it might be true that up until the 2000s the term "community" offered a more reasonable description of how consumers came together to create meaning and value around brands, how people shared and co-created information online (in virtual communities), and how knowledge workers worked together in collaborative communities, whether inside companies or in peer-to-peer networks.

But the term is no longer particularly representative of how collab-orative processes of consumption/production function today. This is so for two principal reasons. First, the shift in consumer culture from a re-productive to a productive phase, in which it is expected of consumers that they make active use of commodities in creating individual lifestyle statements, implies that productive consumer practices have become an ordinary pursuit on the part of more and more ordinary kinds of people. Recent decades have produced a number of detailed studies clearly show-ing that such practices of productive consumption have become part of the ordinary business of at least the "New Class" of knowledge workers. To put it simply, you do not need to be a member of a "community" to engage in productive consumption; you are expected to do this, at some level of activity, as part of your ordinary life course. Naturally the mediatization of consumer culture has facilitated the advance of productive consump-tion, by global consumer culture and global brands by a flourishing DIY (do-it-yourself) culture aided by a plethora of television chefs and reality shows dedicated to home decoration. So has, of course, the diffusion of Internet connectivity. The Internet and social media constitute the second reason for the declining relevance of "communities." These factors have both greatly increased the number of people who participate in productive consumer practices and the ways in which they participate. While in the 1990s the principal way of participating in and creating value for a brand consisted of taking part in forums, mailing lists, and other participatory media that were biased in favor of interpersonal interaction, today it is also possible, and far more common, for consumers to create value for a brand by re-tweeting its communication or simply "liking" its viral com-munications on Facebook. And evidence is accumulating that most forms of online consumer action involve looser and more transitory forms of engagement with brands and products: posting once or twice on a blog, looking up an online forum on motherhood to ask a question about a branded product and then never returning to the site, liking something on Facebook, and so on. While marketing approaches tended to focus on the crucial role played by a small community of influencers (a community in the sense that they interact with each other) in creating and diffusing buzz and opinion, recent approaches that rely on the potential of big digi-tal data, the massive data sets that can be harvested from digital media, have instead pointed toward the role of a large mass of loosely connected individuals. Watts and Dodds, for example, argue that information diffu-sion is driven "not by *influentials* but by a critical mass of easily influenced individuals."[32] Such "accidental influencers" are connected to each other not by strong webs of interpersonal interaction but by weaker forms of mediated association (like re-tweeting a message). Consequently, marketing strategies aim at discovering and promoting the ability of such loosely associated individuals to create buzz in a coordinated way (to enhance the "network value" of those associations).

It is difficult to subsume such loose and fragmented forms of attention under the term "community," because they do not involve sustained interpersonal interaction with other members. (And there is accumulating evidence that when direct forms of interaction do occur, "membership" is highly transitory. For example, only 58 percent of those who have posted one time in a usenet group have subsequently reposted, and *World of Warcraft* guilds lose, on average, 25 percent of their members per month.)[33]

But members might nevertheless care about what such strangers think. They are related to them in some way. Teenagers who post videos of themselves on YouTube might not interact with their viewers, but they are nevertheless interested in what those viewers think about the experience, and that kind of information can be made available to them through comments, number of views, or discussions of their work on blogs and online forums that they care about. So even if content creation does not unfold through the kinds of webs of social interaction that we usually understand as "communities," it is not necessarily an individual pursuit. Instead it is a pursuit that unfolds among strangers with whom one experiences a sense of communion. It is a pursuit undertaken in and by a public. Devotees of brands like Macintosh or Saab not only communicate with each other online but recognize and identify with strangers who endorse the same brand, and experience a sense of ethical affinity with them. People who debate about aliens are united against The Government and other dark forces that try to keep such knowledge secret. Participants in corporate user-driven innovation platforms are united by a strong sense of affective affinity to the brand to which they contribute, and strong expectations that the owners of the brand utilize the productive input that they derive responsibly and give back to or at least "respect" the demands of users. And similar things can be said of other manifestations of participator culture. It might have been possible to speak of the early pioneers of free software as united in a community where everybody interacted with everybody else and trust based on familiarity could develop. But today's free or open-source software production involves tens of thousands of participants who associate in ways that hardly resemble communities.

And as the complexity of such productive pursuits increases, so does the level of integration and coherence of the productive publics devoted to the task at hand. The development of free software has been paralleled by an organizational evolution resulting in sub-publics, written constitutions, explicit reward systems (in the form of reputation metrics), and complex divisions of roles and responsibilities. Contemporary social innovation networks are extended publics that involve a multitude of different actors (social entrepreneurs, NGOs, corporations, investors) who interact on a multitude of different media around a wide range of projects, but who nevertheless experience themselves as a public organized around a common pursuit.

And with the penetration of Internet-based media into everyday life, and in particular with the arrival of a social web, online and offline dimensions of such publics tend to blur as well. Urban creative scenes are publics that are coordinated and held together by social networking sites where events are publicized and where people can locate participants for projects and initiatives. Even so, these publics are heavily dependent on concrete events, gatherings, and face-to-face encounters. Present development toward open material production is paralleled by the emergence of online portals, where designs can be shared and contributions accredited and offline events like makers' faires and hackspaces where members of the public can come together, learn skills from each other, and create things together. Community Supported Agriculture (CSA), the fastest-growing element of the U.S. food economy, coordinates the exchange of farm labor and fresh produce among strangers through the use of online platforms and SMS-messaging systems. At the same time, the popularity of the "movement" rests, at least in part, in the fact that it is firmly rooted in physical space and provides many opportunities for face-to-face encounters as well as for experiencing the materiality of food production in more concrete ways. In other words, productive publics are no longer strictly "online" phenomena; they are acquiring offline spaces as well.[34]

Publics: Toward a Definition

It is now time to insert some rigor into this rather impressionistic narrative by attempting a more solid definition of the term "publics." Concepts like "public" and "public sphere" have been central to modern social and political theory. The consensus has been that the public as a social configuration is distinct to modern society. Indeed, French sociologist Gabriel Tarde thought of publics as *the* modern form of social organization par excellence. Premodern societies had crowds, but only modern societies have publics. What's the difference?[35]

First, at a very basic level, publics are something that happens in the open. Publics are not private; they are not closed off and secluded. (The original meaning of *privatus* in Roman jurisprudence comes from the Latin verb *privare*, more or less "deprive of": a private thing is something that the res publica—the "public thing"—has been deprived of.) This in-the-openness obviously holds for crowds as well, and it holds in principle, although with some modifications, for the productive publics that we have discussed (in the sense that some such publics, like free-software networks, are open to anyone in principle but in practice accept admission only on meritocratic grounds). But it is important to point out the open nature of publics, since that contrasts with the private nature of corporations. In the Fordist model, value creation took place predominantly within the bounds of an organization—inside the factory walls, to use a simplified expression—where particular rules and hierarchies could prevail and where access to non-members was denied, or at least restricted. Corporations could show off a public face or facade, in the form of a brand or a public relations campaign, but the inner workings of value creation remained invisible to the public eye. To the extent that value creation takes place in publics, it obviously challenges and contrasts with the presumption of privacy, and introduces a number of contradictions to which corporations must respond. In particular, corporations that try to constitute themselves as publics generally try to restrict membership, but sometimes have to face the tendency toward publicity inherent in such initiatives, as when employees are encouraged to blog, and those blogs are subsequently read and commented on by outsiders.

But there is more to it. A public is different from a crowd in the sense that a public is in some way organized. A crowd might gather, take shape, and move momentarily in one direction, then disband (as in the case of a market crowd stampeding in a common panic to sell off a particular asset, or a brawl erupting in a crowd of football supporters), but a public is organized around attention to a common *thing* that has a duration in time.[36] This thing can consist of a common focus of attention, as when a theater public goes silent as the curtain opens. It can consist of something more substantial, like devotion to a common cause (as in the case of a working-class public unified by a common political identity). Publics are held together by what moral philosopher Charles Taylor calls a social imaginary, which confers an experience of community, however ephemeral, among members of a public ("we are the citizens of France," "we are the true wine connoisseurs," "we defend open software against corporate profit motives").[37] To the extent that such "social imaginaries" go beyond the superficial level of attention to a theater play, which they do in most productive publics, they imply something like a common worldview and a common sense of ethical obligation.

We have used the term "ethos" to capture this common experience. The original, archaic meaning of "ethos" was something like "dwelling" or "habitat." Later on, the term became central to the Aristotelian tradition, where it came to mean something like "character" or "custom," in two interconnected ways. First, in the rhetorical sense, ethos denotes the emotional character of a speaker that allows her to bond with an audience and affect their interpretation of what she says in a particular way. That is, a public imbued with a particular ethos will interpret the world (slightly) differently than another public will. It might, for example, conceive of Apple products as so superior that it is worth spending a rainy night lining up outside the Apple store to be on hand when the iPad launches. Second, in the ethical sense, "ethos" means something like "moral character," a particular set of vices and virtues that allows a person to coexist with others in a particular way. A virtuous character is a predisposition that enables a person to "live well" with others. A public is united also by such a common ideal moral character, a moral custom. Sometimes this can consist of an explicit set of common values, as in the public of animal rights activists; sometimes it consists of a looser and less articulate ethical disposition, as when Apple users somehow feel that their favored product is superior to others, also in a moral sense, but are not able, perhaps, to explain exactly how. Sometimes this ethos can materialize in explicit codes of conduct, as when a branded corporate organization seeks to make certain values permeate its entire value chain. This moral aspect of publics always entails a set of obligations, or at least expectations as to the conduct of members, that allows a public to make a judgment of their moral worth, or "virtue." Again, such expectations can be strong or weak, implicit or explicit. Publics of free-software developers have strong expectations with regard to the conduct of their members, which are rendered explicit in manifestos, constitutions, and other textual products where values are spelled out. Corporate brands prosper as long as the explicit value statements that they set for themselves are mirrored in the judgments that their stakeholders make as to their actual practice. Brand communities have weaker expectations that are perhaps never spelled out—but just try coming to a Harley-Davidson reunion on your Japanese motorcycle! These two aspects of the ethos of the public—the moral and the cognitive/aesthetic—reinforce each other. As Gabriel Tarde pointed out in his pioneering work, it is the fact that members of a public can share a common sense of community, of mental communion (*communion mentale*), that enables them to harbor a common ethics, a common sense of "truth, beauty and utility."[38]

A third important point about publics is that a public is a relation among strangers. Members of a public need not be physically co-present (although they can be), and they need not even interact with each other (although they can do this too). Instead, members of a public are united precisely by their partaking of the particular ethos that constitutes the public, by their sharing of a particular imaginary. This form of communion enables them to experience themselves as a community, even in the absence of concrete social relations, and consequently it enables them to entertain expectations in relation to their own or other members' actions, without having actually met those members, simply by virtue of being members of a public. Membership in a public allows strangers to know (a little) bit about each other and to entertain (however weak) mutual expectations.

Publics also suggest a different modality of co-creation than a community does. Simply put, in a community members co-create by cooperating with each other directly. And while such forms of co-creation might be a feature of consumer publics, the main modality of creation is different. In a public, the ideal-typical way of co-creating consists of individual or sub-group appropriations and re-elaborations of common resources that are subsequently put back into the common domain. Creation in publics is thus not an interpersonal endeavor as much as it is a common pursuit, uniting a multitude of local and small-scale elaborations that might occur independently of each other, around a common interest or goal. Members of the Apple public, for example, do not co-create the brand experience by working directly with each other. Instead they make contributions (like iPhone apps or advice on technical support forums) individually or in small groups, and put these back into the common domain. This particular modality of value creation is an important foundation for the particular logic of value creation in publics.

Fourth, and finally, publics are self-organized entities. Publics in the modern sense are sovereign in their deliberations (at least in theory), and as such they cannot be entirely controlled by other institutions, like states or corporations. Instead publics are constituted—tautologically—by their ability to organize and maintain the particular ethos that makes them into publics. The public of wine connoisseurs is constituted by a common ethos that emphasizes the cognitive/aesthetic importance of good wine and that contains a number of ethical (in the loose sense) expectations as to the proper behavior of members (not to drink voluptuously but to sniff and swirl and savor the experience, for example). As Michael Warner puts it, "A public is the social space created by the reflexive circulation of discourse"—that is, by the circulation of utterances (in some form or another) that always already understand themselves as addressing the particular public that they are addressing. In this sense the public of, say, a brand community exists as long as discourse circulates that addresses that brand community.

This aspect of "discursive self-organization," as sociologists would say, has at least two important implications. First, it implies that publics are sovereign, that they set their own values, at least in relation to things around which they are organized. The value of free software and of the relative contributions on the part of members of a public oriented around the production of free software is set by that public, more or less deliberatively. The same thing goes for fan fiction, the qualities of football players, or the virtues of participants in reality television programs. This means that publics are (at least in theory) autonomous ethical entities, in the sense of ethics as "the making of value judgments in the absence of universal rules or standards." We write "at least in theory" since this ethical sovereignty of publics naturally clashes with corporate hierarchies when productive publics are included within their value chains, or when corporations themselves try to constitute themselves as publics united by a common ethos or set of values. Such clashes can be understood as an important "driver" behind a number of recent managerial innovations.

The second implication of discursive self-organization is that publics are mediated social forms. They depend on media for their existence. And the media ecology in which they evolve enables them to extend themselves and operate in different ways. In a society where communication is predominantly mediated by direct speech, a public is necessarily restricted to those physically present. Networked information and communication technologies not only extend the scope of a public much further but also enhance and empower it in terms of what it can accomplish. As we will suggest below, the present productive role of publics depends to a large extent on the technological possibilities that this social form can now build on and deploy.

To the extent that publics are constituted by mediated communication, the structure of the media system also influences the structure of the publics. In the modern public sphere, where the media technologies necessary to initiate and maintain mediated communication were expensive and cumbersome, publics tended to be expressions of the consolidated social interests that, like trade unions, employers' associations, or the state, had access to such media institutions (in the form of newspapers or, later, television). Under such conditions it was possible to speak about a unified national (or "bourgeois" or "proletarian") public sphere. One important consequence of the proliferation of networked information and communication technologies is that the ability to initiate and maintain such circuits of mediation becomes fairly widespread. Consequently, the number and diversity of publics begin to proliferate. This means that if modern publics could be considered to be the expression of some common underlying interest or identity, then contemporary publics are understood to be the result of the *activity* of assembling and linking together; for example, the "plastic coalition"—a San Francisco–based coalition of companies, social activists, private individuals, and NGOs that work together for reducing the use of plastic materials—is the result of concrete practices of assemblage through which a diverse multitude of actors becomes constituted as a public by acquiring a common ethos and, as a result, articulates a common interest and identity.[39] The ability to engage in such activities of assemblage on a massive scale has created a proliferation of publics to the extent that this social form has begun to take up the kinds of productive activities that used to be considered the private business of economic actors, outside of the public domain. But this is just one aspect of the emergence of productive publics as a diffuse social form.

WHENCE PRODUCTIVE PUBLICS?

Productive publics are not an entirely new phenomenon. We can find instances of public value creation in the past as well, as when a public of fashion consumers bestows value and popularity on a particular garment or style. Similarly, strong non-economic, ethical motivations for value creation are an ancient phenomenon. Medieval guilds functioned in ways that very much resemble our discussion of productive publics. Members of a guild were recognized as such by other members, even those that they had never met or interacted with. And they were motivated by a common ethical code inscribed in myths and other "secrets" to which one would gain access only through rituals of initiation. This common ethos included prescribed expectations for proper behavior and attitudes. (Indeed, it can be argued that the separation of ethical motivations from purely economic ones, although necessarily incomplete, is a modern tendency.)[40] Similarly,

Max Weber describes the motivations of politicians and scientists as driven to no small extent by a "calling" to contribute to the common cause of their professions. In the 1930s sociologist Talcott Parsons would generalize this argument to apply to most of the important professions of modern society, the members of which, he argued, were strongly motivated by a morally binding professional "ethics."[41] Other predecessors that come to mind are the cooperative movements of the nineteenth and twentieth centuries. Productive publics were also an important organizational form in the postwar counterculture. For example, Stewart Brand's *Whole Earth Catalog* united a public of communes, activists, and small businesses in the common pursuit of an alternative economic model.[42] In the information economy, however, productive publics are becoming more prevalent as a form of economic organization.

This change has a lot to do with the technological features, or affordances, of networked information and communication technologies, although that is not the only factor behind the contemporary proliferation of productive publics. Two basic technological conditions contribute to the current increase. First, the spread of networked media has effectively brought with it a socialization of the means of production and, importantly, organization: the intensification of communication has tended to make knowledge, skills, and other productive resources common. In addition, the automation of production, along with higher rates of education, has created a growing pool of "free," talented labor that is able and willing to participate in the activities of productive publics, a "cognitive surplus," to use Clay Shirky's term. Second, the diffusion of networked digital media has increased the power of association at the disposition of ordinary people. It is now possible to create a public around a particular thing, without the need of large endowments of capital and other resources. It can be done using commonly available tools like computers with Internet access and social media platforms.

Common Resources

At a very simple level, the diffusion of networked computers has made it simpler to make things, whether it be immaterial things like cultural "content" or material things like "fabbed" artifacts. It used to be necessary to have a record studio in order to produce a record; it used to be necessary to have a printing press in order to spread news or opinion. This is no longer the case. And the socialization of this productive potential has put many branches of the old "culture industries," like, notably, music companies and newspapers, in a very difficult situation.

Less obvious perhaps is the fact that networked computers are also a means of organization. We are now seeing a proliferation of collaborative consumer groups or self-organized consumer groups, like GAS (Gruppi autonomi di spesa) that have spread in northern Italy. These groups by-pass supermarkets and purchase (usually organic and local) food directly from growers, then distribute the proceeds among their members. They have arisen for a number of different reasons, among them an awareness of the benefits of organic produce, distrust in supermarkets and the food economy as a whole, and the popularity of local foods, perhaps driven by the success of the Slow Food movement. But they have also been facilitated by networked computers and mobile phones, which allow affordable means of operation for self-organized groups that are not companies and that do not have the wherewithal to employ administrative personnel. Excel spreadsheets tally purchases and payments, e-mail provides an easy way to coordinate orders, and SMS messages coordinate delivery, though some groups deploy more-sophisticated ad hoc software. Similarly, since the arrival of the Internet a virtual boom in alternative currencies has been going on. Some of these currencies operate in geographically bounded communities, some operate within online publics, and some, like bitcoin, are spreading as a generally accepted means of payment. (Arguably the most important of them is the "gold" that World of Warcraft players can trade for dollars and euros at fairly stable exchange rates.)[43] Networked media technologies make this possible because, quite simply, they put powerful means of organization at the disposal of actors who previously did not have such tools. In order to create a currency in the past it was perhaps not necessary to be a bank, but one needed at least a couple of accountants. Now this can be done automatically. (Bitcoin, with all its flaws, is a peer-to-peer currency in which the operating system automatically guarantees the genuine character of the "coins" emitted and safeguards against inflationary pressures.) At a more advanced level, networked media can scale up what used to be the business of local, tightly connected communities (such as the community of firms in a Marshallian industrial district) so that they can involve and coordinate a global public of strangers devoted to the same pursuit (as the 3,000-strong public of Debian developers who do not necessarily interact or know each other but are nevertheless devoted to the creation of a common thing and united by a strong and ethically relevant sense of communion). This increased capacity for assemblage is, as Michel Bauwens has argued, one important factor behind the success of publics as a way of organizing not just opinion making but the creation of artifacts as well.[44]

Both the ability to make things, even quite complex artifacts, and the ability to organize complex processes of production are now common, in the colloquial sense that more people can participate in these activities now than before. But the proliferation of networked information and communication technologies also make resources "common" in a less ordinary sense. When skills, recipes, knowledge, best practices, designs, and technological artifacts are put in the public domain, these resources become common goods that are not owned by anyone but are open to use on the part of anyone. Free software is a common good that can be downloaded and installed for free. (This book, for what it is worth, has been written on Open Office, a free-software package that provides the functionality of Microsoft Office without the price tag or, one might add, the unnecessary complications.) Music is by now virtually a common good: it is no longer necessary to have a huge record collection to become a successful DJ, since most music can be found online. The same is increasingly true for the design and specifications of material artifacts. More important, perhaps, this process of what used to be private becoming common is also a feature of the corporate economy, where outsourcing and inter-firm knowledge sharing makes it much more difficult to protect innovation from spreading to competitors. This process of things becoming common has not been without conflicts and contradictions. The music industry, for example, is quite vigorously resisting the idea that what it considers private intellectual property may end up in the public domain. But the process has created a situation in which skills, know-how, software, design, and so on are no longer scarce. Consequently, access to these resources, while still important, is no longer what determines success, whether business-wise or otherwise. Interestingly, something similar has happened to labor as well.

Free Labor

In a classic essay on the emerging Internet economy, Tiziana Terranova argued that companies like America Online and Amazon.com (this was before Web 2.0) make use of what she called free labor—that is, labor that was not paid a wage and was not subject to direct forms of command and control. In fact, technically qualified labor is no longer that difficult to come by. Take the example of open-source software. To Microsoft, labor is a scarce resource. People have to be paid to code for Microsoft; they do not do this for free. They subsequently have to be managed by paid supervisors. In short, the production of software unfolds in a classic industrial way, through the rational control of commanded labor. For GNU/Linux, on the other hand, labor is not scarce. There are more willing programmers out there who want to contribute to the product than can possibly be admitted. The problem is rather how to keep people out and how to make sure that only those who are sufficiently qualified get a chance to cooperate. Because of this issue, Linux has developed a complex system of entry requirements that starts presumptive programmers off with smaller, less significant tasks to determine whether they are worthy to take a greater responsibility in the project.[45] Indeed, the very management model of Linux is extremely wasteful with respect to labor time. People are allowed to do what they want, to initiate projects of their own. "Management" has neither the interest nor the mandate to intervene. The result is a number of half-finished projects, most of which amount to nothing. Such a management style would be completely inconceivable if labor was scarce.

Admittedly, open-source software is an extreme case, but other productive pursuits encounter similar issues. It is not difficult to find a designer, a manager, an engineer, or a generic knowledge worker who is able to operate the machinery of, say, a call center. The so-called "creative industries," which were held to be the most advanced forms of knowledge production in the 2000s, are particularly swamped with requests for employment. Why is this the case?

One of the reasons is that networked media enhance the possibility of making connections. This is perhaps particularly true for online productive pursuits like open-source software, where, as Yochai Benkler argues, the connectivity of the Internet will ensure that enough interested talent will somehow find their way. (Actually it is not quite *that* simple, as we will discuss later on, in chapter 5.)

Another reason is technological. The programmable nature of computers means that the skills necessary to execute even difficult operations are inherent in the software itself. The computer is a generic device in the information society, a sort of contemporary hoe that can be used for almost anything. With a few elements of basic computer literacy a computer will enable you to write documents and perform calculus, to run automated machinery, coordinate a logistics chain, gather vital information on customer preferences, make suggestions for design or quality improvements, and so on. Moreover, the necessary computer skills are generic.

While teaching workers how to operate in a factory environment was a big problem for early-nineteenth-century industrialists, contemporary computer-literate Indian or Chinese youth have little difficulty in adapting to the environment of the call center or the semi-automated factory. It is important to stress that such basic computer literacy comes as a natural part of a normal socialization process for a large and growing proportion of the world's population: it is a consequence of playing *World of Warcraft* and connecting with friends on Facebook or other social networking sites, at home or in the Internet café.[46]

A further reason has to do with rising levels of education. In Europe and the United States, the educational level of the workforce has increased continuously since the Second World War. In the United States the number of college bachelor's degrees conferred annually has almost doubled, from 840,000 in 1970 to 1,450,000 in 2005. At the same time, the number of master's degrees conferred has increased more than sixfold, from 26,000 in 1970 to 143,000 in 2005.[47] And the scenario is similar for many industrializing countries today. The rise in higher education has been particularly prominent in the so-called creative professions, which now have an oversupply of graduates in relation to available jobs. In Milan, for example, design schools produced 11,000 graduates between 1991 and 2001, but that sector offered only 3,000 jobs; figures for London are similar.[48] This tendency in itself testifies to a value shift within the educated population. We seem to be in the midst of a general Buddenbrooks effect, where people—particularly young people—are prepared to take their chances in difficult professions in hopes of pursuing a career that is rewarding and that allows for self-realization. Indeed, the number of people who self-identify as "artists" on the U.S. census has increased tenfold since the 1960s.[49]

Arguably this value shift is also supported by new forms of institutionalized reward systems in which reputation and social recognition count more than in previous systems. The point here is simply that skilled labor is no longer terribly difficult to come by, and the number of people who seem to be willing to "work for free" is on the increase. (Of course, this means that the definition of "skill" changes, as we will discuss below.)

If skills and labor become abundant, value creation—whether in the traditional capitalist sense of the term or in the sense of being able to create something that stands out as unique and attractive even if it does not have monetary value, like a free operating system—no longer directly depends on access to skills or skilled labor. Rather, such value creation comes to depend on the ability to organize the appropriation and to put to work common resources that are, in themselves, abundant and, essentially, free. In the advertising industry, for example, the proliferation of advertising space and the generalization of the ability to actually produce advertisements have radically altered business models. Advertising agencies used to live off their ability to actually design advertisements, but with desktop publishing "any kid with a Macintosh can do that." This diffusion of skills has led to the emergence of bureaus specializing in event marketing, cool hunting, or viral marketing. All of these practices imply ways of creating value that do not primarily deploy the agency's own skills and resources. Rather they presuppose an ability to connect to developments in the agencies' environment—whether it be new consumer trends, word-of-mouth networks, or artistic talent from the urban "underground"—and put them to work for clients. Indeed, it can be argued that an important aspect of the business model of "creative industries" in general is the packaging and valorizing of creative content that is produced somewhere else. And the ability to identify and connect external resources that presuppose large and diverse networks has become a primary criterion for professional success. In this sense, Richard Florida, whose writings on the "creative class" have been hugely successful among academics and urban policymakers in the last decade, is perfectly correct in identifying the city rather than the firm as the main repository of knowledge and talent. (And before him came a substantial body of literature, although more technical and less popular, on "learning regions" or "districts.")[50]

The point is not that individual skills or "craftsmanship" no longer counts. (Indeed, as Richard Sennett suggests, the generalization of skills can lead to standardization of even medium-quality products, which in itself puts a premium on "craftsmanship." Take the wine industry, for example: there has probably never been as much drinkable, well-made wine available. But at the same time premium prices for uniquely crafted wines have risen to astronomical heights.[51]) The point is actually that the strategic key to success in the information economy shifts from having skills and talent to finding and organizing skills and talent (which is, of course, in itself a talent). Similar arguments have long circulated in the managerial literature, which has emphasized the value of "brokerage" and "closure": the ability to connect resources within a network and the ability to provide coherence to the new productive configurations that emerge from these connections.[52] And increasingly, publics is the organizational form through which this kind of coordination is achieved.

Let us summarize the argument so far. The proliferation of digital media has led to the "becoming productive" of an ever-wider range of aspects of ordinary life. Time, talents, and resources that previously were private have become public and generally available as a cognitive surplus. Within organizations, management now seeks to capitalize on employees' informal relations in raising the productivity of work, particularly knowledge work, and in the public domain, a "participatory culture" has become a feature of ordinary social relations. At the same time, publics have affirmed themselves as a new way of organizing this socialized productivity. While publics are an older model of organization, they have become more common as digital media have distributed and in a sense democratized the means of association. Even though publics are prolific as a way of organizing more "ephemeral" forms of participatory culture, it is a mistake to consider them simply a characteristic of hobbyists or counterculturalists. Rather, productive publics are becoming an integrated and important feature of contemporary business practices.

Brands have evolved from simple "symbols of products" that allowed consumers to distinguish functionally and aesthetically similar products from one another. Today branding attempts to create extended publics that might involve consumers, employees, and subcontractors, and that are united around an ethos that supports a perception of the brand as different and themselves as linked to it and each other in perhaps loose, but ethically binding ways. Companies more and more often turn to user-generated innovation networks, where they can capitalize on the affective bonds between consumers and brands as a motivation for consumers to provide inputs and suggestions, or simply to share their knowledge. And when brands are not strong enough to generate the kinds of affective bonds that can directly support such an initiative, companies trawl online "tribes," in which mothers, reality television enthusiasts, skiers, and other publics discuss the virtues and drawbacks of products and brands.

Inter-firm cooperation increasingly takes the form of publics as well. The concept of an industrial district, pioneered by Marshall but made popular by the success of Italian industrial districts in the 1980s, was based on the notion that physical proximity and a dense web of concrete interaction among firms provided a competitive advantage in terms of social capital that could facilitate trust, knowledge exchange, and flexible coordination. Today, companies like the Italian Arduino, an open-source hardware circuit board creator, derive value from a global public of producers and developers who are not physically proximate and do not regularly interact, but who nevertheless make up a public of Arduino users who share their own improvements and additions to the product and who are united by a strong ethos that emphasizes the values of openness and collaboration. In China "pirate" or *shan-zai* networks are formed by subcontractors to global OEMs (original equipment manufacturers) who share designs and innovations for the electronic consumer goods that they develop (chiefly mobile phones and laptop clones) and who are united by a common ethos combining quirky aesthetics with a spirit of rebellion in relation to established global brands. Even though the *shan-zai* productive public originated in the dense industrial district of Shenzhen, its members are now located across all of China, as well as in other parts of Asia.[53] Indeed, David de Ugarte, from the South American peer-to-peer collective Las Indias, argues that such ethically integrated productive publics, which he calls "phyles," combining businesses and other actors and driven mainly by a commitment to a common ethos, are emerging as the economic organizations of the future.[54] Importantly, companies are increasingly trying to constitute themselves as publics. For extended networked organizations with value chains that stretch across the globe and with complex stakeholder relations, organizations that compete mainly on brand or other "intangible" benefits, it becomes crucial to enable members of the organization to cohere around a common enterprise with its own particular ethos. The growing pervasiveness of concepts like "corporate culture," "corporate brand," "corporate community," or even "corporate social responsibility" all testify to the company-as-a-public development.

Publics have particular features. They are mediated associations between strangers that are devoted to a particular cause. In productive publics the particular cause involves the productive deployment of common resources in ways that feed back into the commonly available pool of wealth. Publics therefore become a way to organize the "circulation of commons," which the Canadian media scholar Nick Dyer Witheford sees as the fundamental dynamic of the information economy.[55] But publics also contain a particular way of evaluating such productive activities, which has the potential to become a basis for a new value logic. We will examine this aspect of productive publics in chapter 4.

4

Value

Since the first decade of the twenty-first century, and in particular follow-ing the onset of a more interactive, Web 2.0 online culture, the possibil-ity of an emerging "third" mode of value creation—beyond markets and hierarchies—has claimed attention in both managerial thought and theo-ries of participatory culture more generally. These theories have indepen-dently arrived at largely converging models of how people come together in self-organized associations of strangers, what we have called "publics," to create wealth using primarily common resources. In recent years much scholarship has documented this trend in contexts as diverse as the kind of large-scale collaborative creativity that unfolds in knowledge-intensive organizations; free or open-source software networks; brand communi-ties, consumer tribes, and other publics of online prosumers; and the cre-ative scenes that have developed in urban centers. Generally, however, the theories that have grown out of these studies have avoided the question of value, of how the relative value of the wealth thus created, and of the indi-vidual efforts required to produce it, is set. The reasons for this blind spot have mainly been ideological: scholars as well as pundits have generally viewed the growth of collaborative public forms of value creation as har-boring the promise of a new, more egalitarian or even altruistic economic arrangement, in which the question of value would matter less as each would contribute to the public domain in accordance with her possibilities and take out according to his needs. Communism, not with a bang but with a whimper, as it were.

The reality of the matter is more complex. Not only does the strongly hierarchical and unequal nature of actual productive publics refute such rather naive egalitarian dreams ,whether clothed in the political ideology of cyber communism or, more recently, in the less overtly political language of "altruistic genes." (As Josh Lerner and Jean Tirole observed in their early study of the economics of open source, "The overall picture that we drew from our interviews and from the responses we received in reaction to the first draft of the paper is that the open source process is quite elitist.")[1] But the growing connection between companies' ability to capitalize on such productive publics and the financial valuation of their intangible assets suggests that what productive publics create should be understood to have monetary value in some way.

We will address this "missing link" by trying to construct a theory of value for productive publics. We believe that this is an essential building block not only for understanding how an emerging new mode of production might work but also for constructing a value regime that would allow this new form of value creation to be governed with greater degrees of justice and legitimacy.

And we believe that such a theory can be constructed, not by positing the existence of some kind of proto-communist "gift economies," nor by reintroducing the Fordist concept of labor, but by starting with the concepts of action, excellence, and reputation. Before we embark on that venture, however, let us briefly examine existing theories of public value creation.

COMMONS-BASED PEER PRODUCTION

Along with the developments in managerial thought and cultural theory, the dot-com boom of the 1990s drove many Internet enthusiasts to argue that valuable and strategically central goods, like software, were now produced in ways that defied the logic of industrial society. Centered on notions like "cooking pot markets," or the "high-tech gift economy" of bazaars instead of cathedrals, thinkers like Rishab Gosh, Richard Barbrook, and Eric Raymond argued that the Internet facilitated the emergence of a collaborative economy in which people would freely share their efforts without the expectation of direct monetary compensation.[2] Many of these thinkers belonged to the cultural environment that had formed around the influential magazine *Wired*, and what Richard Barbrook would later call the "Californian Ideology" of Silicon Valley entrepreneurial networks, and many of them saw the Internet as a medium for a large-scale diffusion of the alternative economic models that had long circulated within the countercultural communes and DIY movements that had proliferated in the United States in the 1970s.[3] To them "the Internet" could be understood as "inherently anti-capitalist" and as the embodiment of actually existing "anarcho-communism." This radical view of social production has been moderated in recent years as influential books like Don Tapscott and Anthony Williams's *Wikinomics* (and many others) have brought the idea of a new collaborative model of production to the attention of the business world. They have stressed the compatibility between productive publics and existing business models by explaining how similar gift- or commons-based models of production can be extended beyond the collaborative production of software, to include popular practices of consumer- or user-led innovation, customer-generated brand communities, or, indeed, the production of culture and information in general.[4] However, the notion of online production networks as a free-for-all persists, even in sophisticated contemporary approaches.

To date, the most famous theorist of wealth creation in productive publics—or as he calls it, "social production"—has been Yochai Benkler. In *The Wealth of Networks: How Social Production Transforms Markets and Freedom*, Benkler stresses that this model of production is new and distinct. Social production is "emerging alongside contract- and market-based, managerial-firm based and state-based production." And he suggests that it is marked by three main characteristics: (1) decentralization—"the authority to act resides with individual agents faced with opportunities for action, rather than in the hands of a central organizer, like the manager of a firm or a bureaucrat"; (2) a frequent use of common resources and public goods; and (3) the prevalence of non-monetary motivations—"Participants to social production use social cues and motivations, rather than prices or commands, to motivate and coordinate the action of participating agents."[5]

And while none of these features is new in itself, all of them have been brought to the fore by three central characteristics of digital media: that "the physical machinery necessary to participate in information and cultural production is almost universally distributed in the population of the advanced economies"; that "the primary raw materials of the information economy, unlike the industrial economy, are public goods—existing information, knowledge and culture" that have an "actual marginal cost of zero"; and that the technical architectures, organizational models, and social dynamics of information production and exchange on the Internet have developed so that they allow us to structure the solution to problems—in particular to information production problems—in ways that are highly modular. This allows diversely motivated people to act for a wide range of reasons that, in combination, cohere into new, useful information, knowledge and cultural goods.[6]

Along with Benkler, Michel Bauwens has suggested the notion of peer-to-peer (or P2P) production. This model coincides with that of Benkler but puts greater emphasis on the ability of peer-to-peer publics to self-organize. The characteristics of such P2P networks are that

> 1) they produce use-value through the free cooperation of producers who have access to distributed capital: this is the P2P production mode, a "third mode of production" different from for-profit or public production by state owned enterprises. Its product is not exchange value for a market, but use value for a community of users.
> 2) They are governed by the community of producers themselves, and not by market allocation or corporate hierarchy: this is the P2P governance mode
> 3) they make use value freely accessible on a universal basis, through new common property regimes. This is its distribution or "peer property mode": a "third mode of ownership" different from private property or public (state) property.[7]

Both Bauwens's and Benkler's models describe the dynamics of wealth creation in public collaborative production rather well: they both focus on how wealth is created by individuals (or small groups) that use common resources to create new things that are subsequently put into the common domain; they both emphasize the diversity of motives—beyond the monetary carrot and the stick of bureaucratic command—that govern these processes; and they both emphasize the (at least theoretical) sovereignty of these networks. However, both also avoid the question of how the value of what is produced or of particular productive efforts is set. In both cases this avoidance of the question of value is, at least in part, the result of a certain idealism. Bauwens clearly sees peer-to-peer production as the building block of a new, more evolved, age of collaboration that will replace capitalism, or indeed Western civilization as such. Benkler sees social production as a seed for the suspension of the market mechanism in favor of collaboration, and in his later work he has discussed the possibility of a collaborative gene that, hitherto suppressed by corporate capitalism, is now allowed to flourish freely, as the costs of such collaboration are radically diminished:

> We need to assume no fundamental change in the nature of humanity. . . . We merely need to see that the material conditions of production in the networked information economy have changed in ways that increase the relative salience of social sharing and exchange as a modality of economic production. That is, behaviors and motivation patterns familiar to us from social relations generally continue to cohere in their own patterns. What has changed is that now these patterns of behavior have become effective beyond the domains of building social relations of mutual interest and fulfilling our emotional and psychological needs of companionship and mutual recognition. They have come to play a substantial role as modes of motivating, informing, and organizing productive behavior at the very core of the information economy.[8]

Even managerial scholars like Paul Adler have had to invoke "altruism" as a deus ex machina in order to solve the apparent paradox of how such productive networks (which he terms "trust-based") can persist despite a meager prospect for monetary rewards.

> Economic theory argues that trust, like knowledge itself, is a public good, and that the spontaneous working of the price mechanism (assumed to be the dominant one) will generate too large a free rider problem [but] people have a propensity for altruism that coexists and competes with the propensity for egoism . . . then there is no reason to believe that trust cannot become an important, or even dominant mechanism of coordination in the right circumstances.[9]

And even though Benkler is sometimes ambiguous on this point (as when he discusses the literature of "social capital" and when he suggests that "social standing" can be taken along with "economic standing" as an "ultimate" economic motivation), he does insist on the diversity of motives that makes people participate in processes of what he calls social production and makes the motivations that drive their participation "not amendable to calculation." In other words, there is no single, rational value logic to social production.

In an alternative model, scholars of Marxist or post-Marxist inspiration have suggested that participation in productive publics could be understood as a form of labor that is exploited by corporations, and in particular by social media companies. This idea was first launched by Tiziana Terranova in a 2000 essay. Discussing the unsalaried productive activity that went into creating and maintaining the wealth of online content that rendered "the Internet" a valuable experience, and drawing on the tradition of Italian "autonomist" Marxism, Terranova concluded that such forms of labor were neither rewarded nor commanded (they were free, as in "free beer" and "free speech," to use Richard Stallman's terms). This insight led her to suggest that such free labor was both subject to extraordinary degrees of exploitation (since the appropriation of surplus value, although limited in monetary terms, was theoretically endless), and, at least theoretically, on the verge of developing new forms of autonomous self-organization. In other words, free labor represented both the most extreme development of the capitalist "subsumption of life" and the most promising candidate for the negation of the capitalist order overall. The notion of free labor has been further developed by authors like Christian Fuchs and Mark Andrejevic, who have applied it to their analysis of value creation and exploitation in the contemporary media economy, and by a long strand of research on contemporary creative or "digital labor."[10]

While the concept of free labor provides an illuminating critique of more enthusiastic narratives of Web 2.0 and "participatory culture," which is able to point out potential injustices and imbalances, it does not "hold water" from the point of view of economic analysis. This is so primarily because, as we argued in chapter 2, in complex networks of collaborative production that use common resources, the linear relation between value and time, necessary for the Marxist critique to work, no longer holds.[11] A less theoretical but more intuitive objection could be that using Facebook, contributing to an open-source operating system, or taking part in a local electronic music scene is rarely experienced as "labor"—at least not in the fairly negative sense that modern social theory has assigned to this term.

Hannah Arendt, who is admittedly extreme in her devaluation of labor, distinguishes between labor, work, and action. The first category, labor, is human activity that is uniquely motivated by necessity, whether external necessity, like the command of factory discipline, or internal necessity, like hunger and other biological forces. Labor in this sense is the condition that marked the lives of slaves in antiquity (and, Arendt suggests, factory workers in modernity). It is the lowest form of human existence. Work, on the other hand, creates an enduring artifact, a computer program, a product of craftsmanship, and it does so as an expression of the individuality of the creator. Work is not entirely driven by necessity. It follows that work is something that one can take pride in; it is the condition of life of the craftsman. Action, finally, describes the deeds and statements by means of which human beings construct a common world together. Action comprises things like political action, enterprise and innovation, and military valor. Like work, action is driven by self-expression and will.[12]

Now, we argue that since participation in productive publics is undertaken freely, since most members of such publics often take pride in their achievements, and since they often understand their participation to be important for their identity, such activity is much more similar to what Arendt calls "work" than to what she calls "labor." (In fact, software creation, knowledge work, and cultural creativity have many traits that resemble traditional forms of craftsmanship.) But since these activities are also self-organizing, they contain an intrinsic "political" or at least "deliberative" element. That is, members of productive publics need not only contribute to the concrete productive "craft" that the public is devoted to (wine connoisseurship, creation of an online encyclopedia, and so on), they need also to participate in the process of collective deliberation whereby the (frequently changing) rules and principles by means of which that particular pursuit is organized are elaborated. And similar things are true for the publics of knowledge workers that operate within corporations.[13] And in doing so, participants in such productive publics make use of their communicative abilities as well as their entrepreneurial courage (in the classic sense of that term). In other words, rather than labor, participation in productive publics should be understood as a combination of work and action.

This observation also gives us a different perspective on value. The value of labor is set according to fixed, external parameters, like time or productivity. The value of work and action, on the other hand, is set according to the *excellence* of these pursuits. But there is no given objective criterion for excellence. Rather, excellence is context-dependent: excellence at creating open-source software is different from excellence at being a deejay. Therefore, the only possible operational measure of excellence is the reputation that an actor can acquire within a particular public: what other people say about his excellence *defines* his excellence. In his empirical analysis of the open-source software public Advogato sociologist Daniel Stewart makes this minor but important point succinctly: "Community members attain status in the Advogato community not necessarily by being good programmers, but by having others say that they are good programmers."[14] Reputation is an inter-subjective measure of excellence, the criteria of which are themselves inter-subjectively elaborated: they depend on the "orders of worth" that are contained in the ethos of a particular public.

Being a good programmer, exhibiting technical excellence, displaying the excellence of the craftsman are obvious ways to acquire a reputation. But those are not the only ways. The many empirical studies of productive publics that have come forth in recent years have also stressed that a good reputation can be gained through one's ability to strengthen the coherence of the public itself in a non-technical way through action rather than work. This can be a matter of socializing new members into the ethos of the public, of elaborating on its values, rules, or norms, or simply of enabling it to do what it does in smoother and more efficient ways. It is clear that such excellent action is an important factor in the kinds of publics that are devoted to non-technical pursuits. In the kinds of self-organized food-buying groups that have sprung up in Europe and in the United States in recent years, for example, engaged consumers are coming together to collectively purchase organic meat, cheese, vegetables, and wine from local producers. The criteria applied for selecting new members of those groups go beyond the potential ability to contribute economically, also considering their reputation as people who are likely to become engaged in and contribute to the strength and vitality of the group.[15] Similarly, in our studies of urban underground scenes, we have found that actors with a certain status often take a calculated interest in actions that can strengthen the coherence of the scene itself, like organizing a party or an event that gives others an opportunity to express themselves. They do this because they understand that such seemingly disinterested contributions to the strength of a local "scene" serve to further their reputation and increase the ethical capital at their disposal.

But excellent action can also be a foundation for reputation in publics devoted to more technical pursuits. Free-software communities also exhibit a strong correlation between the reputation of a member and her ability not only to "write beautiful code" but also to contribute to and reinforce the values and ethos through which the public coheres as a productive unit. In her anthropological work on the free-software project Debian, Gabriela Coleman calls this ability "ethical labor" (an expression that would have made Hannah Arendt cringe!). She intends this in two ways. On the one hand, the term refers to the work of introducing and socializing new members into the Debian community and its values: the creation of an appropriate subjectivity that fits the ideological agenda of the movement. As Chris Kelty argues in his work, participation in free software, as in many other kinds of "movements," entails a process of schooling: "Geeks," as he calls the participants, do not "start out with ideologies, but instead come to them through their involvement in the practices of creating Free Software and its derivatives."[16] On the other hand, Coleman refers to the ongoing and necessary work of contributing to the rules and norms that guide the public, and that are created from below by members of the public themselves—she calls this "jurisgenesis"—as well as the necessary ongoing work of "micro crisis resolution," which results from the self-organization of the productive process that the public undertakes:

> As the number of developers in the Debian project has grown from one dozen to nearly one thousand, crises routinely emerge around particularly contested issues: matters of project transparency, internal and external communication, size, openness, the nature of authority within the project, the role of non-free packages, and the licensing of Debian. Many of these crises have an acute phase in which debate erupts on several media all at once: mailing lists, IRC conversation, blog entries. While the debate during these periods can be congenial, measured, rational, and sometimes peppered with jokes, its tone can also be passionate, uncharitable, and sometimes downright vicious.[17]

The ability to resolve such ever-recurring crises, large and small, contributes strongly to a person's reputation and standing within the public. Indeed, many studies suggest that within productive publics themselves, there is no clear separation between technical and non-technical (or ethical, to use Coleman's term) brilliance as a source of reputation. One acquires reputation through one's ability to contribute to the *cause* of a public, and if that cause is concerned with furthering free software, then reputation is contingent on technical as well as non-technical ability: on work as well as action. One needs to be able to write beautiful code *and* to contribute to the ethos of the public. As Chris Kelty writes in his anthropology of free software,

> Free Software is a public of a particular kind: a recursive public. Recursive publics are concerned with the ability to build, control, modify, and maintain the infrastructure that allows them to come into being in the first place and which, in turn, constitutes their everyday practical commitments and the identities of the participants as creative and

autonomous individuals. In the cases explored herein, that specific infrastructure includes the creation of the Internet itself, as well as its associated tools and structures, such as Usenet, e-mail, the World Wide Web (www), UNIX and UNIX-derived operating systems, protocols, standards, and standards processes.[18]

Reputation in productive publics is contingent on the ability to further the cause of the public. In free-software publics, reputation unfolds through action in crisis resolution and jurigenesis, the creation of norms and rules, and the work of creating a technical object—free software—which is in itself understood to have strong ethical significance, to be a manifestation of the ethos of the public at hand. In self-organized food-buying groups, reputation is built through commitment to the strength and integrity of the group itself, and through the ability to source good suppliers and organize a smoothly functioning process.

The connection between action and ethics can be made more conceptually solid than Coleman's rather unfortunate term "ethical labor" suggests. For Aristotle, on whose thought Arendt builds, action (if not work) is strongly connected to virtue. Indeed, Aristotle's term for virtue, *areté*, also means "excellence," so his term for virtuous character—*ethiké areté*—could also be translated as "excellent character." And character results from action (or rather from habit, which is the accumulated result of past actions). So in this sense we can propose that reputation builds on both the excellent skills of the craftsman and the virtuous character of the social individual. Furthermore, in this tradition such virtue essentially means the ability to adapt and moderate one's passions in order to be able to live well with others. In *Nicomachean Ethics*, Aristotle does not provide a catalogue of virtues so much as he lays out a number of examples of virtuous traits, all of which involve moderation: the ability to find a golden mean between two affective extremes. (Courage, for example, is a golden mean between cowardice and foolhardiness.) Indeed, the kinds of virtues to which Aristotle seems to give the highest importance—magnanimity, wisdom (*phronesis*), justice, and friendship—are all premised on such kinds of affective adaptation. For Aristotle, virtue in the general sense applies primarily to the ability to adapt to and live well with others, so that the *polis* (or in our case the public) can harbor the possibility for a good life (*eudaimonia*). To once again draw on Coleman's work, virtue builds on the ability to contribute to a community where "others can also engage in the life-long project of technical self-cultivation within a community of peers."[19]

A second definition of virtue, perhaps more traditional, is "negative," in the sense that virtue implies not challenging the norms and standards according to which the prevailing ethos of a particular public defines a "life well lived." The strength and rigor of such expectations naturally vary among different publics, but it is a common feature of productive publics that certain behaviors have a negative impact on reputation. In our study of the urban "underground" of Copenhagen, for example, actors were concerned about navigating the difficult interface between creativity and commerce in ways that would not make them appear to be "selling out" to commercial interests, while still being able to do so in practice. Most actors were conscious of the fine-tuned economic dynamics whereby gains in monetary terms could be evaluated against possible losses in reputational terms. Similarly, but in an entirely different empirical context, market researchers have found that members of brand communities who switch to competing brands are seen as "traitors" and suffer heavy reputational losses that can sometimes be damaging to their social lives as well.[20]

So it would seem that in productive publics, reputation is conferred on individuals not only in relation to their brilliance in constructing the artifact (in the widest sense of that term) to which the public is devoted, but also in relation to their virtue, their ability to act in ways that conserve or reinforce the strength and vitality of the public. Even in highly specialized publics, like open-source software developers, people are judged not only for their ability to write "beautiful code" but also for their ability to solve conflicts, socialize new members, and contribute to the cause of the public in general. Such judgments are even more important in publics that require less in terms of technical brilliance, like brand communities or people devoted to a common erotic kink, where the conduct and virtue of individual members often become the main determinant of their standing in the eyes of others. Indeed, in an early study, Don Slater showed that "sex pic traders on IRC"—a breed that by now is presumably defunct—maintained what he called a "moral economy" in which they constantly judged one another's conduct, both in terms of their propensity to "leach" and in terms of the tone of discussion that individual members engaged in.[21] In this sense, reputation can be understood as a measure of the excellence that an individual exhibits in the use of common resources. And it is a comprehensive measure, as it includes both excellence in putting those resources to use in relation to achieving a particular goal or aim (excellent work) and excellence in acting on, strengthening, or preserving the however implicit norms and rules that are contained in the ethos of the public at hand (excellent action). It is the excellence of the "social individual" who is able to draw on and contribute to the value of the common.

As a measure of excellence in the use of common resources, reputation depends on an abstraction of a multitude of value judgments conferred on an individual by a large number of actors who may depart from diverse value horizons. Reputation is the mechanism whereby publics are able to abstract the concrete value judgments that particular members express, and transform these judgments into comparable expressions of a common "substance" or "general equivalent" that embodies the comprehensive judgment of the public itself. Each public has its own "law" of value that enables the conversion of concrete value judgments to a reputation that has general validity. Reputation is the way value is measured and circulates in an economy of commons.

ETHICAL CAPITAL I

But why would people want to acquire a reputation? On a basic level, reputation can be viewed as a form of what sociologists call "social capital," or "the goodwill inherent in social relations"—to use one current definition—that enables people to benefit from others in legitimate ways. But reputation is a distinct form of social capital. While social capital is generally understood to build on the goodwill conferred on an actor by a community to which she is directly related, reputation builds on the goodwill conferred on an actor by a public of strangers. Conversely, reputation supports a public persona that influences attitudes toward someone that one does not know. This way, reputation is the form that goodwill (or ill will) takes in publics.[22] We will call this ethical capital (from ethos, character, custom), in order to emphasize this slight but important difference. The difference consists in the fact that social capital builds on and is reinforced by actual social relations, by concrete interaction between individuals. But ethical capital builds on affective relations—that is, form of identification and experiences of proximity that might act out at a distance without any interaction having to take place. (Of course, such affective relations, such ethos, can subsequently be actualized, when people actually meet. But you do not need to have met Steve Jobs to admire—or hate—his work.) In this sense ethical capital builds on the ability to construct a common sentiment—or better, ethos—that affects the interpretation of a person that one might not know. Ethical capital works at a distance; it can be, and often is, based on mediated relations (like those between a celebrity and his fans, or those between members of the same public of brand enthusiasts who can exhibit goodwill in relation to each other by virtue of their sharing an ethos, even if they have never met). Ethical capital is the form that social capital takes in publics.

Like social capital, ethical capital is a valuable resource that can be put to a variety of different uses. But because of its affective, mediated nature its uses are slightly different from those traditionally associated with social capital.

One way in which ethical capital can be put to use is, however, similar to that traditionally associated with social capital. Within a particular public, reputation allows an individual to mobilize and motivate others. Take the example of software: the greater a person's contribution to a particular public, the higher both the quantity and the quality of her reputation. The stronger the reputation, the higher the position in the hierarchies of the public. It takes reputation to advance from being an ordinary programmer to being a project manager, and onward. And the higher the position, the easier it is to motivate others and create the strong ties that organize productive processes and mobilize resources.

Alternatively, such ethical capital can be monetized in a wide variety of ways (some of which we will explore below). Within urban undergrounds, for example, there is quite a direct relation between the reputation that a person has been able to accumulate and his ability to live off his activities. A lot of participants in free and open-source software publics build on their reputation in those publics to find jobs and advance their corporate careers.[23]

Importantly, accumulation of ethical capital also enhances the experience of self-realization that most participants in productive publics list as the most important motive for participating. This can be a matter of giving expression to one's values and convictions. Many productive publics have strongly articulated ideals or vocations, which to their experience sets them off from what they regard as their "enemy." The free-software world, for example, entertains a strong belief in the virtues of free software, which distinguishes that community from the main enemy, Microsoft. (Sixty-seven percent of surveyed free-software developers stated motivations like "software should not be a proprietary good" or "limiting the power for large software companies" as their main reasons for contributing.)[24] Mainly, however, participation is a matter of experiencing the social recognition of the qualities, talents, and skills that one values in oneself, to be able to experience the direct positive recognition of others. In this sense, ethical capital translates into socially recognized charisma. Steven Weber stresses this point in *The Success of Open Source*. Open-source programming is first of all an aesthetic pursuit, a pleasurable act of self-expression; it is about "the ineffably geeky joys of writing the slickest code you can." But it is important to emphasize that such self-realization is a social activity. It is not enough for me to know that I write excellent code. I need a group of people that I recognize as my peers to, in turn, recognize this fact. So the real motivation consists in developing "code that represents an elegant solution to a complex problem[, which] is a thing of beauty that in the open source setting *can be shared with others*. . . . Open source lets you show the world just how creative you really are. It is the equivalent of putting your best work on display at the national gallery of art as compared to locking it in your basement."[25]

Whatever their other motives might be, one important reason for participation in productive publics is the prospect of acquiring ethical capital that can be "realized" in a wide variety of different ways: as social capital within publics, as a means to enhance individual enjoyment, and as a convention that determines the value of individual skills and labor power. And the more widespread productive publics become as ways of organizing the creation of wealth, the greater the importance of acquiring such ethical capital as a component of overall economic rationality. To understand this better, let us take a look at knowledge work, where productive publics are most prevalent.

Reputation and the Transformation of Knowledge Work

The examples discussed above, like free or open-source software networks or urban creative scenes, are "pure" productive publics in the sense that they remain relatively untouched by the logic of the corporate economy. Or at least this used to be the case. Today we are seeing growing interpenetration of corporate interests in open-source software networks, and, arguably, a similar blurring of the boundaries between creative industries and the "underground," as cities are becoming increasingly branded. In addition, new directions for self-organized productive publics, like social innovation scenes or the social entrepreneurship movement, make it ever more difficult to distinguish between the realm of productive publics and the established corporate economy and perhaps also less useful to demarcate. In any case, it is true that the examples that we have cited remain relatively untouched by the monetary economy in general. In 2002 the FLOSS free-software survey showed that 30 percent of developers made less than 1,000 euros per month, and 50 percent less than 2,000 euros, even though only 20 percent were students or unemployed and 70 percent had a university degree.[26] A similar indication of the amount of money circulating in urban "undergrounds" can be derived from Gregory Sholette's statistics, which show that in 1990, 50 percent of artists in the United States made less than $3,000 a year from their art.[27] Our investigations of the creative scenes of Malmö and Copenhagen support this. Only the absolute top deejays, artists, designers, and, lately, promoters are able to make a living from their creativity. Most live off something else—student loans, state subsidies, their parents, a day job. Some sectors, such as music video production, practically build on and presuppose the free work of participants. As a rule, people do not get paid, or are seriously underpaid (as the head of one of Copenhagen's most successful video collectives commented on how they rewarded the producer of one of their videos, "We paid him with an iPod").

However, value dynamics similar to those we have observed in "purer" forms of productive publics are making inroads into paid forms of knowledge work as well. This development is directly linked to the abundance of skills and skilled labor that we discussed in chapter 3. Among knowledge workers this new situation of "abundance" has had two chief consequences.

First, it has led to a transformation in the kinds of skills that are required from knowledge workers. Recent debates on "knowledge work" have been centered on concepts like teamwork, project management, post-bureaucracy, and "collaborative community."[28] A common theme has been that in an "Internet era," productive cooperation escapes the control of established corporate hierarchies and what really creates value is the ability of knowledge workers to take charge of and organize their own forms of productive collaboration. For example, Susan Christopherson, in her empirical studies of the film and television industry, speaks of a replacement of older skilled craft workers with a new generation of flexible generic workers who are the outcome of the enormous expansion in film and media education in the United States. In these programs, which have proliferated mainly in Los Angeles and New York, students learn a wide variety of production skills and are introduced to new technologies that cross conventional professional and craft boundaries.

They learn how to produce projects on "shoestring" budgets and how to work very rapidly and under severe time constraints. They learn how to work in efficient multifunctional production teams. When they graduate, they are hybrids, writer-directors, director-camera-operator-editors, who make up a flexible independent-contractor workforce.[29]

The point here is not that there might be more-talented or less-talented individuals but that the nature of the talent required is somewhat different. Yes, it is still necessary to be skilled at operating a camera. But a lot of people possess those skills. It is even more important to be skilled at learning new skills and adapting to new situations, to use and deploy common knowledge with excellence. Indeed, Christopherson's analysis shows how the value of television producers increases with their ability to pick up skills from the communities of practice in which they operate, and more generally with their cultivation of social skills, the ability to function as value-adding members of those communities. Studies of knowledge workers show similar results; particularly with the impact of social media, the value of their labor becomes directly related to their ability to participate in inter-firm, social flows of knowledge, while the "stock" of knowledge and skills that they own, their "human capital," counts for less.[30] Similarly, most successful entrepreneurs in the high-tech sector have been able to capitalize on insights that they have developed by participating in networks of knowledge sharing or "collective intelligence," like free software or other publics or by otherwise participating in milieus that cultivate specialized forms of knowledge (Los Angeles for film, New York for advertising, Silicon Valley for software, etc.).[31]

Success in such "collaborative skills" depends less on formal skills and more on an attitude similar to that which we discussed as "virtue" above. In their research on contemporary knowledge work, Charles Heckscher and Paul Adler stress that in new project-oriented and collaborative work processes, virtue, in the sense of "living well" and handling specific situations, is essentially what determines success and worth. They argue that:

> the traditional bureaucratic character type manages to reduce interaction with, and the need for understanding of, those who are different by on the one hand emphasizing conformity, and on the other building walls around different positions. The collaborative sense of self, by contrast, requires constant interaction, taking responsibility for the collective outcome rather than just for doing a job, and it therefore requires the ability to grasp the distinctive contributions that different types can make to a shared project. Individuals need capacity to "see it from the others point of view"—far more than in either traditional or modern forms of community.[32]

Heckscher and Adler go on to suggest that this new importance of virtue is related to the emergence of a new value logic. Comparing the new logic to the standards of value that prevailed in the Weberian ideal-typical bureaucratic organization that emphasized individual achievement according to a fixed standard of goals, they suggest that public contribution is now emerging as the main standard for the social determination of the value of a person. Drawing on social psychologist George Herbert Mead's notion of the "interdependent self," they suggest that participants in such collaborative communities, as they call them, come to foster an ethic in which they understand their own worth as well as that of others in terms of their ability to make a community contribution, either by identifying and creating opportunities for others or by making a contribution to the "collective task" more generally. Participants in social production generally entertain a "sense of worth from contribution rather than from position." As one of their interviewees stated, "If you generate enough value, recognition will come, people understand where the value is being generated."[33] If the corporate career favored individual advancement and status competition—"keeping up with the Joneses," as the dictum went in 1950s America—the new kinds of collaborative production favor a motivational structure in which the individual feels deeply interconnected and interdependent with others and that exhibits a "collaborative sense of self," privileging both the ability to take other people's point of view seriously and integrate it into the processes of coproduction and the ability to create value and opportunities for the people to whom one is somehow affectively attached, like one's coworkers. In other words, the overall ideal is not individual accumulation but the creation of social value, to have a positive impact on the people with whom one has some kind of affective connection.

The literature also suggests that this new mind-set has triggered a transformation of the motivational setup of salaried knowledge workers, away from the organizational climbing associated with the "organization men" of industrial society and on to a cultivation of personal assets, skills, and chiefly, ethical capital in the form of reputation. Knowledge workers have shifted their loyalty and attachments away from the corporation (partly because the prospects of lifelong employment are weaker today) and toward a cultivation of the kinds of ethical capital that are better able to further their success in a more volatile environment. As organizational sociologist Bill Martin observes in a study of managers in networked organizations, "The value of reputations is likely to increase as organizations move away from bureaucratic structures to more hybrid and flexible ones."[34]

The second consequence of the abundance of skills has been the growth of freelance work. Such work can take different forms. It can be a matter of the relatively prosperous and powerful neo-nomads or "sublimes" who are able to capitalize on their reputations and/or their particular skills to move in and out of temporary highly paid employment. They might be working for a couple of months for a software or consulting company and then dedicate the next month to their favorite social enterprise or a hobby project. They might be the serial entrepreneurs who populated the top of the Silicon Valley "food chain" during the dot-com and Web 2.0 booms of the 1990s and 2000s. Like the skilled workers (*les sublimes*) of the industrial revolution, such people are able to combine high economic standards with high degrees of freedom and self-determination. But freelance workers might also include the ever more precarious knowledge workers who populate the "underperforming" knowledge economies of southern Europe, competing against each other for short-term contracts with low pay. They might also mean the hyper-precarious workforce that populates crowdsourcing initiatives like Amazon.com's Mechanical Turk, where creative tasks like Web design or more traditional forms of knowledge work, like translation, are distributed on contracts that might be as short as a single working day. With the continuing overproduction of university graduates and the ongoing economic depression, it is likely that possibilities to maintain high levels of income and gratification while working freelance will become ever more restricted and that levels of precariousness within this group will increase. It is also likely that freelancing, whether precarious or not, will become a more common condition of knowledge work as such. At any rate, a growing number of studies document how the value of freelance skills is ever more directly related to their reputation, and how in particular the status of "elite" freelancers is directly related to the ability to maintain a strong, coherent reputation in the form of a personal brand. As Alice Marwick shows in her study of the San Francisco Web 2.0 scene, the construction of a personal brand, involving the strategic use of technologies from marketing and advertising, was a precondition for economic and career success. However, as she emphasizes, the construction of a successful personal brand was not simply a matter of manipulating a public image, even though that was one ingredient in the process. Rather, the construction of a successful personal brand required the construction (or manipulation) of an entire persona, including activities usually considered private as well and, crucially, a fair amount of "affective" work in which affective relations to a public of peers were instilled and maintained. The creation of such a personal brand involves "presenting a seemingly authentic, intimate image of the self" while crafting communicative strategies that aim at maintaining affective proximity to a public where "popularity is maintained through on-going fan management, and self-presentation is carefully constructed to be consumed by others."[35]

ETHICAL CAPITAL II

To companies, organizations as well as publics themselves, the accumulation of ethical capital serves similar crucial economic functions. As the discussion of value-based management and brands in chapter 3 suggested, the accumulation of such ethical capital becomes ever more important for organizations, as the strategic source of value shifts away from the utilization of proprietary resources to the ability to put common resources to work. In that situation it becomes ever more important for organizations to constitute themselves as extended publics that enable the creation and accumulation of such ethical capital. In many ways the recent popularity of CSR initiatives can be understood to be at least partially driven by this need. Indeed, today, under the heading "Corporate Social Responsibility," virtuous conduct has been progressively positioned as an integrated element to business practice and has become part of "doing well." The growing emphasis on creating ventures with NGOs and other nonprofit organizations can serve to both strengthen and contribute to the ethos that organizes a corporate public and constitutes in itself a source of value creation. For example, the 2006 partnership between the French dairy brand Danone and Grameen Bank was not simply a matter of philanthropy. Rather, Grameen Bank was charged with the task of devising distribution and production models for the experimental high-nutrition yogurt that Danone wanted to develop with the market of the global "bottom of the pyramid" (i.e., the people subsisting on less than $2 a day) in mind. Thus Danone and Grameen Bank did good in helping poor people to gain access to a better livelihood. But they also did well in furthering their respective agendas. Procter & Gamble has made similar use of NGOs to tap in to the market of the rural poor in South America, and these forms of cross-sector partnership are now common in the health industry, particularly in relation to the development of drugs and treatment regimens for HIV and malaria.[36]

As a collective resource, ethical capital has three important functions, similar to those that we have identified at the individual level: as social capital that creates trust, as a convention that undergirds value, and as a kind of "charisma" that sustains creativity.

The value-creating potential of social capital has mainly been explained in terms of its potential to create trust among actors, which in turn enables them to collaborate in relationships that are not subject to either the dynamics of markets or the control of bureaucracies. This freedom becomes increasingly important as productive processes begin to involve a wide range of actors that move outside of traditional mechanisms of coordination—like autonomous firms that work together outside of the control of any particular organization, or employees of a knowledge-intensive company who contribute to a collective knowledge-sharing process. In this sense the development of the concept of social capital has been part of a necessary revision of Ronald Coase's classic model of the firm. That model, first launched in Coase's groundbreaking 1937 article "The Nature of the Firm," suggested that firms can deploy two forms of coordination, markets and contracts. Contracts, or administratively sanctioned agreements with some durability in time, are deployed where transaction costs are too high for markets to work. This way, instead of a company facing costs associated with risks and imperfect information in shopping for supplies, they buy up a supplier, or enter into a long-term contractual agreement with that supplier, in order to reduce transaction costs. However, in today's complex and extended value chains that build extensively on the collaborative construction of a common knowledge pool, markets or bureaucracies are not always feasible alternatives. This puts an increasing premium on the ability to create trust relationships.

Ethical capital has the same function as social capital in that it creates trust, but it does so among actors who do not necessarily meet and interact. For example, eBay builds its business model on its ability to instill a sense of trust among strangers, without social interaction (beyond market exchange) taking place, or at least with very "thin" forms of interaction taking place. The ability to create trust, not just among colleagues or firms that are rooted in the same territory but among strangers as well, of course is enhanced as strangers become ever more frequent participants in the kinds of mediated processes of production that we have called "publics"—like consumers, colleagues in the same organization who are physically located on different sides of the world, or participants in an open production project. In such situations trust creates value in essentially two ways.

First, it facilitates interaction among participants, including consumers, along a value chain. Quite obviously, a brand that is able to instill trust can achieve stable and long-lasting relationships with consumers, which act as a sort of insurance against market risk. But it also facilitates relationships with suppliers and other external stakeholders. This is true in the obvious sense that suppliers and investors who are loyal to a brand might be more inclined to take risks. But a more subtle corollary is also true: a common sense of belonging to the ethos of a brand makes it easier for a company to trust that its suppliers do not engage in the kinds of labor practices or, increasingly, environmentally unsustainable practices that can alienate other stakeholder groups. Indeed, a 2005 survey of 365 companies in thirty countries conducted by the consulting firm Booz Allen Hamilton and the Aspen Institute found that strong brand equity as well as "the robustness of the firm's associations across its value chain, from suppliers to customers' correlate most strongly with a commitment to corporate values.[37]

Second, in networked organizations, such as eBay, trust among strangers is key to enabling efficient transactions and knowledge exchange to take place. Indeed, in today's large networked organizations, most jobs are complex and involve the exchange of tacit knowledge to a great degree. These are the kinds of jobs that create the highest value for companies, but performance varies greatly, particularly in the investment banking industry, where a recent survey found that productivity gains of up to 10 percent resulted from generating such an ethos of trust.[38]

Quite possibly the first sociological description of ethical capital as a source of trust was Robert Merton's analysis of the particular ethos that has kept modern academic science together. There, open access to and free circulation of knowledge was paralleled from the beginning by systems like peer review, collegial reputation, and a strong professional ethic that strongly enforced the formation of relations of trust between scientists who did not necessarily know each other. And in his 2008 work on "post-academic" science, Steven Shapin shows that to the extent that knowledge production unfolds within networks of actors that are located outside the institutions of academia—in cooperative efforts between universities and venture capital, for example—the importance of trust seems to increase.[39]

The importance of trust among strangers is not an entirely new insight. Economic sociology has long stressed the value of trust in reducing transaction costs, starting perhaps with Emile Durkheim's notion of the necessary "non-contractual basis of contract." Our concept of ethical capital makes two important additions to this tradition. The first is quantitative. To the extent that productive publics composed of strangers become more important to value creation, the concept of ethical capital as a source of trust moves from being marginal to becoming central. The second addition is qualitative. For Durkheim, as for Talcott Parsons, who developed his insights into the foundations of modern economic sociology, such trust was given by a morality that was anchored in a more or less fixed set of societal values. It was possible to speak of such a thing as "a natural culture of trust," or of local traditions as a source of social capital.[40] In today's situation such a fixed morality is difficult to find and, in any case, it is not a feature of dynamic and fluctuating publics. Hence value comes to depend on the ability to create the ethos that enables trust to develop in particular and situated forms of cooperation. In other words, the foundation of trust among strangers is no longer a given, but would need to be actually created through concrete practices of association and deliberation, through action, to use Hannah Arendt's terminology.[41]

In addition to creating trust among strangers, ethical capital does two other things that social capital has not yet been identified as doing: it is able to support a shared convention about the nature of reality (that is, an ethos in the rhetorical sense of the term), and it is able to support the charisma whereby an organization or a public can attract "free labor" and other "gifts" from its members as well as from the public at large.

Conventions

A second way in which ethical capital creates value is by organizing a community of interpretation that can sustain a particular perception of a productive process and its value. As we saw in chapter 2, such a common perception can tie in to the formation of value conventions on financial markets. In the form of a brand, it can sustain interpretations on the part of an investor community as to the value of a company and its assets, above and beyond what can be measured with established metrics. This is particularly important in a finance-centered regime of accumulation where ever more often, financial valuations are detached from the value flows that are generated by the creation and sale of commodities, where, as Umair Hacque has suggested, the "game" of value creation plays out on the financial level where perceptions, conventions, or even "fictions" are key.[42]

The importance of the ability to instill such a convention is perhaps particularly pronounced in the case of social media companies. While these might be an extreme category, they do illustrate a common trend. Take Facebook, for example. In 2010 Goldman Sachs purchased shares worth $1.5 billion of the company at an implicit valuation of $50 billion, more or less equal to the GDP of Croatia. This would be an astronomical overvaluation of Facebook's ability to make money by selling advertising space by any standard metric. According to Facebook's own figures, this would imply a price-to-earnings ratio of 143, as compared to the S&P 500 average of 9. And while the events following the Facebook IPO in 2012 suggest that valuations of Facebook have been excessive and speculative, the more stable Google, which does have an established business model around advertising sales (while Facebook has often been accused of being unequivocally *bad* at monetizing its 500 million users), is also valued at 29 times its earnings, or 3 times as much as the S&P 500 average. Twitter has not yet found a reliable business model despite its five years on the market and its 160 million users. Even so, the company acquired an implicit valuation of $4 billion in January 2011.[43] These figures suggest that the real source of value for these companies is not advertising revenue but their ability to initiate and support the formation of an interpretative community or—which is the same thing— the strength of their brands. In simpler terms, at the time of its IPO, Facebook was worth $100 billion not because it could rationally be expected to make a corresponding sum of money from advertising sales but because, on the strength of its brand, other investors could rationally be expected to keep up such valuations.

And this is not unique to social media companies. We can apply the same model to value in the information economy as a whole, which leads us to a different interpretation of the value of advertising, including on-line advertising. The rise of the average price-to-earnings ratio for the S&P 500 from 2 in the 1950s to 9 today has been paralleled by the rise of brands as a component of market value, from virtually nil in the 1950s to on average 30 percent today (and for some companies with strong brands like Coca-Cola or Apple, 40 to 50 percent). This implies that brands have been a key factor in justifying investor valuations that are ever more remote from earnings potential. And it suggests that the valuations of these companies are highly conventional. That is, these figures imply that financial valuations of these companies are not built primarily on their earnings capacity in terms of attracting advertising revenue, but are related to their perceived ability to attract future investments or, to use a more general term, financial rent. The value model deploys the kinds of self-fulfilling prophecies that Keynes argued were typical of financial markets. What is capitalized on in this case is the ability to initiate such a prophecy. But while Keynes never gave us a theory of the origins of those self-fulfilling prophecies, attributing them to the "animal spirits" of the investor multitude as it stampedes in one direction or another, today's brand-centered managerial models suggest that the ability to initiate and support such conventions is increasingly understood as a particular asset, as a form of ethical capital that can be managed and cultivated.[44]

But the ability to instill a convention obviously plays an important role in consumer markets as well. The abundance of labor power and the rapid spread of product and process innovation create a corresponding abundance of high-quality products. When a major Italian fashion brand begins to outsource the production of its bags to small Chinese factories (mostly located in Italy, around Prato and in Campania), these factories quickly learn how to make the bags and can easily churn out identical bags at night. With exploding numbers of engineers and pharmacists and the heightened availability of scientific publications on the Internet, it is now possible for an Indian entrepreneur to gain access to the knowledge and skills necessary to produce generic Viagra in his garage. This means that, at least for the mid-range market, product quality is becoming less relevant as a competitive advantage. In these cases, competitive advantage must build on what cannot be copied: the convention that sustains an experientially tangible difference between a product and its competitors. In Kevin Kelly's words, successful products must be "better than free."[45]

The importance of such conventions is of course even greater with regard to popular ethical, fair, or sustainable consumer products, where what counts is the ability to maintain a convention that supports stakeholder interpretation of the product as ethical or fair. And what is even more crucial is a convention that makes such interpretations robust, so that they can remain operative in the face of the evidence to the contrary that will inevitably arise in a more networked media environment where information circulates with greater ease. Many people still have faith in the Whole Foods chain of supermarkets as an ethical company, despite adverse information that has surfaced as to the company's treatment of its workers or the personal opinions of its CEO. We know that labor conditions in some of the factories to which IKEA subcontracts the production of its furniture are far from "Swedish," and that the company's founder, Ingvar Kampard, was allegedly once a Nazi. Even so, we perceive the company as ethical, fair, and well intentioned. Ethical capital in the form of a convention that maintains itself not only on reasoned opinion and analysis but also to a large extent on faith can act as a filter that affects what information actually enters into decision-making procedures on the part of consumers or other stakeholders. Indeed, as recent research has shown, the ability to maintain such a convention, made robust by the faith (or affective proximity) that it is able to mobilize on the part of consumers or other stakeholders, acts as effective insurance against reputational shocks, minimizing their impact on sales and financial performance.

Charisma

A third way in which ethical capital creates value is by attracting contributions above and beyond what can be motivated by monetary rewards. The importance of the ability to do so of course increases the more a company relies on such "free" efforts. Indeed, it can sometimes be counterproductive to give monetary rewards to actors participating in external processes of innovation or coproduction. The Mozilla Foundation is a good example of this. The foundation was constructed to manage the enormous funds generated by its open-source Firefox browser. The money could not simply be distributed among the developing community, as that would have severely disrupted the peer dynamics by means of which development had prospered. So it is not only the case that monetary rewards are not the prime motivation for many members of productive publics; sometimes the introduction of monetary rewards seriously threatens the workings of a public.[46] Consequently these contributions need to be attracted by the construction of the kind of ethos that members perceive as valuable. The same argument goes for knowledge workers, whose tacit, hidden knowledge needs to be motivated by increasingly immaterial means, what William E. Halal has called a "corporate community."[47] Indeed, there is by now a long tradition of research that has established that beyond a certain point, values and an environment that encourages self-realization count much more than money as a motivational force for many knowledge workers, and that good relations in the workplace are the most important factor in determining whether or not a company is able to retain its skilled personnel.[48] Conversely, emotional intelligence, the ability to establish and sustain good relations with one's peers, has been identified as one of the most important factors in the productivity of knowledge workers. And "cynicism" resulting from the inability of a company to mobilize the affective attachments of its employees has been identified as an important obstacle to performance and organizational change.[49] Ethical capital—the ethos that can support meaningful and durable relations with and among coworkers—has value here because it makes possible the motivation of productive processes that unfold beyond what can be directly commanded or paid for. Ethical capital does this by institutionalizing the moral bases of a functioning "gift economy."

The term "gift economy" has often been tossed around in descriptions of the "new Internet economy," particularly during its earlier, more enthusiastic years. A common misunderstanding of those descriptions has been that gift economies imply that no rules of exchange prevail, that they are "cooking pot markets" each person bringing and taking what she wants.[50] Actually, existing gift economies as studied by anthropologists, beginning with Mauss and Malinowski's work in the 1920s, are highly structured forms of exchange containing strong, if implicit, expectations of reciprocity. A gift calls for a counter-gift and usually that counter-gift must be of at least comparable value. These moral foundations are what enables a gift economy to function over time. Similarly, a brand or a collaborative project in a company needs implicit values and expectations of reciprocity to continue to function over time. (For example, a brand that seeks to involve its consumers in generating brand identity but does not take their desires seriously in developing new products might find it difficult to keep attracting consumer input.) In the past, the moral basis for a functioning gift economy could be instilled through established social values. Today, in a growing number of situations, the moral basis needs to be tailor-made for the particular situation. Ethical capital can create value by enabling such a moral basis to form.

Tying the Knot: Ethical Capital Motivations and Intangible Value

The idea that reputation can be used as a resource, as a form of capital—ethical capital—allows us to complete our theory of value at the levels of both individual motivation and organizational value creation.

At the individual level there is no longer any need to posit "altruistic genes" or "anarcho-communism" to explain participation in productive publics. Instead people can be understood to get involved because of motivations that are perfectly compatible with traditional definitions of economic rationality. That is, whatever other reasons people might have to participate—and most recent studies show that motivations are generally multiple and complex—one common reason is that the ethical capital that they can accumulate by doing so is a valuable resource, a form of capital indeed, that can be "spent" in a variety of ways.[51] Neither is the idea of such "immaterial" motivations entirely new. An established tradition of economic sociology coupled with the recent interest in reputation in economic theory suggests that the prospect of acquiring a good reputation has a long history as an important motivation for economic action. (In fact, Max Weber argued that this was one explanation for the high membership rates that he found in Protestant "sects"—like the Baptists or the Methodists—when he toured the United States in the 1890s.)[52] Today's situation, however, offers three further novelties.

First, the importance of reputation increases as an effect of the general tendency toward a socialization of production. When careers, income, and job opportunities depend less on bureaucratic structures or direct forms of market exchange, it becomes more important for individuals to accumulate ethical capital as a way of justifying the market value of their skills and as insurance against insecurity.

Second, the form that reputation takes also changes in this context. When the strength and importance of institutions like religious sects or professional organizations that have traditionally been identified as the structures within which reputation circulates and is accumulated are diminished, such advantage depends more on the accumulation of the form of reputation that we have discussed as ethical capital. For example, in the 1930s, the career prospects of an architect might have depended a great deal on the social capital that he was able to accumulate among his colleagues and through participation in the local chapter of the professional association of architects. Today, when architects work in teams with other knowledge workers, participate in productive publics that are geographically dispersed, and find that their professional organizations have a much more minor role, ethical capital becomes much more important.

Third, and most significant, the very economic rationality by means of which reputation, or ethical capital, is accumulated changes. Traditional economic action might be understood as "instrumental" in the sense of privileging the maximization of individual utility over social concerns (although contemporary rational choice theory has progressed beyond this rather crude characterization).[53] And traditional reputation economies might have been understood as structured by what sociologists call "value rationality"—that is, individuals accumulated a good reputation by acting in coherence with the established values and norms of a particular institution, like a religious sect or a professional organization. But the accumulation of ethical capital must be understood to be premised on ethics, in a sense that is both highly contemporary and true to its classical roots—that is, the accumulation of ethical capital depends to no small degree on virtuous action, action that contributes to and strengthens the common cause around which a public is organized. But such virtuous action emerges in situations where clear guidelines and principles might be difficult to find and where a number of different, and perhaps conflicting, orders of worth might be present. In such situations, ethics, in the sense of the ability to make a choice in the absence of clear guidelines or to create values in a situation where there are none, becomes the basis of the excellence by means of which an economically valuable asset, ethical capital, can be accumulated. In other words, at the "micro" level of individual conduct, the creation of values and the creation of value—ethics and economics—tend to coincide.

At the collective level, ethical capital explains the creation of what chapter 2 discussed as intangible value. That is, the ability to achieve flexibility in organizations, the ability to constantly innovate by tapping the common knowledge that permeates a company or a public, and the ability to create and maintain a convention, a brand, that can motivate monetary value decisions, depend on the ability to accumulate ethical capital. And the ability to accumulate ethical capital, at the organizational level, depends on excellence in the use of common resources, which, to no small degree, depends on virtuous organizational conduct: the ability to create an ethos that gives coherence and direction to complex networks, or the ability to sustain a convention that supports an interpretation of the organization as socially useful in some way. Such excellence is also what market actors "price in" as intangible assets. So also at the "macro" level, the "circuit of ethical capital" *might* supply a new notion of economic rationality whereby an ever more prevalent intangible basis can be understood to rationally reflect the ability of organizations and publics to accumulate ethical capital by excelling in the use of common resources. "Might" is a key word here, because even though our theory of ethical capital opens up the possibility of such a connection, in the real world this connection, if it exists at all, is far from rational. As chapter 1 argued, we have no way of determining the extent to which actual valuations of intangible assets are rational. (And a similar argument can be made for the rationality of the reputation economies in which individual knowledge workers operate.) In chapter 5 we suggest a way to address this lacuna.

5

Measure

In chapters 3 and 4, we suggested that developments in the real relations of production point toward the possibility of a new conception of value. To revisit this position very briefly: we have argued that the collaborative commons-based production that stands behind the creation of intangible assets tends to happen in a particular institutional form: publics. And we have proposed that such publics also function as highly particular reputation economies. In productive publics, reputation is conferred on actors by their peers, according to a comprehensive judgment of the excellence in the use of common resources and the virtue of their conduct. Furthermore, such reputation can function as what we have called "ethical capital," an asset that has tangible economic value for both individuals and organizations.[1] In other words, value is now becoming public in new ways. The value of a person or a brand is not set according to fixed standards, but determined in more or less open-ended processes of public communication. But one important question remains: Is there a way in which values set in different publics could be compared and evaluated against each other? This is an important question because in the absence of such a common denominator, we remain in a situation of relativism and value fragmentation where the idea that the global economy could be governed in a bottom-up, participatory way remains a fiction—and, less dramatically, where the concrete reputational values remain insecure and precarious.

We believe that it is possible to identify such a common denominator, and that this possibility is related to the ways in which the public sphere has been transformed. Essentially we will suggest that the current transformation of the public sphere, which is accelerating with the impact of social media, is making intensities of affect objective and measurable in new ways. Such objectified affect, which we call general sentiment, can act as a new common denominator, a new general equivalent, by means of which different kinds of reputation can be evaluated and compared. But for this possibility to be realized, we need to construct and institutionalize a new measure.

Measures and standards are aspects of reality that have been ignored by social scientists and historians for a long time.[2] This lack of attention is quite understandable because, insofar as such measures and standards are efficient, they tend to be invisible. We hardly reflect on the politics behind the development of the metric system (national unification in postrevolutionary France) or the hidden agendas behind the TCP/IP protocol (to keep decisions about Internet traffic decentralized) as long as they work. Recently this trend has been reversed as the emergence of networked digital media has highlighted the role of standards (like protocols, software standards, or privacy standards) in enabling or restraining a whole series of actions. Consequently, social scientists and historians have begun to pay attention to standards, to the political dynamics behind their construction as well as their impact on social and economic life. And activist currents have begun to stress the political relevance of standards and the importance of paying attention to their construction. ("Learn a programming language and change the world," as the Anonymous slogan goes!) Measures and standards, these historians and social scientists argue, are important political facts that constrain and enable everyday action in powerful ways. (Some contemporary movements, like the alternative currency initiative, exaggerate in the opposite direction, blaming most of our present predicament on the standard of centralized money alone.)[3] In short, standards are "recipes for reality," as the subtitle of a recent book on the matter claims.[4]

From this perspective it would seem that an important task would be to construct such a recipe for a functioning reputation economy, one in which the measure of economic value would coincide with the measure of ethical value in a new and more relevant way. That task would be important from the point of view of economic rationality. But as we will suggest, its realization would also have important political consequences. In order to achieve this we need a measure that can standardize the notion of reputation that circulates in what we can now begin to call "the ethical economy," and that can create solid connections between such standardized measures of reputation and the processes by which economic values are set—most importantly, although not exclusively, on financial markets.

While the processes of developing a measure and setting a standard have historically been rife with political conflicts—from the controversy about the correct interpretation of units of measure for oil and grain that raged in the medieval peasant economy to the long history of political confrontation that ended in the institutionalization of the labor theory of value as the basis for the Fordist welfare state—such conflicts never happen in a void.[5] That is, measures and standards cannot be freely invented in accordance with what we might find politically or ethically desirable. (And that is why utopian alternative currency projects that build on elements like barter and the direct exchange of labor time are not feasible. It might be nice if we could simply exchange, say, carrots for marijuana with each other, but direct exchange is not adequate to coordinate a complex global information economy, nor is it coherent with the direction in which the relations of production are actually evolving.)[6] Instead, we have to make do with the ingredients and possibilities that history gives us. That is, we need to work with the direction in which things are actually evolving and build upon that, rather than trying to dream up another, perhaps more desirable way. And the tendency that we suggest as a building block—a tendency that has attracted its fair share of criticism and lament in recent years—is the emergence of affect as a new criterion of public value. To put it more precisely: along with the emergence of productive publics and the reputation economies that they entail, recent decades have seen a transformation of the public sphere whereby affective engagements are cut loose from traditional value structures to emerge as intensities that depart from a wide diversity of value horizons but that can nevertheless lead to the formation of common values in a novel and different way.

AFFECT, ETHICS, AND THE PUBLIC SPHERE

The concept of "publics" has been central to modern social thought ever since the circulation of print material, like books, newspapers, magazines, and pamphlets, took off in earnest in the eighteenth century. This material made possible the formation of associations of strangers who all read about and paid attention to the same issues and who could now debate and discuss the correct ways of interpreting and addressing them, either by meeting face-to-face or, as was often the case, by circulating their arguments in print. Around the circulation of printed material there arose a number of concrete institutions and associations, like cafés, learned societies, social movements, trade unions, and other interest groups in which people could come together as members of a public to take part in the creation of a public opinion, where the diverse perspectives of different individuals, social movements, and religious communities could converge. While not necessarily unitary or undivided, that kind of public opinion could allow local forms of protest to develop into organized social movements with a clear political agenda, thus making possible the foundation for modern mass politics: a reading and reasoning public that fostered such typically modern things as nationalism, popular social movements, and fashion and consumer culture.[7]

While the concept of publics is much older, the most influential use of this concept is that of German philosopher and sociologist Jürgen Habermas. In *The Structural Transformation of the Public Sphere* (translated into English in 1989, but originally published in German in 1962), Habermas suggested that modern societies are endowed with a "public sphere," made possible by modern mass media, where citizens can interact freely, exercise their opinions about the common cause (or res publica), and thus form a public opinion that would serve as input for politics and overall societal governance.[8] Habermas insisted that a functioning public sphere that allowed rational debate among equals, or at least an approximation of this ideal, was crucial for modern societies to function. At the same time, his book was a critique of developments in what he called "late modernity" that he understood to be undermining this ideal. In particular he suggested that the combination of a rapidly expanding consumer culture and the administrative power of the Fordist welfare state tended to eliminate rational debate and judgment from different spheres of life, thus undermining the capacity for people to make value judgments and instead transforming them into clients or consumers who simply accepted what was on offer.

Today this critique has progressed even further, and it is common knowledge that the public sphere has been colonized by commercial culture, consumerism, and brands. Naomi Klein makes this point strongly in her work *No Logo*, in which she shows how the physical and media spaces that were originally thought to allow public interaction and discussion have been privatized, turned into commercial media culture or shopping malls and surveyed city centers where only behaviors that are compatible with global consumer culture are allowed. The conclusions of such critiques are that the impact of advertising and branding, and the replacement of mass parties and public service television (none of which were very dear to Habermas) with globalized consumer culture and commercial television, have fragmented the possibilities for rational debates and individualized horizons and worldviews and have made the pursuit of a common rationality almost impossible. But there might be another, more dialectical way of looking at it.

No doubt, the branding of public space and of the media has had the effect of undermining the communitarian dynamics that Habermas viewed as the force and vitality behind the modern public sphere. People participate less in the forms of face-to-face interaction that support shared values, as membership rates of anything from trade unions to PTA associations have declined.[9] At the same time, however, the transformation of the public sphere has enabled a new modality of value formation that is less communitarian and more public, where common values are sustained less by face-to-face interaction and more by mediated forms of affective identification.

A key trend in the processes that Habermas defines as the decline of the public sphere has been an individualization of perspectives and horizons. No longer part of a larger moral community, individuals now choose the causes and identifications that suit them. The modern public sphere was centered around a handful of organizations, mass parties, state media, and cultural institutions that materialized a particular worldview in which values and relations of affective proximity were largely predefined. If one was a member of the Communist Party, one realized that that position came with a number of particular moral standards that were beyond discussion, at least for the individual member, most of the time. Today there are several hundred thousand cause-related NGOs in the world that invite individuals to identify with everything from whales to molested children. (Indeed, Paul Hawken goes so far as to suggest that the proliferation of single-issue organizations means that we need to change the paradigm we use to think about political agency. Politics, he suggests, should no longer be understood in the modern sense, as a campaign or "common struggle" organized around central goals and values and endowed with a common direction. Instead it should be viewed as a sort of moral immune system, where small, single-issue organizations "swarm" around particular problems.) At the extreme end of this fragmentation, the individual herself chooses her own more or less momentary value engagements. These choices need not be based on universal moral criteria, but can also be—and frequently are—based on a *feeling* of affective proximity with a cause or an actor, a feeling that is created by the mediatized experience of the suffering of others.[10]

Such an individualization of value horizons has long been a central part of sociological theories of the impact of modern media. In its most optimistic version, this idea led Marshall McLuhan to suggest that electronic media would undermine the boundaries of nation-states and form a new "global village," where people would be directly linked to each other through the tactile, sensual bonds formed through television. In more pessimistic accounts, like those of Habermas and, more recently, Robert Putnam, it suggests the end of the "common ground" that allowed rational public opinion to form. However, social theorists have begun to take the middle road, suggesting that such processes of "ethical individualization" are not necessarily good or bad, but simply new and different.

In this vein, French sociologist Luc Boltanski has used the term "politics of pity" to argue that our mediated experience with distant sufferers—chiefly on television, but increasingly also via the Internet—creates a new modality of ethical and political engagement, based not on general rules or ideological principles, nor on rational argument, but on the direct affective experience of the sufferings of the other, on what Adam Smith, long ago, termed the human capacity for sympathy.[11] In her 2006 work on what she calls the "spectatorship of suffering," Lilie Chouliaraki develops these insights.[12] She suggests that the very nature of ethics is being reconfigured in the contemporary public sphere. On the one hand, we are seeing a proliferation of corporate responsibility initiatives in which companies enlist suffering others (or at least needy others) not because of general principles but because of a proximity of interest. In the same way that they construct commercial brands, they form a public around a common cause by associating different actors and organizations with it. Such publics can, and often do, span national boundaries. At the same time, a similar way of creating ethical association is spreading outside of the business world proper, as illustrated by social businesses or NGOs that work for a particular cause and by individuals who choose their ethical engagements on the basis of affective (or interest-based) proximity.

This reveals two important things about the contemporary public sphere and the value engagements that it can foster. It suggests that in the contemporary public sphere, where there are both a multitude of potential objects of ethical engagement and a multitude of potential weak links, value engagements are no longer deduced from a priori universal principles, like established ideologies or national interest. Instead they are increasingly formed through the *activity of association*, where weak links are transformed into strong links and affective engagements grow in intensity into links that matter. Relations of value are constructed from below, in ways similar to the procedure by which individuals bond into publics and establish the value horizons or ethoi that should apply to their common pursuits. In other words, ethical horizons and public values are not inherited or handed down from the past; they are built from what media scholar Zizi Papacharissi calls a connection of private spheres.[13] Not only has the contemporary public sphere produced an individualization or privatization of ethical horizons, but, in ways similar to the productive publics discussed earlier, it has also cohered a different way of associating such private horizons into public affective intensities that can support new values.

This raises an important, somewhat philosophical point. To Habermas, as well as to most modern (in the sense of "industrial," Fordist) moral philosophers, the values that grounded people's ethical choices were inherited from the past and were transcendent in relation to the particular situation. True, they could change, and one of Habermas's points was that they did so as new actions tested their practical relevance (values were quasi-transcendent, he claimed). But the kinds of ethical choices that we have described are not transcendent, not even quasi-transcendent: They do not depart from a somehow modified version of some common values that have been inherited from tradition; on the contrary, they depart from a wide diversity of individual experiences (whether mediated or not). This means that there is no common ground from which these ethical choices depart (since each individual experience is singular and irreducible—a point made by feminist "standpoint theorists" in the 1970s).[14] And this means that there can be no common agreement on value. (Habermas instead argued that however diverse the actual conduct of individuals might be, the quasi-transcendent nature of the value horizons that guided their conduct meant that if only they argued long enough, common values would eventually be arrived at.) But at the same time, the fact that these values are supported by the same substance, by intensities of public affect, means that they can be measured and compared against each other, in terms of the strength and direction of those intensities.[15]

GENERAL SENTIMENT

In order for relations of affective proximity to become measurable and objectified, they need to be separated from the ideas and representations to which they are tied. Like "heat," "force," and "speed," "affect" needs to emerge as a particular dimension that can be isolated and measured in its own right. This process of objectification of affect has been under way for a long time, and it has been part and parcel of the very same developments that are often understood to have undermined the feasibility of a modern, rational public sphere.

Ever since the onset of modern consumer culture, social theorists have suggested that phenomena like fashion, celebrity culture, and the mobility of a new, mediated public opinion testify to a new objective and economically important role for affect. Indeed, Gabriel Tarde, writing in the early 1900s, went so far as to say that the value of modern consumer goods depended mainly on their ability to sustain public perceptions of their "truth, beauty and utility," which in the end depended on the affective investments that they were able to attract in public communication.[16] Arguably this process is presently being intensified through the impact of social media.

Social media are rapidly becoming the default application of the Internet and the "normal" way to communicate (in the sense of transferring ideas as well as in the sense of fostering affective "communion" with others). For example, during the first eight months of 2009, Facebook grew by 100 percent, from 100 million to 200 million users; at the time of this writing it has surpassed 800 million. Twitter grew by 1,440 percent in 2008 and is presently targeting one billion users. Already today more people use social media than e-mail.[17]

What happens when social and affective relations are remediated by social media? Social media have two central properties that are relevant to this issue. First, as we have already suggested in discussing the formation of publics, social media facilitate the construction of affectively significant connections between strangers. As many media scholars have emphasized, the result is a more interdependent, or even "networked" subjectivity, where one's public identity (or reputation) and in particular the way it is evaluated by "proximate strangers" (that is, people one might not know in the traditional sense of that term, but nevertheless feels affectively proximate to, like one's followers on Twitter, or the members of an online forum to which one regularly contributes) become central not only to one's sense of self-worth but also, and increasingly, to one's objective value as a professional, networker, or "micro-celebrity."[18]

Second, social media add to the process of the becoming public of affect by introducing a new dimension of objectivity. Affective relations now become tangible in a wide variety of manifestations: the links that tie a blog to its network, friends on a social media page, re-tweets, or even explicit ratings of the truth, beauty, or utility of a person, object, or service. In this way, social media are "phatic media" in the double sense of both fostering the formation of public affective relations through "non-dialogic and non-informational" practices of "keeping in touch" and enabling such manifestations of public affect, of *phatos*, to serve as an objective criterion of the value of individuals and other actors.[19]

This process has been further enabled by the development of new methods of measurement in which affect has emerged ever more clearly as a criterion of economic value.

Measuring Affect

The development of instruments for measuring affect independently of representations and ideas has occurred within the tradition of audience research, and significantly, it has been driven by the growing importance of brands as devices that translate public affect into economic value. During the first three decades of modern audience research, from its inception in the 1930s—when radio became the main advertising medium—until roughly the 1960s, the paradigm was values-based. That is, it was understood that the audience was naturally divided into sociodemographic segments that harbored particular values that guided their consumer behavior. But the 1960s saw the birth of what was known as lifestyle segmentation. This technique built on the use of large-scale surveys that mapped consumers according to a wide range of affective attachments that, like the AOI (attitudes, opinions, interests) and later VALS (values, attitudes, lifestyles), went far beyond what was directly related to purchases or attitudes toward consumer goods. These data were subsequently subjected to inductive multivariate analysis (or "cluster analysis"), and the resulting correlations were represented as "lifestyles."

The reasons behind the success of psychographics were many. The 1960s had seen a transformation of the media environment, driven by the establishment of television, that demanded new kinds of audience segmentation; the computers necessary to perform the complicated forms of data processing now became affordable for mid-sized companies like advertising agencies and market research companies; the previous decade had seen a rising popularity of qualitative audience research that supplied new and interesting kinds of information. Most important, however, there was a perception of a general transformation of consumer culture, and a sense that the affective makeup of consumers, their desires, was being delinked from class structures. In other words, there was a perception that consumers were already creating their own forms of affective association, their own publics, which were less dependent on the persuasive power of advertising, and that these affective intensities could support ever more important brand values.[20]

The methodology of psychographics involved a number of important innovations. First, it pioneered the kinds of inductive statistics that have become a basis for the data-mining techniques still in use today. Second, lifestyle segmentation created a picture of the market in which consumer demand was understood to be determined by a number of affective concerns that appeared to be independent of the position of consumers vis-à-vis the industrial economy. Third, and of special significance, psychographics introduced, if only in an embryonic form, a new definition of economic value. As lifestyle analysis was used to determine the value of advertising space in terms of how well the value structure of a particular medium coincided with the "lifestyle" of a targeted consumer group, it introduced, for the first time, a notion of "value distance" or affective proximity as a measure of economic value.

In the 1970s psychographic segmentation was based on large-scale surveys. Beginning in the 1980s the proliferation of credit cards and bar codes created vast data banks that were generated "naturally," so to speak, at the point of purchase in stores and supermarkets. This information was subjected to data-mining techniques that were essentially refined versions of the multivariate cluster analysis deployed in psychographics, to generate the kinds of information that went into Customer Relationship Management programs and eventually into brand valuation instruments. More recently, the arrival of the Internet, and especially social media, has greatly expanded the range of naturally occurring data that can be submitted to data-mining techniques, and social media in particular have provided a wide range of data on public affect that lends itself to such statistical profiling.

The most popular methods for processing social media data have been, on the one hand, network analysis and sentiment analysis, and on the other hand, user-generated ratings through public forms of tagging, bookmarking, and/or "social buttons" like Facebook's "Like" button or Twitter's "re-tweet" function.

Network analysis has been employed with the social sciences since the 1960s, but the arrival of networked communication media gave a boost to this methodology as a wide range of meaningful large relational data sets are now available. In the field of value measurement, network analysis has been used for some time by managerial scholars in computing inter- and intra-firm "social capital," and more practically, by companies, including IBM, as a knowledge management tool: calculations of the centrality of employees to communication flows were taken as a valid measure of their economic productivity.[21] In calculating the value of public affect, the main application of network analysis has been that of identifying "influencers," people who have a central position in relational networks and communication flows, and who are therefore "worth more" as communication channels. Yahoo has been using this approach for a long time in order to identify "influencers" to be used in marketing campaigns, and Facebook has developed a similar approach to enable advertising to be placed on the basis of preferences expressed in personal networks (the "page rank algorithm"). In the growing business of applying data mining to the measurement of brand strength and return on investment (ROI) in viral marketing campaigns, network analysis is used in identifying the degree to which a certain campaign has managed to influence actors that are central to communication networks as one dimension of ROI. A second dimension is provided by sentiment analysis.

Sentiment analysis is based on the automatic recognition of the affective valence of words or patterns of words used in text. The challenge consists in overcoming the ambiguity and polyvalence of natural language. This issue can be addressed by machine-learning approaches that train an algorithm on independent data sets.[22] However, such approaches have become feasible only with social media, for two reasons. First, only social media platforms supply the vast amounts of data needed to even out errors and reach reliability rates comparable to those generated by human observers. Second, only social media provide large enough sets of training data, such as movie or product reviews, where text is linked to quantitative estimates of value (in the form of number of "stars" or other kinds of ratings). In practice, sentiment analysis is used to quantify the intensity of affective investments in an object. Brand valuation services such as Radian6 or Sysomos, for example, use sentiment analysis to determine whether a branding campaign has generated a shift in the positive or negative intensity of affect invested in the brand on the part of the public, or, to use the current term, in sentiment.[23] Similarly, sentiment analysis is growing in importance as a component of information systems for financial operators and other kinds of asset valuators. The company StreamBase, for example, generates trading recommendations on the basis of a sentiment analysis of online news. Covalence, another company, mines a wide range of sources on corporate social responsibility and subjects them to sentiment analysis, the output of which is presented as an indicator of the "ethical status" of an asset.[24] More recently, Derwent Capital Markets has launched a Twitter-based hedge fund that uses Twitter to gauge the mood of the stock market.

Many more of these applications are emerging, particularly around Twitter because it has (so far) permitted public access to its data and is rapidly becoming a fairly representative platform of Internet traffic in general.

Finally, "social buttons" allow for transforming intensive social and affective dynamics into comparable metrics by aggregating bottom-up expressions of affective proximity (I like it or I don't like it) on the part of users.[25] Social media platforms like Facebook are currently orienting their business models around their users' collaborative valuation of topics or individuals through the use of such social buttons.

The use of network analysis, sentiment analysis, social buttons, or some combination of these is emerging as a new paradigm for measuring the value of assets, communication campaigns, or individuals in terms of what is increasingly talked about as their "reputation." In most models, reputation is defined as some combination of three measurements: the number of times that an object is mentioned or "liked," the network centrality (or influence) of the actors mentioning it, and the affective intensity (sentiment) with which they mention it. All of these variables measure affect independently of ideas. Instead, the value of affect is defined in terms of proximity. Network analysis defines influence (or network centrality) according to a number of measures that describe the distance of influencers from other nodes in the network, regardless of what that particular network is *about*. (Facebook is of course not about anything; it is a place for the formation of affective, "phatic" relations.) Sentiment analysis defines sentiment according to two dimensions: "valence," or the sum of the affective valence of the words occurring in a message, and "arousal," or the sum of the absolute values of the valences. Here too the affective valence of words is defined according to a variety of lists that report their affective charge in natural language use, independent of the ideas that they might convey, individually or in combination.[26]

General Equivalent

This emergent common approach is built on a distinct way of objectifying affect. First, it is based on inductive statistics like cluster analysis and other forms of pattern recognition that are able to find regularities in large data sets without departing from any a priori presuppositions about the nature of those regularities. This means that general sentiment is represented as an emergent variable that does not appear to be caused by any other factors. Like labor for the classical economists, it can be a kind of deus ex machina: the commodity (or in this case, the artifact) by means of which the value of all other commodities (assets or communication channels) is established. Second, general sentiment is quantified in terms of value distance, or affective proximity, which is the same thing. This was already an element in psychographic clustering where clusters were defined according to vector distances in a multivariate space, and it is a basic presupposition in both network and sentiment analysis. The criterion of "distance" can generate a measure of general sentiment that is independent of particular ideas and representations that might be the foundation of individual value judgment. Regardless of whether I am a Christian or a Muslim, the tweets that I produce can be judged in terms of a universal, if temporary, scale of positivity and negativity. The same thing goes for my position in a network, or for my expression of preferences in rating systems. However, like the general equivalent of money, and unlike the universals of modern morality, the standard of judgment does not refer to any fixed values; it refers only to the status of the system as a whole. It is not a matter of moral universality. Positive or negative sentiment is judged according to a word list that is itself derived empirically from natural language use. And different word lists are constructed through algorithms being trained on different data sets, such as movie reviews, financial data, or ratings of various kinds of consumer products. Network centrality is calculated in relation to the network itself.[27] So it seems that we are acquiring a new standard—general sentiment—that is measured according to three dimensions: the strength of the affective charge of a message (sentiment), its influence (network centrality), and the numerical size of its occurrence. Incidentally, these dimensions coincide precisely with the factors that Gabriel Tarde thought would determine the strength of the mental communions that he argued underpinned perceptions of immaterial value: "le plus ou moins grand nombre: le plus ou moins poids social (ce qui veut dire ici considération, compétence reconnue) des personnes qui s'accordent à l'admettre, et le plus ou moins d'intensité de leur croyance en elle."[28]

Toward a Politics of Standards

Our argument is that the convergence of social media platforms and data-mining techniques, bottom-up indicators like "social buttons," and methods like network and sentiment analysis are combining to create a common standard for the measurement of public affect, or general sentiment. This common standard is emergent: it has already established itself in some sectors, like brand valuation and the estimation of ROI on viral marketing campaigns. What's more, this approach has a history that goes back to the 1970s and the impact of psychographic segmenting. In other words, it has been emergent for a long time, and its emergence has had a natural relation to the overall transformation of the public sphere.

At the moment of writing, a standard similar to what we have called general sentiment is affirming itself as a component of social media business models. In this sector many successful applications, like Kickstarter, for example, build on some version of a reputation economy. And this seems to become even more consolidated as various notions of "reputation-based currencies" are used to conceptualize and measure individual contributions to such publics. For example, social currency provides a system for valuing individual contributions to open innovation systems in non-monetary ways, by counting the "value and sentiment that stem from the exchange of words, videos, reactions and links." "Relationship capital" is another system that aims at the parameters on which the value of online relations in business ventures can be estimated. And there are many more around.[29]

Significantly, a similar standard is making inroads in practices of financial asset valuation, especially through the diffusion of sentiment trading. The number of companies offering services related to trading on sentiment in some way is growing rapidly. Some services provide flows of sentiment data gathered from the mining of social media traffic that can be combined with other data flows, more traditional ones as well as those that are mined from other online sources (like news). This information can subsequently be integrated into personalized information systems sold on a subscription basis to large and small investors. Alternatively, it can be directly connected to automated trading bots, the architecture of which can now be directly customized by clients using object-oriented programming environments, like StreamBase's event processing platform. To date it seems that sentiment-based data are mostly employed as a way of reducing the complexity inherent in a financial system that is in "value crisis." That is, the demand is high for data sources that can provide, however fleetingly, alternative interpretations of existing data, and sentiment data is one such source of non-obvious and hence valuable angles. However, there seems to be a development toward sentiment data as a standard for estimating the value of corporate social responsibility and conduct in a wider sense. In that sector, established standards—like IRIS promoted by the Global Impact Investing Network—that build on the periodic collection of company information are now being supplanted by companies and organizations that use sentiment analysis of online data as a parameter of value. Bloomberg, for example, has launched an environmental, social, and governance (ESG) performance investment analyst tool that, in 2009, evaluated performance on "extra financial" issues like human capital, risk management, brand, carbon exposure, and capacity for innovation for 2,250 firms. The data are organized in seventy-two data points visible on the Bloomberg terminal, and gathered from Web sites, CSR reports, SEC filings, and surveys.[30] Similarly, the Swiss company Covalence extracts information on companies from media, company reports, blogs, and other online sources and classifies it into positive and negative sentiment. The result is represented graphically as a curve showing the shifting ethical impact (measured as positive or negative sentiment around a variety of diverse values).

But should we simply accept a standard that originates in market research as a universal value measurement? At first glance it would seem that we have few alternatives. While other standards, mainly in the form of alternative currencies, might seem attractive in theory, they lack the kind of broad backing that might turn them into practical suggestions. (Traded emission rights might be one exception to this. But that system has also been heavily criticized.) Reputation metrics, on the other hand, are backed by a broad coalition of actors—from traditional corporations via media companies and Web start-ups to alternative publics and activist networks. And while members of this broad "coalition" might disagree strongly on how reputation should be defined, they agree that if correctly defined, it is an acceptable measure of value in a networked information economy. In many ways this situation looks like that of eighteenth-century Britain, where many diverse actors—employers, the emerging labor movement, progressive social planners, and so on—agreed that the productivity of labor should be a measure of economic value, but disagreed strongly on how such productivity should be defined and how the value thus measured should be distributed.

A second similarity to the eighteenth century is that now, as then, the design of the measurement standard depends on how it is defined by members of the coalition that supports it. Since reputation has not yet consolidated into a standard, since it has not yet been made into "furniture," in the sense of becoming taken-for-granted hidden assumptions for thought and action, the field remains open for activist intervention that defines what it will eventually look like. Again, what consolidated as the Fordist value regime was the result of some two centuries of political struggles whereby the institutions of a new value regime—corporations, banks, insurance companies, financial entities, but also labor unions, literary saloons, cafés, and social movements—were constructed. In a sense our task is similar. We need to engage in the construction of a new public sphere that can support and give vitality to a new standard of value, making it something that people participate in, developing and shaping it as they do so.

And perhaps the process will be quicker this time, since the preconditions for such intervention are singularly good today. First, the spread of open standards to political and, increasingly, economic governance has set the stage. Platforms and applications, like Open Politics, openDemocracy, and most famously, of course, WikiLeaks, actively strive to make previously private and secluded information public. Similar standards are emerging for accounting, like open-book accounting, where all stakeholders are invited to view and share information. In short, openness, making information publicly available and open to public scrutiny, seems to be one such new standard that is being advocated by activists who make a difference by constructing Web applications and platforms and promoting their diffusion and use.

Second, there is an ongoing democratization of the skills necessary for building such devices. We are seeing a proliferation of hackers, makers, and nerds that come together to construct a new infrastructure in fields as diverse as communications, gaming, money transfers, social media, transports, food systems, and even open biotech. In addition, the necessary programming skills are ever more often inscribed in computer applications and thus rendered easier and more accessible. It is no longer essential to know how to use html in order to build a Web site, or even start a blog; a wide range of available applications can do that for you. And similar things are happening in mash-up and design software. The result is a virtual flood of new applications built from below (like iPhone and iPad apps that have seen an explosion in numbers in recent years). Around social media, particularly Twitter, we are seeing a steady stream of applications that measure reputational value in some way, most famously perhaps, Klout. Indeed, venture capitalists now suggest that the integration of some kind of reputation-based currencies into social media platforms might be "the next big thing."[31] And the past decade has seen an accelerating boom in alternative, peer-based currency systems or systems for making payments, like, famously, Bitcoin.

It is important to note that this development is also driven by corporations themselves. Companies like Apple, Google, and IBM depend on socialized innovation communities for their business models. Consequently they finance and support these communities and provide them with tools. But they cannot entirely control what is being produced on those platforms. They are in a sense taking the risk of opening up a Pandora's box that may prove to contain very surprising forms of content.

There is also growing interest in alternative value systems on the part of corporations. From our experience as consultants we have learned that one of the main problems that companies, particularly large multinational companies, face is that while they do realize the need to cater to alternative values and "orders of worth," they have no way of measuring such alternative values and hence no way of inserting them in the performance standards that guide day-to-day operations on the part of managers. At the same time, they are aware of the value of doing so, also in the strictly economic sense. What they need is a system that can measure and visualize performance in terms of, for example, environmental sustainability, and in particular the economic value of such performance, in ways that are as solid and objective as those that can now visualize performance in terms of shareholder value creation.

Our suggestion is therefore a call for a politics of standards whereby the widespread capacity to construct technological interfaces, particularly social media devices, is mobilized to build a new kind of value infrastructure by means of which a standardized representation of virtue, in the form of online general sentiment, is connected to the places in which values are set. This can be a matter of financial values, other kinds of asset valuations, or even decisions about the distribution of public welfare. We believe that the time is propitious for embarking upon such a constructive effort for the reasons listed above, as well as, perhaps more fundamentally, because we do not have any reliable, commonly accepted systems for measuring value. This presents a historical opportunity to build new systems, with the expectation that they are likely to spread and gain network power.

However, the success of such a politics of standards depends on a number of conditions that need to be defended by traditional parliamentary politics. The open and neutral Internet is presently under threat from both political and commercial forces. Large commercial operators like telecommunications and media companies are interested in introducing biased standards that threaten Net neutrality by allowing certain kinds of information to travel better than other kinds. Social media companies are growing very large very fast, and a situation similar to that which developed in the radio market in the 1930s, when a multitude of small operators were engulfed by a couple of very large ones, seems imminent.[32] Such large social media companies have little interest in providing access to data on their traffic, thus limiting the scope for the construction of the kinds of value infrastructure that we have discussed above. Facebook, for example, keeps most of its data secret and is very difficult to "mine" for significant information. Twitter has kept access to its traffic partially open and as a result an archipelago of measurement services has developed around the device. But such access is being closed down as we write. Finally, present plans for a next-generation "Internet of things" tend to privilege closed standards, whereby individuals have no influence on the amount of data they give off—as they walk around with their cell phones turned on, for example—or on how that information is used. This of course represents a dangerous challenge to basic notions of privacy.

In the light of this developing situation, a bottom-up initiative needs to be paralleled by traditional political lobbying and activism that seek to attain and safeguard two important things: (1) Net neutrality that makes it impossible for states and commercial operators to privilege certain kinds of traffic at the expense of other kinds, a crucial step if we are to maintain the diversity and openness that make the Internet a productive environment for innovation; and (2) the regulation of social media companies, which need to be treated like public utilities and regulated so as to ensure that they satisfy a public interest. It is particularly important that they provide open access to data that track the traffic on their platforms, which can be used as input for a new value architecture. To do this without threatening basic levels of privacy, they need also to be required to allow users to decide the amount of data they want to disclose to the platform. Do users want all their tweets to be publicly visible, for example, or all their tweets except the ones where they tweet about their particular sexual preference? And so on. Social media companies also need to ensure the portability of identity, so that users can migrate from one platform to another without losing information like friends and their addresses, links, and previous conversations in the process. This is a fundamental component of enabling competition in this field. At present, developments point in a different direction. It is crucial that progressive forces raise awareness on these issues and act to change the current trajectory. If that does not happen, what is, to our mind, the most important direction for progressive action, the construction of a new and more participatory value infrastructure, runs the risk of being blocked, or at least delayed.

A New Rationality?

Why then would it be desirable to work toward the construction of a new standard for measuring online affect? What could be achieved if such a standard was indeed institutionalized as a powerful parameter for value decisions?

First, a new standard would offer a way to connect the evaluation of intangible assets (principally on financial markets) to rational estimates of the excellence in the use of common resources that we have defined as their real underlying value. While these assets build on what we have termed ethical capital—that is, a capacity to motivate and mobilize "free" productive resources and common wealth via the creation of bonds of affective proximity—they lend themselves poorly to measurement systems that depart from the notion of productive time as the central criterion of value. But value measurements based on general sentiment are better suited to this task since they take as their point of departure precisely the *sentiment* or the affective proximity that is the "active ingredient," so to speak, of such ethical capital. And this criterion measures affective proximity according to a common standard that can transcend particular value horizons. From an economic point of view this approach would be rational because general sentiment is able to measure precisely what creates value in the processes in which these intangible assets are produced. And this measurement yields results that are generally valid, since with general sentiment we have a common denominator by which diverse forms of ethical capital could be compared and valued.

It would of course be crude to suggest that the price of assets would simply be an effect of the general sentiment that a given asset has been able to accumulate. After all, neither were prices in the industrial economy simply an effect of labor time (although that was the most influential theoretical definition of value). The relationship between pricing decisions and general sentiment rather depends on how the devices and institutions that support a new value regime are constructed; in other words, these are *political* questions. Would it be desirable for the EU to force brand valuation companies to take a measure of public reputation into account? Should sustainability initiatives be certified by measuring the sentiment that they have been able to accumulate around certain sustainability-related values? These are questions that need to be resolved through the kinds of constructive politics that we are suggesting. What we would have would be a basis for rendering different value estimates comparable. Today the elaboration of the conventions that undergird intangible values is split into diverse and weakly connected publics of deliberation. There is the public of producers, who elaborate on the values that give coherence to a productive network. There is the public of consumers, who create on the convention that underlies the distinctive nature of a brand. There is the public of investors and analysts, who deliberate on the conventions that support the valuation of intangible assets. The establishment of a new standard could be a way to connect these publics and render their value decisions comparable, against the backdrop of a common value horizon in the form of measurable general sentiment. It could be argued that social media are already providing such a common space in which diverse deliberations can be compared and valued. The proliferation of social buttons on social media platforms like Facebook suggests that these devices are already becoming important channels by means of which affective investments by publics can be translated into objectified forms of affect that support consumer decisions and, increasingly, financial valuations. Hence social media is a "utility," not only in the sense that these platforms enable social relations to form and unfold in new ways but also in the sense that it allows for new ways for the conventions that support intangible valuations to stabilize. A new standard like general sentiment would further contribute to connecting such diverse publics into a "networked multitude," able to set its own values and, as a consequence, make the process more rational.

Second, general sentiment is a bottom-up measure. It consists in aggregations of subjective affective investments that derive from a multitude of different actors. And, according to the model of publics and reputation economies described earlier in this volume, such affective investment would correspond to diverse estimations of the overall conduct or "virtue" of an organization or individual. A value measure based on general sentiment would be based on universal notions of right and wrong that would enable universally valid value decisions. However, unlike the modernist universalist solutions, these universals would be temporary and dynamic; they would change in the same way that the "universals" of the market change, in a real-time adaptation to actual events. And they would be based not on a privileged perspective or on any supposedly universal rationality but on an aggregation of affective judgments made on the basis of a plurality of such perspectives and rationalities.[33] This would create a measure of value that is able to persist in a situation where a plurality of orders of worth pertains within a diversified globalized economy. It would also be a measure of economic value that would be ethical in a sense that is both highly contemporary and close to its classical roots. By this we mean that value in terms of general sentiment would be based on real-time aggregations of how a multitude of actors make value judgments in situations of insecurity where no single standard prevails, like, for example, how they evaluate monetary prices on an everyday basis in relation to, say, environmental sustainability or impact on the communities or publics to which they adhere.

This arrangement can of course be criticized on many points. One can argue that it amounts to a trivialization of the issue of ethics, its transformation into the complete opposite of what ethics is supposed to mean, the mindless following of objective patterns on a chart, like popularity. One can suggest that this results in nothing less than the tyranny of vox populi, and the consequent reduction of all values to what the hoi polloi prefer—celebrity, pornography, glitz, and schmaltz. But we already have that. With a new standard we would have that *and* a new way of making value judgments that would be able both to confer an inter-subjective relevance on ethics once again and to make ethical decisions matter in determining the course of political and economic events. Again, we have never suggested that this would be a perfect arrangement; we've suggested only that it is a possible arrangement.

It can also be argued that the objectification of affect and its transformation into general sentiment risks transforming what were once supposedly "hot" affective relations, the kinds that really mattered, into managed forms of what Eva Illouz has called "cold intimacies."[34] It is true that the present mediation of affective relations changes their nature. The freeing of them from their foundations in communities and, more generally, "values" has popularized a specific kind of inter-subjective relation. People can now be affectively concerned, if in a limited way, with others that they do not know and have no intimacy with. In this sense, the transformation of the public sphere, in particular the diffusion of social media, fosters a new kind of social relations, between those of "kin" and those of "stranger"—what we can call "proxy relations." Proxy relations are public relations that entail limited, calculated, and instrumental forms of affective investments. (A proxy generally has a limited affective investment in a company, compared to, for example, a parent's affective investment in her child, which is calculated in the sense that it is directly related to the performance of a company in the areas that touch on her life. It is not unconditional, like that between parents and children, or between lovers.) Such limited affective investments might very well be perceived as "cold" in Eva Illouz's terms. However, we should also note that similar forms of disciplined affect are precisely what Aristotle describes as the basis for the practice of ethics. In his view, the persistence of the *polis* is contingent on the citizens' ability to enter into binding relations with other citizens who are not members of their *oíkos*. This presupposes their ability to balance and discipline their affects with those of other citizens In other words, the "cold intimacy" fostered by social media and the new culture of public intimacy of which they are part signifies not only a deterioration of once supposedly "hot" forms of human affect; it also implies a return of disciplined affect, or *ethics*, as a principle for the public conferment of value on companies and other actors.

And valuations of ethical capital in terms of general sentiment are made primarily by proxies because they are the actors most likely to talk about a public or organization in ways that lend themselves to measurement in terms of general sentiment. This is rational because they are also most likely to have access to the kind of information that allows them to make more rational decisions about how to value a company or organization. The proxy network also constitutes a "natural" limit to the ethical responsibility of an organization. Nobody can be responsible for everything, but everybody is forced to be responsible in relation to the actors that constitute one's proxies, for the simple reason that these proxies have the power to add or subtract investments or general sentiment and thus affect valuation. Beyond the proxy network, attitudes matter less.

On its own, the proxy network risks fostering a parochial culture in which companies or organizations are evaluated mainly by the people who are their friends or who are like them. A well-designed standard of value would also give people and organizations an incentive to expand their proxy network.

While nobody can satisfy everybody in every respect, the brands or organizations that satisfy most people in most respects should be rewarded. The positive correlation between size of the proxy network and monetary value of ethical capital would be rational in two ways. It would constitute a rational valuation of real productivity. Since the people who produce the most value in the ethical economy are the kinds of movers and shakers who touch and transform the most people's lives, it is rational that the ability to expand one's social impact as far as possible will translate into higher valuations. By fostering such a principle of expansion and universality, an economy based on general sentiment would also effectively create its own motivational structure. It would make sense for companies and other actors to act in a way that maximizes the reach and scope of their social impact, that enables them to have a positive social impact for as many people as possible, across as many value horizons as possible. While this goal is impossible to realize in the absolute, it does create a particular direction for actors' ambitions. The present default motivation of continuous capital accumulation would be paralleled by a new default motivation, an "ethical iron cage" dictating that we all must strive to maximize our social impact, lest we go out of business.

So to the extent that this measure of value could be made to "count" in economic decisions, it would result in a rationalization and a democratization of the fundamental axis of the information economy. This is particularly important at the level of financial markets. After all, financial markets are a functional mechanism of value distribution in a situation where value creation is ever more socialized and based on appropriations of common resources. In the information economy value creation is ever more a matter of productive publics that utilize common resources and put them to work in socialized processes that unfold beyond the control of single actors. Already today the value that derives from these processes is distributed on financial markets in the form of intangible assets. If the mechanisms of distribution could be rationalized and connected to a value parameter—general sentiment, which is itself determined in participatory, bottom-up ways—the basis for a new way of reconnecting economy and society could possibly be found. This arrangement would confer a new rationality and stability upon financial markets, enabling them to take into account alternative orders of worth like sustainability or social responsibility in more transparent ways, and creating more comprehensive value measures that would, in all likelihood, reduce present levels of volatility, and by implication the scope for speculation. It would also reintroduce the judgment that Amar Bidhé, among others, has called for as a necessary component of what he refers to as sensible financial order.[35] However, such judgment would not depend solely on the virtue and good sense of financial operators. Rather, they would have at their disposal a dynamic and universal representation of the comprehensive judgment of the "networked multitude" of proxies who contribute to the formation of general sentiment.

6

Ethical Economy

The financial expansion that has marked the last three decades signals the end of the industrial/consumerist model of capitalism that we have gotten used to in the postwar years. This has been a long-standing argument on the part of "unorthodox" economists like Robert Brenner and Andre Gunder Frank. Already in the 1990s they suggested that underneath the financial expansion that fueled the dot-com boom, and subsequently the housing boom, there was a persistent decline in the rates of profit of virtually all non-financial sectors of the U.S. economy (and tendencies are the same for Western Europe). To put it very simply, profits from the industrial production of commodities—the backbone of the industrial economy—are now so low that capital tends to migrate into financial markets, where prospective gains are much higher, at least in the short run. Indeed, Robert Brenner suggests that the financialization of the economy should be seen as a reaction to the long downturn in non-financial profitability that has plagued the world economy since 1973. (And in his earlier work, Brenner documents a decline in U.S. manufacturing profitability of 40 percent between 1965 and 1973.)[1]

The decline in U.S. and European manufacturing profitability is of course partly the result of the opening up of the Chinese and other Asian economies and the subsequent availability of a vast "reserve army of labor" that has increased competition and pushed profits down. In part it is the result of tightening consumer markets: it is simply more difficult to sell things like refrigerators and television sets than it was in the 1950s, because people already have them. And as for the potentially huge Chinese market for consumer goods, there is a growing awareness that lifting the Chinese to Western standards of living would quite simply be impossible, for reasons related to ecological sustainability and the impact that such a change would have on resource prices.

Most importantly, however, the declining profitability in the manufacturing economy has resulted from technological change, notably the impact of networked digital technologies. These have made possible the networking and outsourcing of production; they have supported new flexible and collaborative production systems and, by putting previously private knowledge in the common domain, they have made the skills and "intellectual capital" needed to engage in basic material production common. Once again, it would be wrong to reduce everything to the impact of networked digital technologies. (Political factors like the opening up of the Chinese economy, the wave of labor militancy that shook the West in the 1970s, which made automation seem an attractive choice, and neoliberal policies that have favored trade deregulation and financialization are other important causes.) It would also be wrong to attribute the arrival of networked digital technologies to some mysterious technological "force." (Like all other technologies, these are "socially constructed": they are the effect of a number of choices made at different levels and by different actors, that have impacted the concrete realization of these technologies. The political history of the Internet is indeed a fascinating read.)[2] But that said, networked digital technologies are the necessary backbone that has enabled these political and social forces to converge into a series of structural transformations that have undermined the viability of the Fordist mode of development. They have supported the creation of a systemic overcapacity of international dimensions, where manufacturing companies have more capital and more productive capacity than they can put to lucrative use under existing market conditions.

Drawing on Soviet economist Nicolai Kondtratieff's work on "long waves" in economic development, Carlota Perez has developed this connection between technological innovation, financialization, and crisis in more detail. In brief, Perez suggests that each new disruptive technology goes through four phases. In the first, "irruption" phase, the technology enters the existing mode of production and transforms the way things are done. This happened in the 1880s as the combination of electricity, combustion engines, and railroads paved the way for what is known as the "second industrial revolution"; it began to happen again in the 1970s as microcomputers entered offices and automation began to be used in factories. In the second phase, the "frenzy" phase, the gains in productivity from this transformation create massive amounts of new wealth. But in the absence of an overall model of economic regulation that is able to put this new wealth to productive use and in the absence of an adequate value regime, the wealth is channeled into speculative activity, leading to a speculative boom that eventually bursts. What follows is a prolonged period of crisis that is resolved by the construction of a new regulatory regime that permits the channeling of the productivity resulting from the new technology into a "synergy" phase of balanced and sustained growth. The cycle ends in a "maturity" phase, in which the political contradictions resulting from a period of sustained growth (essentially an increasing militancy on the part of a empowered working class) come to the fore.[3]

With this interpretation, it is possible to suggest, as Perez herself does, that the expansion of financial markets that has marked the last three decades should be viewed as a result of the changes brought about by networked digital technologies entering their frenzy phase. Along with the argument presented in chapter 2, the introduction of networked digital technologies in the production process has enabled great advancements in the ability to produce wealth (as is manifested in the declining prices of consumer durables that result from new kinds of global supply chains).[4] But this productive expansion unfolds within a regulatory framework that has remained largely unaltered since the 1930s, when the last crisis—resulting from the conclusion of the frenzy phase of what Perez calls "the age of oil, automobiles and mass production"—was resolved through the New Deal and the institutionalization of expansionist mass consumerism as an overall paradigm of economic growth. This framework is now unable to absorb the excess productivity unleashed by information and communication technologies and the new kinds of productive publics that they have made possible. It cannot open up the markets through which the new productive power could be channeled and transformed into measurable expressions of what economists call "productivity." And it remains difficult to see how this opening could be achieved with the existing institutional framework: even with a more equal global distribution of income it is difficult to sustain a continuous demand for products like washing machines and television sets, not to mention the environmental costs of such a continuous expansion. The result is a profit squeeze in manufacturing and a diversion of the profits actually realized into speculative activity, in our case the expansion of financial markets taking the form of a series of boom-and-bust cycles: the mergers and acquisitions boom in the 1980s, the dot-com boom in the 1990s, and the housing market boom in the 2000s. In the same way, corporate bureaucracies are inefficient at harvesting and motivating the efficiency of productive publics and are limited in their ability to channel the new ethical demands, which have themselves developed as a consequence of the proliferation of such productive publics, into factors that can have a tangible impact on economic value decisions. Thus a legitimacy crisis is added to an ever more obvious economic decline.

In this interpretation, the flight of capital away from the "productive economy" and to financial markets is essentially a manifestation of the inability of the present economic regime to put the capacity it generates to productive use. This is an important point. It is not that there are no more needs to be met in the world; it is simply that the prevailing political-economic paradigm is unable to open up the markets by means of which capital could be productively deployed to meet those needs. Although a number of efforts are being made in this direction, like venture capital investing in alternative energy systems, or companies cultivating the "bottom of the pyramid"—that is, the market of the global poor—these represent isolated results of mostly private enterprise, not the coordinated outcome of systemic initiatives. From this point of view, such a coexistence of unmet needs and excess capital, and the financial expansion that results from that combination, is a classic symptom of the imminent transition from one system to another. Similar progressions have occurred before, for example in the financial boom of the 1920s that marked the transition from a nineteenth-century English-style industrial capitalism to an American-style consumer capitalism. The resolution of that crisis consisted in a series of systemic measures—the New Deal and resulting welfare systems—that managed to realize a more democratic mass consumer society, thus opening up a range of new markets where capital could be deployed to address hitherto unmet needs and desires, and institutionalized a new, Fordist paradigm of capitalist development. Indeed, in his masterful history, *The Long Twentieth Century*, Giovanni Arrighi argues that periods of financialization of the economy, like ours, usually constitute the last phase of a "systemic cycle of accumulation" and signal the imminent emergence of another one. This implies that such a crisis will go along until a new regulatory framework—a new "new deal"—is found that can connect efficiency gains made possible by new technologies, and the new relations of production that they support, to unmet needs and thus enable continuous growth and productivity gains.[5]

In short, we need a new institutional framework built around a new conception of value, a new value regime, in order to exit the present crisis and give a new direction to development that can open up the markets in which the potential of networked digital technologies can be fully realized. Only that way can we achieve a new period of economic growth and, in the longer perspective, support the emergence of a new political subject able to radicalize global politics. But where can we find the components of such a new institutional framework? In this book we have argued that networked digital technologies have not only undermined the feasibility of the Fordist mode of development but also have supported the development of the fundamental building blocks for a new paradigm. The first two of these building blocks are productive publics as a way of organizing wealth creation in an economy of commons and financial markets as a way of making value decisions and distributing wealth in a situation of networked and global value chains. (And here our interpretation obviously differs from Perez's characterization of finance as mere "speculation." As we have stressed before, the financialization of value is also a rational response to the new importance of processes of wealth creation that rely on common resources.) The third building block consists in a new reputation economy that has emerged as a "natural component" in the development of productive publics and that is currently acquiring a new objectivity, chiefly through its remediation by means of social media. This way, this new reputation economy is developing its own general equivalent, what we have called general sentiment, by means of which value decisions that are made against the backdrop of diverse value horizons can be compared to one another and evaluated accordingly. We have suggested that these components, taken together, point to the possibility of a new ethical economy in which economic value would be directly related to virtuous conduct.

"Possibility" is of course a key term here. What is missing is an institutional framework that can connect these components into a coherent "value regime," a coherent way of making value decisions that is inscribed in a wide range of different institutions. As always, such an institutional framework needs to be built by political action. Building this new value regime is, we suggest, the most urgent political task that we are facing. But it will require a different kind of politics than that with which we are traditionally acquainted.

Dingpolitik!

When we think about political agency, we tend to think about contrast and confrontation. This view is something that we inherited from the twentieth century, when the main paradigm of politics was conflict between opposing social forces—capitalism and communism, democracy and totalitarianism. Politics in this modern sense occurred in a pre-constituted arena where the forces were known and the spaces of conflict were evident. Such predictability no longer applies today. Now the main challenge is rather to constitute the political forces that can act, by associating a diverse range of individual, or at least particular, perspectives and concerns. And such new forms of association are certain to cut across the boundaries established by modern oppositional politics. For example, while there are many evil corporations around, we also need to recognize that work toward sustainability takes place mostly in hybrid initiatives that feature cooperation between corporations and other organizations. So we can no longer view politics and political agency as a matter of one pre-constituted force battling another. Rather, we need to construct a new public sphere in which politics can play out and its forces can be constituted.

This suggestion is not as strange as it might seem. We are used to a public sphere that is already in place and that can serve as an arena for political processes and the formation of public opinion. But this public sphere itself was once constructed, built by the people who invented new techniques for printing books, who kept salons and founded learned societies, who organized unions and social movements. Since the public sphere that they built is now being fragmented by the transformations that this book has (in part) discussed, we need to build a new one. Indeed, in his recent work, French sociologist Bruno Latour suggests that to build the things that can found a new public sphere (what he calls a politics of things or a *Dingpolitik*) is the most important direction for contemporary progressive politics.[6]

A *Dingpolitik* could encompass many different things. It could be a matter of the clever use of geolocalization software and mobile phones to render garbage recycling more efficient; it could be a matter of using art in new ways to create areas of public debate and discussion. For our purposes, the most pressing kind of *Dingpolitik* is that of constructing new devices whereby value can be represented in new ways: to construct the infrastructure for a new value regime. Again, in itself this is not an entirely new thing. The notion of productive time, with which the industrial economy operated, was itself a "constructed" thing. Even though the medieval historian Jacques le Goff dates an emerging conception that "time has value" to the commercial revolution of the fourteenth century, the notion of productive time as a standard way to conceptualize economic value emerged out of the turbulent struggles of the seventeenth century, and became operative only with the managerial revolution and the rise of modern corporations in the late nineteenth century.[7] It became operative not through any sovereign decisions on the part of a central actor, but through the construction of a multitude of devices, each serving very minute and modest purposes, like modern cost accounting, Taylorist principles of scientific management, and bureaucratic job descriptions that institutionalized time as a measure of value across the economy. Of course, the basic principle of these devices, that time had value, could not simply be plucked out of the blue; it needed to be already realized in the concrete day-to-day operations of the economy to such a degree that it "made sense" to the actors concerned. But the gap between time making sense as a measure of value in some abstract and intuitive way and time actually operating as the institutionalized, objective, or even "scientific" measure of economic value was bridged by a diffuse *Dingpolitik*.

This example illustrates another feature of *Dingpolitik* that sets it apart from modern confrontational politics. While modern politics tends to address ideas and actions, *Dingpolitik* focuses mainly, although not exclusively, on the infrastructure by means of which such ideas and actions are communicated and carried out. It rests on a belief that the technical standards or, to use a term in vogue right now, "protocols" of this infrastructure can have a decisive impact on the ideas and actions that it conveys. Protocol denotes a "way of doing things" that is accepted as a matter of course, as in "military protocol" or "diplomatic protocol." The term has acquired a new salience as media theorists have focused on the technical protocol of the Internet and the effect that it has had on the nature of online communications. For example, the TCP/IP protocol, which has become the basic infrastructure of the Internet, was developed in ways that shifted control over the network from central computers to the multitude of devices that participated. Developed in the early 1970s, it was shaped by technical concerns, like the need to develop a more efficient way to interlink the original Internet, ARPANet, with radio and satellite networks. It nevertheless had profound political and social consequences as it effectively institutionalized the centrifugal nature of the Internet and limited possibilities for centralized control over communications, allowing for a wide diversity of devices to connect to the Net and to each other in ways that had not been centrally set.[8]

But even though "protocol" is a term used in computer science—to designate the affordances of communication infrastructures, like the TCP/IP protocol, and how they shape communications themselves—a similar perspective can be applied to other standards as well. For example, legal scholar David Singh has shown how common standards like the global use of the English language or the affirmation of gold as a default definition of monetary value shape the globalization process.⁹ It is possible to suggest that the introduction of modern paper money worked in a similar way. Money is not simply a measure of value, or a way to transfer value from one person to another (or to store it for the future). It is also an embodiment of value; its social diffusion tends to create a new default definition of what value is, or, to put it in more general terms, what sorts of goals are socially desirable. Moreover, like any other medium, money has particular properties, or "affordances." It is endowed with a protocol—that is, a set of biases toward certain actions. For example, when the medium spreads to the masses, as modern money did with the invention of paper money and modern "fractional reserve banking," it tends to actually make certain actions more likely than others (saving and investing instead of spending, for instance). Its capillary spread in the social fabric caused a massive "value change" (in the cultural sense of that term). From this point of view, the protocol of money, essentially its ability to render absolute values relative and exchangeable and its bias toward accumulation, made an important contribution toward the mass diffusion of a capitalist mentality. We are of course not arguing that the spread of money was the sole cause of the gigantic social transformation that the transition to a modern capitalist society entailed. But we are suggesting that the diffusion of the medium of money, with its particular protocol, played an important part in achieving this transition at the level of values or *mentalités*. It had two important consequences. First, it contributed to extending the participation in economic life and included ordinary people as important actors in the practice of establishing values through their exercise of choice on markets. Second, it fostered a particular capitalist mentality, by embedding the new set of capitalist values in the very mechanisms by means of which a growing share of the relations and activities that made up everyday life could unfold. As the great French historian Fernand Braudel argued, the eighteenth century saw the generalization of a "bourgeois mentality" geared toward business, trade, and risk taking, across virtually all social strata, including the once snobbish aristocracy.¹⁰

Protocols, Singh suggests, have "network power"—that is, the more people use them, the more influential they become. But, unlike sovereign mechanisms like law, they need not originate in any decision on the part of an identifiable actor or group of actors. Rather, the dominance of a standard is the outcome of a large number of small decisions that often follow from each other in a cascading way. To put it simply, when more people use a standard, more other people are likely to start using it as well. We have seen the proliferation of standards and their network power in the accelerating diffusion of social media platforms like Facebook and Twitter, which have quite profoundly changed the ways in which we interact and relate to each other. The suggestion of a *Dingpolitik* is thus to learn from these viral processes to construct and diffuse different kinds of applications that can *make into a standard* a new way of making value decisions. This of course does not mean that traditional political actors should be ignored. Government—from the transnational to the local level—as well as state agencies of different kinds can be important partners in this development, and working traditional parliamentary politics is important in order to secure the kinds of legal frameworks that can facilitate, rather than obstruct, the construction of a new public sphere. But it implies that the construction and diffusion of standards constitutes the main political strategy through which to involve government, corporations, and other actors.

ETHICAL ECONOMY

What would the outcomes of a successful *Dingpolitik* be? What could an institutionalized ethical economy achieve? While it is unwise to speculate in excessive detail about the future, to "write the recipes for tomorrow's soup kitchens," to use Karl Marx's phrase, a number of very general points seem obvious to us.

First of all, a functioning ethical economy would probably be able to relaunch economic growth, as it would result in a redefinition of value, thus opening up new markets and possibilities for expansion (like those involved in creating more-sustainable energy, transport, and production systems), connecting new actors (like social ventures and entrepreneurs) to financial capital, and enabling productive publics of various kinds to monetize their efforts in more rational and transparent ways and facilitate their access to markets and capital (as well as rendering participation in such pursuits economically sustainable for individuals). It would do this simply by expanding the range of orders of worth that could count in economic decision making. Overall, the new collaborative productive processes that remain partially blocked by the neoliberal corporate institutional framework in which they presently unfold would be allowed to evolve on more favorable and proper terms, much as early manufacturing freed itself from the remains of the medieval guilds during the eighteenth century.

Second, a functioning ethical economy would introduce a new econom-ic rationality. If indeed the intangible assets that are strategically central to the information economy are produced in productive publics, deploying the kinds of ethical capital that is the central asset of the ethical economy, then it is rational that their value be measured in relation to the virtuous conduct by means of which such ethical capital is created and accumu-lated. (In the same way, it was rational that the material goods that were strategically central to the industrial economy were valued in relation to the productive time through which the then central machine capital was put to work and reproduced itself.) Thus steps toward the realization of an ethical economy are also steps toward the re-creation of an economic rationality that has been lost. And by reflecting a wider range of value concerns, that new economic rationality would also be ethical in a new, and potentially more up-to-date way. Its development would no doubt help in overcoming both the legitimacy crisis from which contemporary capitalism suffers and the existential crises that plague its more ethically conscious participants.

Third, the ethical economy would introduce a new source of *stability*. In its absence, asset valuations are ever more self-referential and thus prone to strong fluctuations. With an established external measurement that an-chors their value in notions of performance that pertain to areas outside of the market itself, valuations become more predictable. Stability of values would initiate a virtuous cycle in which prospects for short-term specula-tion (like that performed by today's automatic financial trading "bots") would be reduced and hence the long-term investment necessary for ef-ficient stewardship of common resources (like the environment) would assume renewed importance.

Fourth, the ethical economy would redefine democracy. Today econom-ic values are considered to be outside the domain of political deliberation. But, as we have suggested in this book, there is no reason for this to be so. The values of intangible assets are already set in deliberative processes, but these deliberations are restricted to highly limited circles of experts. Just as the development of a market economy in the eighteenth century facili-tated a more widespread popular participation in the processes through which economic values were set—and was heralded as a great harbinger of democracy by its proponents—the development of an ethical economy will connect not only more people, but also more communities, publics, and value horizons to the deliberative processes in which economic values are set. This has the possibility of deepening economic democracy even further, because it now becomes possible to connect a multitude of orders of worth to the economic system in ways that enable them to have a more direct impact on market prices. True, most of these actors would not actually participate in deliberation over, say, how to price in the environmental performance of a company. That would probably not even be desirable, as it would generate excessive complexity. But they would participate in setting the value standard, the general sentiment, against which such deliberation could be settled.

Fifth and finally, a functioning ethical economy would create a new version of what sociologist Max Weber called the "iron cage." With this term he referred to the process by means of which the values of capitalist development were inscribed in a series of institutions, from commercial law to the functioning of markets and the monetary system, that forced actors to maximize their profits regardless of their subjective will or intentions. This way the values of continuous capital accumulation were inscribed in the objective framework of everyday action. In a similar way, a fully functional ethical economy would create a direct link between virtue, in terms of overall social impact, on the one hand, and legitimate claims to wealth, on the other. This connection would make it compelling to act in ways that ensure that such virtue is maximized. In other words, it would create an alternative overall iron cage.

While it is not for us to speculate on the precise nature of the institutions that could achieve this, at least not at this point, we would like to give a couple of hints in the directions that we think are most important.

Finance and the Commons

As we have suggested throughout this book, the expansion of financial markets should not only be understood as a sign of crisis. Finance should also be seen as a possible building block of a new, more rational mode of development, because the financialization of value is a rational component of the development of an increasingly commons-based mode of production. In the industrial economy, value could be primarily based on the putting to work of proprietary capital in productive processes that unfolded within the privately controlled space of the factory. Thus the valorization of private capital could constitute the main mechanism of accumulation. Today value creation is ever more a matter of utilizing common resources and putting them to work in socialized processes that unfold beyond the control of single actors. And the value that derives from these processes is distributed in financial markets in the form of return on assets and, even more important, differentials in interest rates. (Given present tendencies toward increases in household debt, the latter dimension is perhaps most important for ordinary people.)[11] Empirically this presents itself as a combination of, on the one hand, diffuse and global value chains that involve a large diversity of productive practices, and on the other hand, financial markets as the key institution through which the social surplus is distributed and values are set. But what is valued on financial markets is not just wealth that is created during work time; what is valued increasingly includes wealth that is created in a wide range of life practices—consuming, viewing, working for a wage, working without a wage, contributing to a maker public, being engaged in a social enterprise, and so on. Financial markets thus extract and redistribute value not just from the restricted range of practices that used to be considered "the economy," but from the whole *bíos* of the population. Therefore, decisions about financial valuation become decisions about the value of our life in common.

This situation of "complete subsumption" of life as a source of economic value has often been criticized as an expression of the excessive power of capitalism in its present, financial phase. But it can also be viewed as the embryo of a new arrangement. After all, to the extent that value-producing processes and life processes come to coincide, to the extent that we operate in what Andrea Fumagalli calls a bioeconomy, it is rational that the determinant of a person's wealth be related to his or her entire life process, and not just to the parts of that life process that have been spent in activities formally designated as productive labor.[12] But for this to be a functioning arrangement, the value of life, of *bíos*, must find its just measure. Today its value is generally determined according to the risk that it poses for investor profits (as in the credit ratings that determine the access to and cost of credit for ordinary people). A better measure would be based on its overall productivity, or the virtue of its conduct. (To put it in other, more formal terms, the correct measure of the value of *bíos* is ethics.) And the same is of course true of the conduct of organizations. (Some, however rudimentary, notion of conduct is already operating in the systems that determine the creditworthiness of individuals or the reputation of companies.)[13]

From this point of view, there is, as Robert Schiller argues in his recent book, *Finance and the Good Society*, nothing wrong with finance per se.[14] Instead we should see the financial system as something that needs to come to age and maturity. But in order for it to do so, financial innovation needs to be expanded. We need to develop new instruments that are better able to connect the complex forms of cooperation and pooling of resources that financial instruments orchestrate to a wider and more realistic set of needs. The institutionalization of an ethical economy would be a way to inspire and drive such financial innovation.

If the deliberations of value on financial markets, in a variety of instances that go from the automated processes that determine credit scores and process mortgage applications up to the decisions made on bond markets, could be connected to more general and participatory measures of the virtue of conduct, in the form of general sentiment, then the capacity to determine what the values would be would be greatly democratized. This would mean that the distribution of wealth, in the form of the prices of or access to credit, would vary for different kinds of actors according to criteria that are broader than those presently in place with regard to such decisions. The consequence would be that a wider range of concerns that reflect the concrete experiences that people have had with companies, as expressed in the strength and positivity of the sentiment that the multitude nurtures toward them, would directly determine the price of money that corporations and other actors would have to pay. It would probably also facilitate access to financial capital for actors that have agendas that appear risky or unprofitable today, but that nevertheless have important environmental and social consequences, like NGOs and nonprofit investments in the green economy. Indeed, a movement in that direction is already under way as impact investing is gaining momentum through the agency of organizations like the Global Impact Investing Network or the San Francisco–based venture capital firm Good Capital. However, in the absence of a transparent and rational measure of "impact," this movement remains weaker and less coherent than it could be. Only with such a measure in place will it be possible to transform impact from an immeasurable add-on to a measurable and tangible feature of corporate performance among others.

Most importantly, such a rationalization of finance would create a direct link between virtue, in terms of overall social impact, and endowments of wealth. This would introduce a dimension of judgment and ethics in the setting of financial values. But, contrary to Amar Bidhé's recent call for judgment, it would be a kind of judgment that relies not only on the individual wisdom of financial operators but also on a new kind of objectified ethical wisdom, the general sentiment of the networked multitude. The fact that this general sentiment would reflect a wide diversity of points of view would also mean that the concrete values assigned to particular assets would provide a realistic reflection of the impact that those assets have on actors that are concerned with or touched by their conduct. This would introduce a fundamental channel by means of which the diversity of real impacts of an asset could be reflected in its price. It would give us a way to transform finance in the direction of the kind of stewardship of common resources that Schiller sees as its role in what he calls "the Good Society."

Publics and Stewardship

The concept of stewardship has acquired a new salience in progressive social thought. As the London-based organization Tomorrow's Company defines it, stewardship is "the active and responsible management of entrusted resources now and in the longer term, so as to hand them on in better condition."[15] As an overall goal, stewardship is about not the short-term maximization of profit from private resources, but the long-term management of common resources. And as Elinor Ostrom, the 2009 winner of the Nobel Prize in economics, suggests, successful stewardship (a term she does not use herself), or long-term management of common resources, develops in situations where "individuals communicate and interact with each other in a localized physical setting [so that they develop] shared norms and patterns of reciprocity." In other words, it is by developing shared norms and values, what Ostrom calls "social capital," through weighing their individual concerns and interests against each other that a common understanding of the values of long-term management and preservation of the commons develops. Common resources that are not handled by communities that have developed such common norms tend instead to be subject to the "tragedy of the commons" that traditional economic models depict (i.e., actors have incentives to maximize the benefits that they can derive from their individual use of the commons at the expense of others).[16] To Ostrom, communities that are able to develop the kinds of shared norms that can support long-term stewardship represent an alternative to both state intervention and markets in the management of common resources. Her research was based on communities that were organized around physical proximity and dense interaction. However, today the challenge is also to achieve stewardship around common resources that are of interest to actors that are not physically present and do not interact with each other. We have global commons that need to be safeguarded, like information and knowledge, the earth and its ability to sustain life, the biopolitical rights of life itself. Obviously these cannot be guarded by communities. But publics can function as an institution that can achieve stewardship of such global commons. Indeed, it is possible to argue that brands have already begun to evolve in that direction.

Brands are already being transformed from empty signifiers like "Just do it!" that are controlled and owned by companies and brand managers. They are evolving into publics that are united around values and ethoi that are, to a large extent, influenced by participants. To date, however, this control remains superficial and quite powerless. If there are ways in which members of branded publics can articulate common values that are able to generate strong affective attachments, there is really no way in which such publics can reach down into the depths of production to value the real virtue of a brand in terms of the conditions that guide its material production and what this really does to the surrounding environment. While such publics can and do imagine what stewardship of the process to which they are affectively tied might look like, they have no way of actually exercising that stewardship. Once again, the institutionalization of an ethical economy could increase the power of publics, and not just communities, to actually exercise stewardship of common resources, branded or not. Indeed, there is much research suggesting that such commitments, as well as their ability to actually have an impact, could be strengthened through the construction of material devices that both give greater coherence to publics themselves and strengthen the compelling force that a public ethics has on individual and corporate behavior. For example, sociologist Noortje Marres has shown how devices for carbon accounting in homes work to promote both an awareness of global warming and a propensity to take that awareness into account in everyday actions. In this sense the carbon-counting device renders an abstract problem, that of global warming, public and concrete at the same time. Similar devices could most certainly be used to address the gap between ideals and actions that marks both socially responsible corporations and ethically aware consumers. Indeed, the proliferation of smartphones and mobile devices provides a promising platform for achieving this, even in poorer contexts. (The market for mobile apps is growing rapidly in countries like India and Nigeria, and they are already being used for social purposes, like advising the public on the authenticity of malaria drugs.)[17] Together with the expansion of RFID tagging, such apps could support the introduction of some form of communicative, non-monetary dimensions in a growing number of commercial relations. After all, the process of introducing communicative dimensions to commercial interactions has already been under way for some time as Customer Relations Management, and contemporary brand management have, since the 1990s, worked to strengthen the enduring relational components to commercial transactions. The integration of consumers into the production process, through increased reliance on customer-centric brand equity and user-led innovation, is likely to further blur the relations between consumers and production, reconfiguring their relative roles as participants in a productive public with some kind of ethical coherence. This would enable a development of global brands into the kinds of global, interconnected publics that are necessary to counterbalance the globalization of production and of the economy. A functioning platform for measuring and communicating the value of social impact could create a common space in which people who are proximate to a particular brand all along its value chain—from the American consumers of a particular sports shoe to the Thai seamstresses who make the actual material product—could influence its value, by making known their judgments as to the extent to which the brand lives up to its announced values. And the overall impact or virtue of the brand or the common resource would be visible through its general sentiment score. (Such ratings could be accessed by simply sweeping one's mobile phone over the branded object in question.) This would create a concrete economic incentive for good stewardship, since the overall virtue of a brand or a productive public would directly affect its economic value. And just as in the case of impact investing, it would transform loose "ethical" concerns into tangible and measurable features of commodities and brands, akin in nature to their functional attributes.

It would also make members of the public evaluate the conduct of the brand in terms of its long-term sustainability. As Ostrom describes it, this kind of evaluation would happen because communitarian norms themselves build on the sedimentation of affective ties that constitute individuals into a community or a public organized around a common interest. These also constitute that public as an object of affective proximity, of passionate engagement for its members. Thus, once a public has been constituted, its members tend to articulate an interest in its long-term sustainability, and it becomes recursive; indeed, such recursivity often becomes the overarching goal. In other words, stewardship tends to be the natural outcome of an ethics born out of collaboration and affective proximity.

A Rationalized Reputation Economy

Another urgent need today is a process that is able to confer rationality and transparency upon the reputation economy that is becoming ever more important as a component of productive pursuits. Until quite recently, productive activities with little or no market value, like writing free software code or contributing to an urban creative scene, could be sustained without individual remuneration because of open labor markets or generous welfare systems. (It was possible to find a reasonably relaxed day job to support one's career as an artist; Berlin used to be full of Danish artists living on the generous student grants of the Danish welfare state.) Today those possibilities are diminishing as job markets tighten and states, even the Scandinavian welfare states, are forced to cut back on their generosity. Indeed, welfare is perhaps the component of a functioning economy that is most lacking today. Two decades of neoliberal policies have been preoccupied with the dismantling of welfare systems. And what remains of the welfare systems developed in industrial society is exceptionally bad at meeting the needs that arise with more diffuse production processes that blur the distinction between life and work and create a greater number of unstable working conditions and more mobile and project-based careers.

Instead, reputation economies seem to be developing as a new mechanism for the monetization of collaborative, non-market production. This evolution works well for privileged knowledge workers who have achieved high levels of reputation, which enables them to start companies and move in and out of employment or other forms of engagement with the capitalist economy.[18] But for the overwhelming majority of freelancers, creatives, and to an increasing extent also knowledge workers, the "pie" is so small that living on their reputation alone is not enough. Here a rational and transparent reputation economy could support a number of progressive developments.

It could make the pie larger by creating better connections between financial capital and the commons produced by a particular public. This could be achieved by enabling freelancers to come together in guilds or "phyles" that can bank on their collective reputation as collateral for investments. More realistically, states or local governments issuing bonds and other financial instruments could team up with such publics and issue bonds that capitalize on future financial gains created by their activities—in terms of the gentrifying effects of social entrepreneurship or the likely tax gains that might result from social innovation processes as these enter into corporate value creation down the line. Here, too, a rational measure of reputation would be useful in pricing such bonds.

Indeed, a similar question has surfaced in recent discussion about the feasibility of a guaranteed minimum income at the municipal level. This suggestion is reasonable, given that it is quite easy to prove that many productive pursuits that are not valued by the market, like participating in the production of free software or taking part in a creative scene that contributes to a gentrification process, actually create tangible forms of economic value further down the value chain. However, the problem with such a measure is finding a mechanism that can determine whom to pay and how much. Should everybody be paid such a minimum income, or only the unemployed? Should the unemployed who engage in activities that are socially useful be paid more than those who do not? In that case, how do we determine what is socially useful? Some institutionalization of a reputation economy along the lines of what we have discussed might well provide a solution to these problems. One could imagine a two-tiered minimum income, where a basic income was conferred on everybody, while a top tier was dependent upon people's reputation in terms of their accumulation of general sentiment in open and transparent platforms of deliberation. Indeed, to reform welfare states in ways conducive to maximizing the productivity and innovativeness of new forms of socialized production, while still respecting basic concerns for inclusion and equality, would be an interesting challenge for what remains of European social democracy.[19]

What Kind of Ethics?

The ethics that is emerging with the transformations that we have documented is at the same time radically new and quite ancient. It is different from the two most important ethical paradigms that have characterized modern societies. It is not a rules-based ethics, since unlike Christian ethics or, more generally, Kantian ethics, it does not depart from universally valid rules of good conduct (whether these rules were given by God or arrived at through rational argument). And it is not a communitarian ethics, since even though it emphasizes the power of particular forms of association (publics) to create their own values, it still retains the notion that the values thus created could be compared with each other and evaluated. In other words, it is neither a universalist nor a relativist ethics. Instead we like to think of it as a *public* ethics.

We understand the source of this kind of ethics to be public action, the ability to create values and, more generally, bonds and ties with others. In this sense it is quite similar to Aristotelian ethics, which, rather than being a meditation on right or wrong in the absolute sense, was more like a theory of how citizens can live together and realize the good life (*eudai-*

monia) in common. We think this ancient conception of ethics is coming back as a component of the new kinds of productive publics that we have discussed in this book. But it is coming back in a quite different, and dare we say improved, version. The differences are obvious.

First, Aristotle reserved the ability to engage in ethical behavior for propertied, male citizens. This was because the social structure of Athens in the fourth century B.C. was that of a slave-owning patriarchal society where only male heads of household could be considered sufficiently freed from the slavery of material needs to be able to engage in ethical deliberation. Obviously, this condition of exclusion does not apply to productive publics. In part, of course, this is a result of historical progress—we no longer consider slavery or the subordination of women acceptable. But it also results from the fact that the resources around which publics are organized tend to be common, and hence abundant, to the members of such publics. Thus the problem of material need, at least in the narrow sense of need for the resources that are necessary for participating in a public pursuit (like skills in software writing), is solved. And just as the Aristotelian ethics that was developed by people who were free from material need tended to emphasize the virtues of moderation and prudence, so this new ethic of abundance is geared toward emphasizing the sustainability and stewardship of the sources of such abundance (common knowledge, the common world).

Second, Aristotelian ethics was an ethics of the leisurely. To labor and work in the creation of wealth was the condition of slaves, who, because they were not free, could not be ethical subjects. (The relation to craft—*techné*—was more complex: indeed, Aristotle defines ethics as the "craft of living well.") The new kind of public ethics that we understand to be emerging today is instead intrinsically fused with wealth-creating activity. It is by taking part in productive publics, dedicated to the creation of things that also have economic value, that one becomes engaged in the kinds of ethical action that we have described. In productive publics, ethics and economics, two domains that have remained tragically separated in modernity, come together again. In this sense productive publics can be understood as basic elements of a new public sphere that can give expression to the ethical, or even political nature of collaborative knowledge work that has constituted a common discovery of management scholars on the one hand and Italian autonomist Marxists on the other.[20] In productive publics, collaborative productive practices can create their own values, and participating individuals can express their own individuality, without the situation degenerating into the collective cynicism observed in corporate frameworks and the empty individualism associated with consumer culture. Conversely, the intrinsically ethical or civic nature of such forms of wealth creation suggests that the proliferation of productive publics can contribute to explaining the present diffusion of a new "ethical mentality" in the form of ethical consumerism, fair trade, and philanthropic engagements. In this sense productive publics represent the practical convergence of ethics and economics; they are the micro-level building blocks of the ethical economy.

In contrast to communitarian ethics, the public ethics that we are proposing is open and universalistic. Productive publics are extended forms of association that reach beyond physical co-presence and that tend to be open to a wide diversity of individuals. Or rather, publics tend to accept or reject people on the basis of their achieved qualities (like technical excellence) rather than their ascribed qualities (like membership in a particular ethnic group). This openness probably operates partly because policies of a priori exclusion tend to limit the productivity of large-scale cooperative networks. Similarly, this public ethics is open to a wide variety of different values: publics constitute themselves around the values that they create and there is no a priori limit to the proliferation of those values. At the same time, this public ethics contains a mechanism for evaluating the relative worth of the values created by different publics. It contains the possibility of an ethical measure. But this measure is not transcendent. It is not derived from any common higher principles (God, reason, morality). Rather it is immanent. The universal measure of ethical value is general sentiment, a mediated aggregation of the concrete value judgments that a multitude of actors, publics, and individuals have made, independently of the concrete values that have motivated them in making such judgments. Thus this new public ethics is able to avoid the Scylla of universalism and the Charybdis of relativism: it is able to confer universal value on things without privileging one perspective over another. And what's more, this universal is dynamic. Like market price, general sentiment constitutes a real-time estimate of the affective intensity, the sentiment, that the multitude has in relation to a particular thing. And as this sentiment changes, the value of the thing changes, in time, and this new public ethics evolves with the evolution of the concrete ethical concerns of the actors that support it. Therefore it is much more adaptable to a social framework made up of complex chains of cooperation and rapidly shifting trends and values. And the source of ethics is the excellence of action, which manifests itself in the ability to make a value judgment in the absence, or rather the overabundance, of rules and guidance. Such excellence requires courage and enterprise; it requires the courage to express one's own individuality and, together with others, to create one's own values. What we have then is a vitalist ethics: the values that it arrives at result from the strength of the life processes that express and support them.

Finally, our ethics is an ethics of the common good. The mediatized and open-ended nature of the publics that create values means that they tend to extend relations of sympathy beyond the geographically proximate or the parochially similar. The recursive nature of these publics, the fact that they are primarily devoted to the continuation of the particular thing to which they are devoted, tends to cause them to privilege values of stewardship and sustainability. In other words, the public ethics that we propose might well become a building block of a new "empathetic civilization" constructed around the stewardship of global commons.[21]

What Kind of Value?

Like our ethics, our notion of value is new. Modern social thought has tended to "naturalize" value, to link it to some objective, quasi-natural mechanism, thus rendering it close to a natural fact that, like, say, the weather, cannot be affected by discussion and deliberation. But as we have seen throughout this book, the mechanisms that have been invoked in such attempts at naturalization—the market and labor time, chiefly—are continually losing their relevance. Instead we suggest that value be opened up to deliberation, and that the deliberative basis of particular value decisions (or their socially constructed nature, which is the same thing) be recognized and the judgments thus made (whether human of algorithmic) be forced to potentially legitimate themselves.[22] Naturally such deliberations cannot extend to everyone; their concrete extension will be the empirical results of the artifacts built to enable them. But the value horizon against which such deliberations can be settled—general sentiment—can have universal validity as a representation of the concrete value judgment made by the actual multitude of interested parties. And contrary to the modern conceptions of value, general sentiment would be genuinely popular and naturalistic: it would not be related to some predetermined parameter, which inevitably would reflect the interest of a particular group. Instead it would approximate a situation in which economic value reflects the intersubjective balance of the passions of the multitude as these evolve over time.[23] Thus economic value would be a truly participatory construct, a peer-to-peer artifact, like the objects on which value is conferred. Just as the creation of wealth ever more builds on cooperation and common resources, so the determination of the value of that wealth would ever more build on the strength and association of the passions that are common to us all.

NOTES

PREFACE

1. dannon.com/dannoncares.aspx.
2. See J. Grant, *The Green Marketing Manifesto* (London: Wiley, 2007); U. Hacque, *The New Capitalist Manifesto: Building a Disruptively Better Business* (Boston: Harvard Business Review Press, 2011).
3. forceforgood.com/.
4. See, for example, R. Schiller, *Irrational Exuberance*, 2nd ed. (Princeton, NJ: Princeton University Press, 2005); S. Hart, *Capitalism at the Crossroads: Aligning Business, Earth, and Humanity* (Upper Saddle River, NJ: Wharton School Publishing, 2007); Grant, *Green Marketing Manifesto*; Hacque, *New Capitalist Manifesto*.
5. S. Turkle, *Alone Together: Why We Expect More from Technology and Less from Each Other* (New York: Basic Books, 2011).

1. VALUE CRISIS

1. L. Campetti, "Quattro domande a Napolitano" *Il Manifesto*, January 4, 2012.
2. For an excellent collection of figures like this, see D. Harvey, *The Enigma of Capital and the Crisis of Capitalism* (London: Enigma Books, 2011).
3. See, for example, A. R. Sorkin, *Too Big to Fail: The Inside Story of How Wall Street and Washington Fought to Save the Financial System* (New York: Viking, 2009); G. Soros, *The Crash of 2008 and What It Means: The New Paradigm for Financial Markets* (New

York: Public Affairs, 2009); L. G. McDonald and P. Robinson, *A Colossal Failure of Common Sense: The Inside Story of the Collapse of Lehman Brothers* (New York: Crown Business, 2009).

4. R. Schiller, *Irrational Exuberance*, 2nd ed. (Princeton, NJ: Princeton University Press, 2005).

5. A. Bidhé, *A Call for Judgment: Sensible Finance for a Dynamic Economy* (Oxford: Oxford University Press, 2010).

6. R. Sennett, *Together: The Rituals, Pleasures, and Politics of Cooperation* (New Haven, CT: Yale University Press, 2012), 171.

7. P. Kedrovsky, "The Run on the Shadow Liquidity System," *InfectiousGreed*, July 5, 2010, http://paul.kedrosky.com/archives/2010/05/run_on_the_shad.html (accessed May 25, 2011).

8. Bidhé, *Call for Judgment*, 25.

9. See, for example, C. Kelly, P. Kocourek, N. McGaw, and J. Samuelson, *Deriving Value from Corporate Values* (Washington, DC: Aspen Institute and Booz Allen Hamilton, 2005).

10. M. Morsing, "Conspicuous Responsibility: Communicating Responsibility—to Whom?" in *Corporate Values and Responsibility: The Case of Denmark*, ed. M. A. Morsing and C. Thyssen, 145–154 (Copenhagen: Samfundslitteratur, 2003).

11. See, for example, S. M. Barraclough, "A Grim Contradiction. The Practice and Consequences of Corporate Social Responsibility by British Tobacco in Malaysia," *Social Science Medicine* 66, no. 8 (2008): 1784–1796.

12. J. Hruska, "Apple's Record Profits Build on Grinding Employees into Dust—and Then Blowing Them Up," *ExtremeTech*, January 26, 2012, http://www.extremetech.com/computing/115833-apples-record-profits-built-on-grinding-employees-into-dust-then-blowing-them-up (accessed January 29, 2012).

13. See M. G. Gallazara, I. Gil-Suara, and M. Holbrook, "The Value of Value: Further Excursions on the Meaning and Role of Customer Value," *Journal of Consumer Behavior* 10 (2011): 179–191.

14. D. Stark, *The Sense of Dissonance: Accounts of Worth in Economic Life* (Princeton, NJ: Princeton University Press, 2009).

15. See A. Badiou, *Ethics* (London: Verso, 2001).

16. A. MacIntyre, *After Virtue: A Study in Moral Theory* (Notre Dame, IN: University of Notre Dame Press, 1984).

17. B. Lev, *Intangibles: Management, Measurement, and Reporting* (Washington, DC: Brookings Institution, 2001).

18. Figures from T. Philippon, "The Future of the Financial Industry," blogpost, *Stern on Finance*, October 16, 2008, http://sternfinance.blogspot.com/2008/10/future-of-financial-industry-thomas.html (accessed May 10, 2010); "Corporate Profits by Industry, 1959–2007," *Economic Report of the President*, 2008, as cited in J. Bellamy-Foster, "The Financialization of Capital and the Crisis," *Monthly Review* (April 2008), http://www.monthlyreview.org/080401foster.php (accessed May 10, 2010). See also G. Epstein, ed., *Financialization and the World Economy* (Lon-

don: Edward Elgar Publishing, 2006); G. Krippner, "The Financialization of the American Economy," *Socio-Economic Review* 3 (2005): 173–208; D. Harvey, *A Brief History of Neoliberalism* (Oxford: Oxford University Press, 2007).

19. C. Hulten and J. Hao, "Intangible Capital and the 'Market to Book Value' Puzzle" (New York: The Conference Board, June 2008). On the market-to-book-value ratios of Google and Facebook, see A. Arvidsson and E. Colleoni, "Value in Informational Capital and on the Internet," *The Information Society* 28, no. 4 (2012): 135–150.

20. P. Adler and C. Heckscher, Introduction to *The Firm as a Collaborative Community*, ed. C. Heckscher and P. Adler, 28 (Oxford: Oxford University Press, 2006).

21. J. Gerzema, "Brand Bubble Presentation on Slideshare," http://www.slideshare.net/johngerzema/5201brand-bubble-presentation (accessed May 20, 2011).

22. The first figure, $153 billion, comes from the Millward Brown BrandZ ranking (http://www.millwardbrown.com/Libraries/Optimor_BrandZ_Files/2011_BrandZ_Top100_Chart.sflb.ashx); the second, $33 billion, comes from the market leader Interbrand (http://www.interbrand.com/en/best-global-brands/best-global-brands-2008/best-global-brands-2011.aspx).

23. G. Salinas and T. Ambler, "A Taxonomy of Brand Valuation Practice: Methodologies and Purposes," *Journal of Brand Management* 17 (2009): 39–61.

24. Ibid.

25. This operation is generally attributed to Jean-Baptiste Say, one of the founders of mathematical economics, who simplified eighteenth-century discussions about value by equating value with price, thus making possible more-complex mathematical models.

26. J. Cassidy, "Rational Irrationality: An Interview with Eugene Fama," *New Yorker*, January 13, 2010, http://www.newyorker.com/online/blogs/johncassidy/2010/01/interview-with-eugene-fama.html (accessed February 1, 2012). Fama does concede that markets can misprice assets, but this is the effect of external intervention, like regulation that distorts the rationality of markets.

27. Cf. F. Hayek, *The Road to Serfdom* (London; Routledge, 1944).

28. Fama's hypothesis does allow for different levels of information access. The weak hypothesis states that markets price in publicly available information, while the strong hypothesis states that all information, including private information, is already priced in. The strong version means that profits, or at least sustained profits, from practices that aim at circumventing markets, like insider trading, are impossible.

29. To Braudel, the historical development of capitalism has built on the monopolization of markets. See F. Braudel, *Civilization and Capitalism: 15th–18th Century* (New York: HarperCollins, 1981).

30. A classical reference for this approach is M. Callon, *The Laws of Markets* (Oxford: Blackwell, 1999); for a good application to financial markets, see M. Pyrke, "Money's Eyes: The Visual Preparation of Financial Markets," *Economy and Society* 39, no. 4 (2010): 417–459. A recent volume that puts together a number

of empirical studies of pricing is J. Beckert and P. Aspers, eds., *The Worth of Goods: Valuation and Pricing in the Economy* (Oxford: Oxford University Press, 2011).

31. See R. Knight, *Risk, Uncertainty, and Profit* (Cambridge, UK: Riverside Press, 1921).

32. V. Cook, "Interbrand Value and Market Cap: A More Meaningful Comparison," *Seeking Alpha,* http://seekingalpha.com/article/47276-interbrand-value-and-market-cap-a-more-meaninful-comparison (accessed September 29, 2010).

33. On "postmaterial values," see R. Inglehart, *Modernization and Postmoderniza-tion: Cultural, Economic, and Political Change in 43 Societies* (Princeton, NJ: Princeton University Press, 1997); P. Ray and S. Anderson, *The Cultural Creatives: How 50 Million People Are Changing the World* (New York: Crown, 2001).

34. Z. Bauman, *Postmodern Ethics* (Oxford: Blackwell, 1993).

35. For the original argument about the "death of Grand Narratives" in "post-modernity," see J. F. Lyotard, *La condition postmoderne: Rapport sur le savoir* (Paris: Editions de Minuit, 1979).

36. Z. Bauman, *Does Ethics Have a Chance in a World of Consumers?* (Cambridge, MA: Harvard University Press, 2008), 28–29.

37. MacIntyre, *After Virtue*; Badiou, *Ethics.*

38. See A. Arvidsson, "Quality Singles: Internet Dating and the Work of Fantasy," *New Media and Society* 8, no. 4 (2006): 671–690.

39. Sennett, *Together.*

40. For a more detailed development of this argument, with a better rendering of the actual historical complexity, see M. Aglietta, *A Theory of Capitalist Regulation* (London: New Left Books, 1978).

2. INTANGIBLES

1. A. Danielsson, *Företagsekonomi: En Översikt* (Lund: Studentlitteratur, 1975).

2. C. Hulten and J. Hao, "Intangible Capital and the 'Market to Book Value' Puzzle" (New York: The Conference Board, June 2008).

3. C. Lury and L. Moor, "Brand Valuation and Topological Culture," in *Blowing Up the Brand*, ed. M. Aronczyk and D. Powers, 3 (New York: Peter Lang, 2010).

4. On ideal types, see M. Weber, *Economy and Society* (Berkeley: University of California Press, 1978), 18–22.

5. On the notion of a "knowledge economy," see P. Drucker, *The Age of Discontinuity* (New York: Harper and Row, 1969), and D. Bell, *The End of Ideology* (Glencoe, IL: Free Press, 1960); on "information economy," see M. Castells, *The Information Age*, vols. 1–3 (Oxford: Blackwell, 1996–1998); on "immaterial labor," see M. Lazzarato, *Lavoro immateriale* (Verona: Ombre Corte, 1997), and A. Negri, *Crisi dello stato piano-Comunismo e organizzazione rivoluzionaria* (Milan: Feltrinelli, 1974).

6. See E. Rullani, *Economia della conoscenza: Creatività e valore nel capitalismo delle reti* (Rome: Carocci, 2004); J. Moykr, *The Gifts of Athena: Historical Origins of the Knowledge Economy* (New Haven, CT: Princeton University Press, 2003).

7. A. Arvidsson, *Brands: Meaning and Value in Media Culture* (London: Routledge, 2006).

8. See M. Aglietta, *A Theory of Capitalist Regulation* (London: New Left Books, 1978); R. Boyer, *Théorie de la régulation*, vol. 1, *Les fondamentaux* (Paris: La Decouverte, 2004); Y. Mourlier-Boutang, *Le capitalisme cognitif: Comprendre la nouvelle grande transformation et ses enjeux* (Paris: Editions Amsterdam, 2007) ; D. Harvey, *The Condition of Postmodernity* (Oxford : Blackwell, 1990).

9. See A. Chandler, *The Visible Hand: The Managerial Revolution in American Business* (Cambridge, MA: Belknap Press of Harvard University Press, 1977); D. Landes, *The Unbound Prometheus: Technical Change and Industrial Development in Western Europe from 1750 to the Present* (Cambridge: Cambridge University Press, 2003).

10. On the "de-skilling of work," see Harry Braverman's classic *Labor and Monopoly Capital* (New York: Monthly Review Press, 1974). Braverman's "de-skilling" thesis served as a foundational hypothesis for the direction of sociological inquiry known as labor process theory. Critics have argued that the de-skilling thesis applies only to some industries, not all, that Braverman places too much emphasis on manual skills as opposed to "social" skills, and that he romanticizes the reality of nineteenth-century craft production (for an overview, see P. Meiksins, "Labor and Monopoly Capital for the 1990s: A Review and Critique of the Labor Process Debate," *Monthly Review*, November 1994, 45–59). As Paul Thompson suggests, however, it is difficult to contest the idea that some form or another of de-skilling is a common experience to most forms of modern industrial labor; see P. Thompson, *The Nature of Work* (London: Macmillan, 1983), 118.

11. S. Clegg, "Organization and Control," *Administrative Science Quarterly* 26, no. 4 (1981): 545–562.

12. On the history of mass consumption, see R. Sassatelli, *Consumer Culture: History, Theory, Politics* (London: Sage, 2007).

13. On the rise of the private sphere as a fundamental category of modernity, see J. Habermas, *The Structural Transformation of the Public Sphere* (Boston: Beacon Press, 1989).

14. Chandler, *The Visible Hand*; cf. J. Burnham, *The Managerial Revolution* (New York: John Day, 1941).

15. M. Weber, "Bureaucracy," in *From Max Weber: Essays in Sociology*, ed. H. Gerth and C. W. Mills, 196–198 (London: Routledge, 1948); F. W. Taylor, *Principles of Scientific Management* (New York: Harper, 1911).

16. G. Giroux, *A Short History of Accounting and Business* (1999), http://acct.tamu.edu/history.html (accessed May 10, 2010).

17. G. Boer and D. Jeter, "What's New About Modern Manufacturing? Empirical Evidence of Manufacturing Changes," *Journal of Management Accounting Research* 5 (Fall 1993): 61–83. On the notion that wages should be linked to productivity,

see F. W. Taylor, *The Adjustment of Wages to Efficiency: Three Papers* (London: Schonnen-shein, 1896).

18. See J. Hagel, J. Seely Brown, and L. Davison, *The Shift Index: Measuring the Forces of Long-Term Change* (Deloitte, 2010), http://www.deloitte.com/assets/Dcom-United-States/Local %20Assets/Documents/us_tmt_ce_ShiftIndex_072109ecm.pdf (accessed May 20, 2011).

19. For a comprehensive, if somewhat dated, synthesis of these trends, see Harvey, *The Condition of Postmodernity*; on the notion of "core" and periphery, see I. Wallerstein, *The Modern World System* (New York: Academic Press, 1974).

20. See G. Arrighi, *The Long Twentieth Century* (London: Verso, 1994).

21. S. Sassen, *The Global City: New York, London, Tokyo* (Princeton, NJ: Princeton University Press, 2001).

22. N. Popper, "Ikea Not Alone in Its Labor Troubles in the U.S.," *Los Angeles Times*, April 11, 2011, http://latimesblogs.latimes.com/money_co/2011/04/ikea-not-alone-in-its-american-troubles.html?cid=6a00d8341c630a53ef0147e3f5c6f0970b (accessed April 12, 2011).

23. A. Fumagalli, *Bioeconomia e capitalismo cognitivo: Verso un nuovo paradigma di accumulazione* (Rome: Carocci, 2007); M. Piore and C. Sabel, *The Second Industrial Divide: Possibilities for Prosperity* (New York: Basic Books, 1984); G. Beccattini, *Distretti industriali e sviluppo locale* (Torino: Rosenberg and Seller, 1989); G. Bertin, *Multinationjales et propriété industrielle: Le controlle de la technologie mondiale* (Paris: Presses Universitaires du France, 1985).

24. See C. Gopal, "Global Automobile Industry: Changing with Times," http://www.outsource2india.com/kpo/site/includes/Global_Automobile_Industry11.pdf (accessed May 7, 2010); F. Veloso and R. Kumar, "The Automotive Supply Chain: Global Trends and Asian Perspectives" (working paper, Asian Development Bank, January 2002); on Toyotism, see Tessa Morriz-Suzuki's groundbreaking essay "Robots and Capitalism," *New Left Review* (1984), I/147: 109–121.

25. H. Arnold, "The Recent History of the Machine Tools Industry and the Effects of Technological Change" (working paper 2001–14, Institute for Innovation Research and Technology Management, University of Munich, November, 2001).

26. On the declining share of labor costs in automated production, see Boer and Jeter, "What's New About Modern Manufacturing?"; on the iPod, see E. Conway, "What the iPod Tells Us About Britain's Economic Future," telegraph.co.uk, November 29, 2009, http://blogs.telegraph.co.uk/finance/edmundconway/100002310/what-the-ipod-tells-us-about-britains-economic-future/ (accessed May 9, 2010); on the "commoditization" of component production, see E. Hunting, "How Open Manufacturing Is Related to the End of Neoliberal Globalization," P2PFoundation, January 20, 2010, http://blog.p2pfoundation.net/how-open-manufacturing-is-is-related-to-the-end-of-neoliberal-globalization/2010/01/20 (accessed May 9, 2010).

27. E. Wenger, *Communities of Practice: Learning, Meaning, and Identity* (Cambridge: Cambridge University Press, 1998).

28. See S. Shapin, *The Scientific Life: A Moral History of a Late Modern Vocation* (Chicago: University of Chicago Press, 2008), 93–95.

29. Veloso and Kumar, "The Automotive Supply Chain," 6–12.

30. E. von Hippler, *Democratizing Innovation* (Cambridge, MA: MIT Press, 2006); L. Huston and N. Sakkab, "Connect and Develop: Inside Procter & Gamble's New Model for Innovation," *Harvard Business Review*, March 2006, 1–8.

31. T. Davenport, "Enterprise 2.0: The New, New Knowledge Management," *Harvard Business Review*, February 19, 2008.

32. N. Masami, "The Myths of the Toyota System," *AMPO Japan-Asia Quarterly Review* 25, no. 1 (1995): 18–25.

33. Arvidsson, *Brands*; C. Lury, *Brands: The Logos of the Global Economy* (London: Routledge, 2004).

34. P. F. Drucker, *Post-Capitalist Society* (New York: Harper, 1993), 17.

35. A. Smith, *The Wealth of Nations* (New York: Random House, 2010), 11. The figures are hypothetical; Adam Smith probably never visited a pin factory, much less studied actual improvements in productivity; see A. Zanini, *Adam Smith: Economia, Morale, Diritto* (Milan: Mondadori, 1997).

36. K. Marx, *Grundrisse* (1939; London: Penguin, 1973), 699–706.

37. Ibid., 705.

38. J. Mokyr, *The Gifts of Athena: Historical Origins of the Knowledge Economy* (Princeton, NJ: Princeton University Press, 2002).

39. See D. Archibugi and B. Lundwall, eds., *The Globalizing Learning Economy* (Oxford: Oxford University Press, 2001).

40. P. Virno, *A Grammar of the Multitude* (London: Verso, 2004).

41. A. Preda, "Socio-technical Agency in Financial Markets: The Case of the Stock Ticker," *Social Studies of Science* 36, no. 5 (2006): 753–782.

42. C. Zaloom, *Out of the Pits: Traders and Technology from Chicago to London* (Chicago: University of Chicago Press, 2006); D. McKenzie, *An Engine, Not a Camera: How Financial Models Shape Markets* (Cambridge, MA: MIT Press, 2006).

43. D. Harvey, *A Brief History of Neoliberalism* (Oxford: Oxford University Press, 2005).

44. A. Glyn, A. Hughes, A. Lipietz, and A. Singh, "The Rise and Fall of the Golden Age," in *The Golden Age of Capitalism: Reinterpreting the Postwar Experience*, ed. S. Marglin and J. Schor, 39–73 (Oxford: Clarendon Press, 1990).

45. G. Arrighi, *The Long Twentieth Century* (London: Verso, 1994), 300–324.

46. For a sociological explanation of the emergence of shareholder-oriented corporate governance, see W. Lazonick and M. O'Sullivan, "Maximizing Shareholder Value: A New Ideology for Corporate Governance," *Economy and Society* 29, no. 1 (2000): 13–35.

47. See, for example, A. Leyshon and N. Thrift, "The Capitalization of Almost Everything: The Future of Finance and Capitalism," *Theory, Culture, and Society* 24, nos. 7–8 (2007): 97–111.

48. Harvey, *Brief History of Neoliberalism*; for the case of Sweden, see D. Forslund, *Hit med pengarna! Sparandets genealogi och den finasiella overtalningens vetandekonst* (Stockholm: Carlssons, 2008).

49. R. Blackburn, "The Subprime Crisis," *New Left Review* 50 (March 2008): 71.

50. On the changing structure of income of U.S. middle-class households, see J. Edwards, M. Crain, and A. Kallenberg, eds., *Ending Poverty in America: How to Restore the American Dream* (New York: New Press, 2007).

51. For an overview, see K. Knorr Cetina and A. Preda, eds., *The Sociology of Financial Markets* (Oxford: Oxford University Press, 2005).

52. D. Beunza and R. Garud, "Securities Analysts as Frame-Makers," *Universitat Pompeu Fabra Economics and Business Working Papers Series* 73 (2004): 3.

53. Ibid., 36.

54. D. Stark and D. Beunza, "The Cognitive Ecology of an Arbitrage Trading Room," in D. Stark, *The Sense of Dissonance: Accounts of Worth in Economic Life*, 124 (Princeton, NJ: Princeton University Press, 2009).

55. H. Wilmott, "Creating Value Beyond the Point of Production: Branding, Financialization, and Market Capitalization," *Organization* 17, no. 5 (2010): 517–542.

56. P. Holdsworth, "John Murphy Walks Out the Retreads," *Brand Management*, May 1, 2001, http://www.highbeam.com/doc/1G1-74336433.html (accessed February 7, 2011).

3. Publics

1. P. Kane, *The Play Ethic: A Manifesto for a Different Way of Living* (London: Macmillan, 2004).

2. T. Levitt, "The Globalization of Markets," *McKinsey Quarterly* (Summer 1984): 4–20.

3. A. Marchetti and E. Gramigna, *Produttori di stile: Lavoro e flessibilità nelle case di moda milanesi* (Milan: Franco Angeli, 2007), 42.

4. A. Burns, *Blogs, Wikipedia, Second Life, and Beyond: From Production to Produsage* (New York: Peter Lang, 2008).

5. F. Reichheld, *The Loyalty Effect: The Hidden Forces Behind Growth, Profits, and Lasting Value* (Cambridge, MA: Harvard Business School Press).

6. B. Cova. "Community and Consumption: Towards a Definition of the Linking Value of Products and Services," *European Journal of Marketing* 31, nos. 3/4 (1997): 297–316.

7. See, for example, D. Edelman, "Branding in the Digital Age: You're Spending Your Money in All the Wrong Places," *Harvard Business Review*, December 2010, 64–69; B. Cova and D. Dalli, "Working Consumers: The Next Step in Marketing Theory?" *Marketing Theory* 3 (2009): 315–339; A. El-Amir and S. Burt, "A Critical Account of the Process of Branding: Towards a Synthesis," *Marketing Review* 10, no. 1 (2010): 69–86.

8. See, for example, D. Aaker, *Managing Brand Equity: Capitalizing on the Value of a Brand Name* (New York: Free Press, 1991).

9. R. Coase, "The Nature of the Firm," *Economica* 4, no. 16 (1937): 386–405.

10. F. Roethlisberger and W. Dickson, *Management and the Worker* (Cambridge, MA: Harvard University Press, 1939).

11. T. Peters and R. Waterman, *In Search of Excellence: Lessons from America's Best-Run Companies* (New York: Harper, 1982).

12. P. Adler, "Market, Hierarchy, and Trust: The Knowledge Economy and the Future of Capitalism," *Organization Science* 12, no. 2 (2001): 215–234; W. G. Ouchi, "Markets, Bureaucracies, and Clans," *Administrative Science Quarterly* 25, no. 1 (1980): 129–141; E. Wenger, *Communities of Practice: Learning, Meaning, and Identity* (Cambridge: Cambridge University Press, 1998).

13. See, for example, P. Du Gay, *Organizing Identity* (London: Sage, 2007).

14. C. Grey, "Career as a Project of the Self and Labour Process Discipline," *Sociology* 28, no. 2 (1994): 479–497.

15. M. Maccoby and C. Heckscher, "A Note on Leadership for Collaborative Communities," in *The Firm as a Collaborative Community*, ed. C. Heckscher and P. Adler, 472–473 (Oxford: Oxford University Press, 2006); J. R. Galbraith, *Designing Organizations* (San Francisco: Jossey-Bass, 1995).

16. L. Peacock, "IBM Crowd Sourcing Could See Employed Work Force Shrink by Three Quarters," *PersonnelToday*, April 24, 2010, http://www.personnel-today.com/articles/2010/04/23/55343/ibm-crowd-sourcing-could-see-employed-workforce-shrink-by-three-quarters.html (accessed March 12, 2011).

17. P. Adler and C. X. Chen, "Combining Creativity and Control: Understanding Individual Motivation in Large-Scale Collaborative Creativity," *Accounting, Organizations, and Society* 36 (2011): 63–85.

18. I. Castello and J. Lozano, "Searching for New Forms of Legitimacy Through Corporate Responsibility Rhetoric," *Journal of Business Ethics*, February 10, 2011, http://www.springerlink.com/content/n68q5x17n78tv276/ (accessed March 2, 2011); cf. J. Calton and N. Kurland, "A Theory of Stakeholder Enabling: Giving Voice to an Emerging Postmodern Praxis of Organizational Discourse," in *Postmodern Management and Organizational Theory*, ed. D. Boje, R. P. Gephart, and T. Thatchenkery, 154–180 (London: Sage, 1966).

19. On the concept of participatory culture, see H. Jenkins, *Convergence Culture: Where New and Old Media Collide* (New York: New York University Press, 2006); on creative consumer styles in the sixties, see T. Frank, *The Conquest of Cool: Business, Counterculture, and the Rise of Hip Consumerism* (Chicago: University of Chicago Press, 1997); T. O'Reilly, "What Is Web 2.0?," O'Reilly.com, September 20, 2005, http://oreilly.com/web2/archive/what-is-web-20.html (accessed February 10, 2011).

20. A. Lenhart, M. Madden, A. Smith, and A. McGill, "Teens and Social Media," *Pew Internet and American Life Project*, December 19, 2007, http://www.pewinternet.org/PPF/r/230/report_display.asp (accessed July 21, 2008); M. Madden and S. Fox, "Riding the Waves of Web 2.0," *Pew Internet and American Life Project*, May 5, 2006, http://www.pewinternet.org/PPF/r/189/report_display.asp (accessed July

21, 2008); A. Smith, "Online Participation in the Social Media Era," *Pew Internet and American Life Project*, http://www.pewinternet.org/Presentations/2009/RTIP-Social-Media.aspx (accessed February 15, 2011).

21. M. Stepanek, "The Year Ahead," blogpost, *CauseGlobal Social Media for Social Change*, January 1, 2010, http://causeglobal.blogspot.com/2010/01/social-enterprise-2010.html (accessed January 17, 2010).

22. See R. A. Gosh, *Economic Impact of Open Source Software on Innovation and the Competitiveness of the Information and Communication Technologies (ICT) Sector in the EU*, Final Report, http://ec.europa.eu/enterprise/sectors/ict/files/2006-11-20-flossimpact_en.pdf (accessed September 10, 2010).

23. See http://fashionstake.com/signup.

24. L. Alter, "3D Printers Now as Cheap as Laser Printers in 1985," *TreeHugger*, October 28, 2008, http://www.treehugger.com/files/2008/10/3d-printers-getting-cheap.php (accessed May 5, 2010).

25. On RepRap, see http://reprap.org/wiki/Main_Page; on Fab Lab, see http://fab.cba.mit.edu/.

26. http://www.biocurious.org/index.php?title=Main_Page; on Open or DIY Biotech, see A. Delfanti, *Biohackers: The Politics of Open Science* (London: Pluto Press, 2013).

27. M. Lennert, "The Open Minded Professor: An Interview with Eric von Hippel, MIT's Sloan School of Management," *Deloitte Review*, January 19, 2010.

28. For a scenario, see K. Carson, *The Homebrew Revolution: A Low Overhead Manifesto*, http://homebrewindustrialrevolution.wordpress.com/2010/06/14/hard-copy-books-now-available/ (accessed February 15, 2011).

29. H. Jenkins, K. Clinton, R. Purushotma, A. Robinson, and M. Weigel, *Confronting the Challenges of Participatory Culture: Media Education for the 21st Century* (Chicago: The MacArthur Foundation, 2005), http://digitallearning.macfound.org/atf/cf/%7B7E45C7E0-A3E0-4B89AC9E807E1B0AE4E%7D/JENKINS_WHITE_PAPER.PDF (accessed February 12, 2011).

30. R. Kozinets, *Netnography: Doing Ethnographic Research Online* (London: Sage, 2010), 15.

31. J. Jacobs, *The Death and Life of Great American Cities* (New York: Random House, 1961). In an early article on what he calls "community without propinquity," Craig Calhoun criticized the unreflective use of the term "community" by Internet researchers. Rather than the web of direct social relations that "community" usually implies, electronic media are likely to "encourage the proliferation of indirect relationships . . . that could in principle be directly interpersonal." That is the kind of relations between strangers that we have suggested as a defining feature of "publics." Cf. C. Calhoun, "Community Without Propinquity Revisited: Communications Technology and the Transformation of the Urban Public Sphere," *Sociological Inquiry* 68, no. 3 (1998): 373–397.

32. D. J. Watts and P. S. Dodds, "Influentials: Networks and Public Opinion Formation," *Journal of Consumer Research* 34, no. 4 (2007): 441–458.

33. J. Arguello, B. S. Butler, L. Joyce, R. E. Kraut, K. S. Ling, C. P. Rosé, and X. Want, "Talk to Me: Foundations for Successful Individual-Group Interaction in Online Communities," in *Proceedings of the 2006 ACM Conference on Human Factors in Computing Systems*, 959–968 (New York: ACM Press, 2006); N. Ducheneaut, N. Yee, E. Nickell, and R. J. Moore, "Building an MMO with Mass Appeal: A Look at Gameplay in World of Warcraft," *Games and Culture* 1, no. 4 (2006): 281–317.

34. B. McKibben, *Deep Economy: The Wealth of Communities and the Durable Future* (New York: Times Books, 2007).

35. G. Tarde, "The Public and the Crowd," in *On Communication and Social Influence: Selected Papers*, ed. T. N. Clark, 277–294 (Chicago: University of Chicago Press, 1969); see also J. Habermas, *The Structural Transformation of the Public Sphere* (Boston: Beacon Press, 1989).

36. See G. Schnapp and M. Tiews, eds., *Crowds* (Stanford, CA: Stanford University Press, 2006).

37. C. Taylor, *Modern Social Imaginaries* (Durham, NC: Duke University Press, 2004).

38. G. Tarde, *Psychologie économique* (Paris: Félix Alcan, 1902).

39. See, for example, I. Castello and J. M. Lozano, "Searching for New Forms of Legitimacy Through Corporate Social Responsbility Rhetoric," *Journal of Business Ethics Online*, February 10, 2011, http://responsiblebusiness.haas.berkeley.edu/documents/Castello_JoBE_2011.pdf (accessed May 20, 2011).

40. V. Zelizer, *The Purchase of Intimacy* (Princeton, NJ: Princeton University Press, 2005).

41. See M. Weber, "Politics as a Vocation," in *From Max Weber: Essays in Sociology*, ed. H. Gerth and C. W. Mills, 77–128 (New York: Oxford University Press, 1946); T. Parsons, "The Professions and Social Structure," *Social Forces* 17, no. 4 (1939): 457–467.

42. F. Turner, *From Counterculture to Cyberculture: Stewart Brand, The Whole Earth Network, and the Rise of Digital Utopianism* (Chicago: University of Chicago Press, 2006).

43. E. Castronuova, *Synthetic Worlds: The Business and Culture of Online Games* (Chicago: University of Chicago Press, 2006).

44. M. Bauwens, "The Political Economy of Peer Production," *CTheory*, December 2005.

45. S. Weber, *The Success of Open Source* (Cambridge, MA: MIT Press, 2004); M. O'Neil, *Cyber Chiefs: Autonomy and Authority in Online Tribes* (London: Pluto Press, 2009).

46. J. Dibbell, *Play Money* (New York: Basic Books, 2006); P. Kane, *The Play Ethic: A Manifesto for a Different Way of Living* (London: Macmillan UK, 2005).

47. See National Center for Educational Statistics, U.S. Department of Education, http://nces.ed.gov/fastfacts/display.asp?id=37 (accessed July 23, 2008).

48. See A. Arvidsson, G. Malossi, and S. Naro, "Passionate Work? Labor Conditions in Italian Fashion," *Journal for Cultural Research* 14, no. 3 (2010): 295–309.

49. R. Lloyd, *Neo-Bohemia: Art and Commerce in the Postindustrial City* (New York: Routledge, 2006), 66.

50. For a development of this argument, see A. Arvidsson, "Creative Class or Administrative Class: On Advertising and the Underground," *Ephemera* 7, no. 1 (2007): 8–23.

51. M. Beverland, "Uncovering 'Theories-in-Use': Building Luxury Wine Brands," *European Journal of Marketing* 38, nos. 3–4 (2004): 446–466.

52. D. Stark, *The Sense of Dissonance: Accounts of Worth in Economic Life* (Princeton, NJ: Princeton University Press, 2009), 169; cf. R. Burt, *Brokerage and Closure: An Introduction to Social Capital* (Oxford: Oxford University Press, 2005).

53. Y. Shi, *Shan-zhai: Alternative Manufacturing—Making the Unaffordable Affordable* (Cambridge: University of Cambridge, Center for International Manufacturing, 2009), 1.

54. D. Uguarte, *Phyles: Economic Democracy in the Network Century*, available at http://deugarte.com/gomi/phyles.pdf (accessed March 15, 2011).

55. N. Dyer-Witheford, "The Circulation of the Common" (paper presented at the workshop Immaterial Labour, Multitudes, and New Social Subjects: Class Composition in Cognitive Capitalism, King's College, Cambridge, April 29–30, 2006).

4. VALUE

1. J. Lerner and J. Tirole, "Some Simple Economics of Open Source," *Journal of Industrial Economics* 50, no. 2 (2002): 206; on "altruistic genes," see Y. Benkler, *The Penguin and the Leviathan: How Cooperation Triumphs Over Self-Interest* (New York: Crown Business, 2011).

2. The kind of gift economy that Barbrook and others have proposed is curious, for several reasons. First, it completely does away with the condition of reciprocity, which is fundamental to classic theories of gift exchange, beginning with Mauss's own writings and continuing as developed by the MAUSS (Mouvement anti-utilitariste en sciences sociales) collective in France. In the classic view, the *economic* aspect of gift exchange consists in the fact that a gift requires a counter-gift, that there is a moral, if not legal, obligation to reciprocate, (even if reciprocity might occur much later on). And the counter-gift must be "in kind"; that is, it must be an object of comparable value. This implies that traditional gift economies operate with a perhaps implicit law of value that allows them to determine the comparative value of, say, a seashell and a ton of pork cracklings. And this reciprocity is compelling at the individual level. That is, person A must reciprocate the gift given by person B, to person B, by giving her an object of comparable value within a reasonable time frame, lest person A lose face. It is because of this condition of individual reciprocity that gift economies can be understood to create and reinforce social relations and "social capital." In the "high-tech gift economy," an

individual gives something not to another identifiable individual but to the "community of the Net" as a whole, without directly expecting something in return. He then just takes what he needs from "the Net," when he needs it, regardless of what he has given to "the community of the Net" before. While this describes the actual dynamic of commons based production, it is pretty far from any classical notion of "gift economies." Indeed, Barbrook posits that there is no law of value at work that structures expectations of reciprocity. The absence of a law of value means that this way of organizing the distribution of useful things is not a gift economy, in the sense that it is not an *economy* at all. It looks more like actually existing anarcho-communism, which is characterized precisely by its not being an economy, since the law of value has been suspended. See E. Raymond, *The Cathedral and the Bazaar* (Sebastopol, CA: Gravenstein Media, 1999); see also R. Gosh, ed., *CODE: Collaborative Ownership and the Digital Economy* (Cambridge, MA: MIT Press, 2005); R. Barbrook, "The High-Tech Gift Economy," http://subsol.c3.hu/subsol_2/contributors3/barbrooktext2.html (accessed December 1, 2011). M. Mauss, *Essai sur le don: Forme et raison de l'échange dans les sociétés primitives* (L'Année Sociologique, 1923–1924).

3. R. Barbrook and A. Cameron, "The Californian Ideology: A Critique of West Coast Libertarianism," *Science as Culture* 26 (1996): 44–72; F. Turner, *From Counterculture to Cyberculture: Stewart Brand, the Whole Earth Network, and the Rise of Digital Utopianism* (Chicago: University of Chicago Press, 2006).

4. D. Tapscott and A. Williams, *Wikinomics: How Mass Collaboration Changes Everything* (London: Portfolio Press, 2006).

5. Y. Benkler and H. Nissenbaum, "Commons-Based Peer Production and Virtue," *Journal of Political Philosophy* 14, no. 4 (2006): 400.

6. Y. Benkler, *The Wealth of Networks: How Social Production Transforms Markets and Freedom* (New Haven, CT: Yale University Press, 2006), 106–107.

7. M. Bauwens, "Peer Property" (wiki-entry, P2P Foundation, http://p2pfoundation.net/Peer_Property).

8. Benkler, *Wealth of Networks*, 91–92. While Benkler is right in pointing to an increase in the relative salience of social sharing and exchange as a modality of economic production, he is wrong about the historical role of such "neighbourly relations" in material production. Most of the wealth produced in the medieval European peasant economy, for example, relied not on money but on social sharing and exchange within the moral economy of the village or the extended family.

9. P. Adler, "Market, Hierarchy, and Trust: The Knowledge Economy and the Future of Capitalism," *Organization Science* 12, no. 2 (2001): 215–234.

10. T. Terranova, "Free Labor: Producing Culture for the Digital Economy," *Social Text* 18, no. 2 63 (2000): 33–58. For some other influential Marxist exercises, see M. Andrejevic, "The Work That Affective Economics Does," *Cultural Studies* 25, nos. 4–5 (2011): 604–620; C. Fuchs, "Labour in Informational Capitalism and on the Internet," *The Information Society* 26, no. 3 (2010): 179–196; for a critique, see A. Arvidsson and E. Colleoni, "Value in Informational Capitalism and on the Internet," *The Information Society* 28, no. 1 (2012): 1–16.

11. This happens primarily because the productivity of "free labor" does not lend itself to measurement in terms of the labor theory of value, for both analytical and empirical reasons. Analytically, the Marxian labor theory of value presupposes that exploitation happens within the wage relation. Consequently it cannot be applied to productive activity that unfolds outside of the wage relation. This analytical problem could possibly be overcome by drawing on Dallas Smythe's application of the Marxian Labour Theory of Value (MLTV) to audience participation, arguing that the audience is both dominated by the medium (by having its attention captured) and paid a wage (so to say) in terms of the use value that it receives from the media product that it is watching (its entertainment value). But this approach runs into the second empirical problem. It might be possible to argue that, say, Facebook users are "dominated" by Facebook (in the sense that they are compelled to use that platform to structure their ongoing social lives) and that they receive a wage for using Facebook (in terms of the utility or "experience" that the platform can provide). But on the other side of the equation we must recognize that the creation of value in social production—whether a trend through social media conversation or an artifact like the Debian operating system through more organized forms of collaboration—unfolds through complex forms of productive collaboration where it is extremely difficult if not impossible to identify the contribution of one single actor. Often exchanges build on the ability to mobilize common resources, collective intelligence, and General Intellect, which makes the productivity of such labor independent of investments of labor time. Consequently, the MLTV (which presupposes a linear relation between time and value) cannot apply. The main inspiration for Terranova's thinking, Antonio Negri, arrived at this conclusion in the late 1970s, speaking of the "becoming complex of labour" that occurred in new socialized relations of production (like the Italian "industrial districts"). About the same time, the labor theory of value was abandoned in practice as Taylorist cost accounting was supplanted by post-Fordist accounting methods like value flow analysis and Total Quality Management. In short, the notion of "free labor" does not hold because "free labor" is not labor, at least not in the Marxist sense of that term, neither analytically nor empirically.

12. H. Arendt, *The Human Condition* (Chicago: University of Chicago Press, 1958); R. Sennett, *The Craftsman* (New Haven, CT: Yale University Press, 2008).

13. For an excellent analysis of the political dimension inherent to knowledge work, see P. A. Virno, *Grammar of the Multitude* (London: Verso, 2004); M. Lazzarato, *Lavoro immateriale* (Verona: Ombre Corte, 1997).

14. D. Stewart, "Social Status in an Open Source Community," *American Sociological Review* 70 (2005): 838.

15. C. Cafagna, *Gruppi di aquisto solidale: Nuove frontiere per una società in evoluzione*, (Tesi di Laurea, Corso di Laurea in Comunicazione Politica e Sociale, Università di Milano, Anno Academico 2008–2009).

16. C. Kelty, *Two Bits: The Cultural Significance of Free Software* (Durham, NC: Duke University Press, 2008), 8; G. Coleman, *Three Ethical Moments in Debian*, http://anthropology.usf.edu/cma/ssrn-id805287 (accessed June 10, 2010).

17. Coleman, *Three Ethical Moments*, 5.

18. Kelty, *Two Bits*, 7.

19. Coleman, *Three Ethical Moments*, 13.

20. A. Muniz and T. O'Guinn, "Brand Community," *Journal of Consumer Research* 27, no. 4 (2001): 412–432.

21. D. Slater, "Trading Sexpics on the IRC: Embodiment and Authenticity on the Internet," *Body and Society* 4, no. 4 (1998): 91–117.

22. See D. Solove, *The Future of Reputation: Gossip, Rumor, and Privacy on the Internet* (New Haven, CT: Yale University Press, 2007).

23. A. Arvidsson and D. Tjader, *Laboratorium for Spontankultur: Slutraport*, (Malmö: Kulturforvaltningen, 2009).

24. R. A. Gosh, R. Glott, B. Krieger, and G. Robles, *Free/Libre and Open Source Software Survey and Study*, Part 4, *Survey of Developers* (International Institute of Infonomics, University of Maastricht, The Netherlands, June 2002), 45.

25. S. Weber, *The Success of Open Source* (Cambridge, MA: MIT Press, 2004), 136–137.

26. Gosh et al., *Survey of Developers*, p. 45. J. Hagel, J. Seely Brown, and L. Davison, "Tomorrow's Talent Networks," blogpost *The Big Shift, Harvard Business Publishing*, March 18, 2009 (blogs.hbr.org/bigshift/2009/03/tomorrows-talent-networks.html (accessed October 2, 2012). Even when participants are paid directly for their input, like the iStockphoto community of stock photo producers, peer recognition and the ability to create contacts figure as important motivations for participation; see D. Brabham, "Moving the Crowd at iStockphoto: The Composition of the Crowd and Motivations for Participation in a Crowdsourcing Application," *First Monday* 13, no. 6 (2008).

27. G. Sholette, "Heart of Darkness: A Journey into the Dark Matter of the Art World," www.gregorysholette.com/essays/docs/04_dark (accessed May 9, 2007).

28. P. Drucker, *The Future of Industrial Man* (New York: John Day, 1942). P. Du Gay, *Organizing Identity* (London: Sage, 2007); see also P. Johnson, G. Wood, C. Brewster, and M. Brookes, "The Rise of Post-Bureaucracy: Theorist's Fancy or Organizational Praxis?" *International Sociology* 24, no. 1 (2009): 37–61.

29. S. Christopherson, "Beyond the Self-expressive Creative Worker: An Industry Perspective on Entertainment Media," *Theory, Culture, and Society* 25 (2008): 83.

30. J. Hagel, J. Seely Brown, and L. Davison, *Measuring the Forces of Long-Term Change: The 2009 Shift Index* (Deloitte, 2010), http://www.deloitte.com/assets/Dcom-UnitedStates/Local%20Assets/Documents/us_tmt_ce_ShiftIndex_072109ecm .pdf (accessed May 20, 2011).

31. Gosh et al., *Survey of Developers*, 44.

32. C. Heckscher and P. Adler, eds., *The Firm as a Collaborative Community* (Oxford: Oxford University Press, 2006), 58.

33. Ibid., 57.

34. B. Martin, "Managers After the Era of Organizational Restructuring: Towards a Second Managerial Devolution?" *Work, Employment, and Society* 19, no. 4 (2005): 752.

35. A. Marwick and D. Boyd, "To See and Be Seen: Celebrity Practice on Twitter," *Convergence* 17, no. 2 (2011): 139–158.

36. M. J. Le Ber and O. Branzei, "Towards a Critical Theory of Value Creation in Cross Sector Partnerships," *Organization* 27, no. 5 (2010): 599–629; C. K. Prahalad, *The Fortune at the Bottom of the Pyramid: Eradicating Poverty Through Profits* (Pittsburgh, PA: Wharton School Publishing, 2004); M. Yunnus, *Creating a World Without Poverty: Social Business and the Future of Capitalism* (New York: PublicAffairs Books, 2007).

37. C. Kelly, P. Kocourek, N. McGaw, and J. Samuelson, *Deriving Value from Corporate Values* (Washington, DC: Aspen Institute and Booz Allen Hamilton, 2005).

38. S. C. Beardsley, B. C. Johnson, and J. M. Manyika, "Competitive Advantage from Better Interactions," *McKinsey Quarterly* 2 (2006): 53–63).

39. S. Shapin, *The Scientific Life: A Moral History of a Late Modern Vocation* (Chicago: University of Chicago Press, 2008).

40. F. Fukuyama, *Trust: The Social Virtues and the Creation of Prosperity* (New York: Free Press, 1995).

41. See R. Coase, "The Nature of the Firm," *Economica*, 4, no. 16 (1937): 386–405; T. Parsons and N. Smelser, *Economy and Society* (London: Routledge, 1956).

42. U. Hacque, *The New Capitalist Manifesto: Building a Disruptively Better Business* (Boston: Harvard Business Review Press, 2011).

43. B. Parr, "Twitter Now Worth $4 Billion," *Mashable*, January 25, 2011, http://mashable.com/2011/01/25/twitter-now-worth-4-billion/ (accessed February 20, 2011).

44. J. M. Keynes, *The General Theory of Employment, Interest, and Money* (New York: Harcourt, 1936); cf. C. Marazzi, *Capital and Language* (Los Angeles: Semiotext(e), 2008).

45. K. Kelly, "Better Than Free," *The Techium*, January 31, 2008, http://www.kk.org/thetechnium/archives/2008/01/better_than_fre.php (accessed July 10, 2009).

46. See "Mozilla Foundation," htttp://p2pfoundation.net/Mozilla_Foundation (accessed September 15, 2010).

47. W. E. Halal, *The New Management: Bringing Democracy and Markets Inside Organizations* (San Francisco: Berrett-Koehler Publishers, 1996).

48. See, for example, J. H. Dulebohn, "Thinking for a Living: How to Get Better Performance and Results from Knowledge Workers," *Human Resource Planning* 29, no. 1 (2005): 52–53; L. K. Johnson, "Debriefing Thomas Davenport: Are You Getting the Most from Your Knowledge Workers?" *Harvard Management Update* (2006): 3–4.

49. H. Gardner, *Good Work: Aligning Skills and Values* (New York: Basic Books, 2002); A. E. Reichers, J. P. Wanous, and J. T. Austin, "Understanding and Man-

aging Cynicism About Organizational Change," *Academy of Management Executive* 11 (1997): 48–59.

50. For a critical version of this argument, see R. Barbrook, "The High Tech Gift Economy," http://subsol.c3.hu/subsol_2/contributors3/barbrooktext2.html (accessed June 10, 2010).

51. S. O'Mahoney and F. Fernando, "The Emergence of Governance in an Open Source Community," *Academy of Management Journal* 50, no. 5 (2007): 1079–1106.

52. M. Weber, "The Protestant Sects and the Spirit of Capitalism," in *From Max Weber: Essays in Sociology*, ed. H. H. Geerth and C. W. Mills, 302–322 (London: Routledge, 1948). On reputation in economic theory, see G. Brennan and P. Pettit, *The Economy of Esteem* (Oxford: Oxford University Press, 2004).

53. See, for example, M. I. Lichbach, ed., *The Cooperator's Dilemma* (Ann Arbor: University of Michigan Press, 1996), in particular 89–121.

5. Measure

1. For an overview, see R. D. Raggio and R. P. Leone, "Drivers of Brand Value, Estimation of Brand Value in Practice, and Use of Brand Valuation: Introduction to the Special Issue," *Journal of Brand Management* 17, no. 1 (2009): 1–5. S. E. Abraham, B. A. Friedman, R. H. Khan, and R. J. Skolnik, "Is Publication of the Reputation Quotient (RQ) Sufficient to Move Stock Prices?" *Corporate Reputation Review* 11, no. 4 (2008): 308–319. B. Barber and T. Odean, "All That Glitters: The Effect of Attention and News on the Buying Behavior of Individual and Institutional Investors," *Review of Financial Studies* 21, no. 2 (2008): 785–818.

2. For a notable exception, see W. Kula, *Measures and Men* (Princeton, NJ: Princeton University Press, 1986).

3. For an example of such money fetishism in critical thought, see C. Eisenstein, *Sacred Economics: Money, Gift, and Society in the Age of Transition* (Berkeley, CA: Evolver Editions, 2011).

4. See L. Busch, *Standards: Recipes for Reality* (Cambridge, MA: MIT Press, 2011); D. S. Grewal, *Network Power: The Social Dynamics of Globalization* (Ann Arbor, MI: Sheridan Books, 2008); A. Galloway, *Protocol: How Power Exists After Decentralization* (Cambridge, MA: MIT Press, 2004).

5. On the struggles around labor as a measure of value, see P. Linnebaugh and M. Rediker, *The Many-Headed Hydra: The Hidden History of the Revolutionary Atlantic* (London: Verso, 2000).

6. See, for example, M. Albert, *Parecon: Life After Capitalism* (London: Verso, 2004).

7. See J. Israel, *Radical Enlightenment* (Oxford: Oxford University Press, 2002); C. Tilly, *Social Movements, 1768–2004* (London: Paradigm, 2004); B. Anderson, *Imagined Communities* (London: Verso, 1983).

8. J. Habermas, *The Structural Transformation of the Public Sphere* (Boston: Beacon Press, 1989).

9. R. Putnam, *Bowling Alone: The Collapse and Revival of American Community* (New York: Simon and Schuster, 2001).

10. R. Silverstone, *Media and Morality: On the Rise of the Mediapolis* (Cambridge: Polity Press, 2007); P. Hawken, "The New Great Transformation" (address presented at the Long Now Foundation, San Francisco, June, 8, 2007), http://blog.longnow.org/2007/06/09/paul-hawken-the new-great-transformation/ (accessed June 10, 2010).

11. L. Boltanski, *Distant Suffering: Morality, Media, and Politics* (Cambridge: Polity Press, 1999).

12. L. Chouliaraki, *The Spectatorship of Suffering* (London: Sage, 2006).

13. Z. Papacharissi, *A Private Sphere: Democracy in the Digital Age* (Cambridge: Polity Press, 2010), 131.

14. On "standpoint epistemology," see S. Harding, *The Science Question in Feminism* (Ithaca, NY: Cornell University Press, 1986).

15. See also S. Lash, *Intensive Culture: Social Theory, Religion, and Contemporary Capitalism* (London: Sage, 2010); B Massumi, *Parables for the Virtual* (New York: Zone Books, 2002).

16. G. Tarde, *Psychologie économique* (Paris: Félix Alcan, 1902), 1–2.

17. D. MacMillan, "Twitter Targets One Billion Users, Challenging Facebook for Ads," *Bloomberg Businessweek*, October 12, 2010, http://www.businessweek.com/technology/content/oct2010/tc20101012_048119.htm (accessed December 7, 2010); J. Rayport, "How Social Networks Are Changing Everything," *Bloomberg Businessweek*, May 7, 2009, http://www.businessweek.com/magazine/content/09_20/b4131067611088.htm (accessed June 12, 2009).

18. A. Marwick and D. Boyd, "'I tweet honestly, I tweet passionately': Twitter Users, Context Collapse, and the Imagined Audience," *New Media and Society*, Online, July 7, 2010. A. Hearn, "Meat, Mask, Burden: Probing the Contours of the Branded 'Self,'" *Journal of Consumer Culture* 8, no. 2 (2008): 163–183.

19. V. Miller, "New Media, Networking, and Phatic Culture," *Convergence* 14, no. 4 (2008): 388, 395.

20. T. Frank, *The Conquest of Cool* (Chicago: University of Chicago Press, 1997).

21. S. Baker, "Putting a Price on Social Connections," *Bloomberg Businessweek*, April 8, 2009, http://www.businessweek.com/technology/content/apr2009/tc2009047_031301.htm?link_position=link1 (accessed December 16, 2010).

22. See, for example, K. Dave, S. Lawrence, and M. Pennock, "Mining the Peanut Gallery: Opinion Extraction and Semantic Classification of Product Reviews," in *WWW'03: Proceedings of the 12th International Conference on the World Wide Web*, 519–528 (New York: ACM, 2003); B. Pang, L. Lee, and S. Vaithyanathan, "Thumbs Up?: Sentiment Classification Using Machine Learning Techniques," in *Proceedings of the 2002 Conference on Empirical Methods in Natural Language Processing*, 79–86 (Stroudsburg, PA: Association for Computational Linguistics, 2002);

B. Pang and L. Lee, *Opinion Mining and Sentiment Analysis* (Boston: Now Publishers, 2008).

23. http://www.radian6.com/; http://www.sysomos.com/.

24. http://www.streambase.com/; http://www.covalence.ch/.

25. C. Gerlitz and A. Helmond, "Hit, Link, and Share: Organizing the Social and the Fabric of the Web in a Like Economy" (paper presented at the DMI mini-conference, Amsterdam, January 24–25, 2010), 3, 25.

26. See, for example, M. Bradley and P. J. Lang, *Affective Norms for English Words (ANEW): Stimuli, Instruction Manual, and Affective Ratings* (Technical Report, Center for Research in Psychophysiology, University of Florida, Gainesville, Florida, 1999).

27. See, for example, N. O'Hare, M. Davy, A. Bermingham, P. Ferguson, P. Sheridan, C. Gurrin, and A. Smeaton, "Topic-Dependent Sentiment Analysis of Financial Blogs," (paper presented at TSA'09, First International CIKM Workshop on Topic Sentiment Analysis for Mass Opinion Measurement, Hong Kong, November 6, 2009).

28. Tarde, *Psychologie économique*, 62.

29. B. Solis, "A Conversation About You, Social Currency, and Social Capital," BrianSolis.com, December 22, 2010, http://www.briansolis.com/2010/12/a-conversation-about-you-social-currency-and-social-capital/ (accessed March 18, 2011); D. Robles, "Social Currency: The Real Value of Conversations About Your Brand," Conversationalcurrency.com, August 13, 2010, http://www.conversationalcurrency.com/10672/social-currency-the-real-value-of- conversations about-your-brand/ (accessed March 18, 2010); R. Peters, "Relationship Capital—Accounting for Your Success," http://www.slideshare.net/RPeters59/relationship-capital-accounting-for-your-success (accessed March 18, 2010).

30. C. Marquis, D. Beunza, F. Ferraro, and B. Thomason, "Driving Sustainability at Bloomberg L.P." (Harvard Business School Case N9–411–025, August, 10, 2010).

31. A. Rosenblith, "New Currency Frontiers," blogpost, April 12, 2009, http://newcurrencyfrontiers.blogspot.com/2009/04/reputations.html (accessed June 16, 2009).

32. See T. Wu, *The Master Switch: The Rise and Fall of Information Empires* (New York: Atlantic Books, 2011).

33. J. Friis, N. Peitersen, and J. M. Skibsted, "Actics—A Dynamic Ethical System of Proximity" (Kesera Working Paper 3, 2004).

34. E. Illouz, *Cold Intimacies: The Makings of Emotional Capitalism* (Cambridge: Polity Press, 2007).

35. A. Bidhé, *A Call for Judgment: Sensible Finance for a Dynamic Economy* (Oxford: Oxford University Press, 2010).

6. Ethical Economy

1. R. Brenner, "New Boom or New Bubble?" *New Left Review* 25 (January–February 2004): 57–58; *The Economics of Global Turbulence: A Special Report on the World Economy*, *New Left Review* 229 (May/June 1998): 93.

2. See, for example, J. Ryan, *A History of the Internet and the Digital Future* (New York: Reaktion Books, 2010).

3. C. Perez, *Technological Revolutions and Financial Capital: The Dynamics of Bubbles and Golden Ages* (Cheltenham: Edward Elgar, 2002).

4. On how declining consumer prices have compensated for declining wages, see E. Warren, "The Vanishing Middle Class," in *Ending Poverty in America: How to Restore the American Dream*, ed. J. Edwards, M. Crain, and A. Kallenberg (New York: New Press, 2007).

5. G. Arrighi, *The Long Twentieth Century* (London: Verso, 1994), x–xi.

6. B. Latour and P. Weibel, eds., *Making Things Public: Atmospheres of Democracy* (Cambridge, MA: MIT Press, 2005).

7. See J. Le Goff, *Le Moyen Age et l'argent: Essai d'anthropologie historique* (Paris: Perrin, 2010); P. Linnebaugh and M. Rediker, *The Many-Headed Hydra: The Hidden History of the Revolutionary Atlantic* (London: Verso, 2000).

8. Ryan, *A History of the Internet and the Digital Future*, 31–44.

9. J. Galloway, *Protocol: How Control Exists After Decentralization* (Cambridge, MA: MIT Press, 2004); D. G. Grewal, *Network Power: The Social Dynamics of Globalization* (Durham, NC: Duke University Press, 2008).

10. F. Braudel, *Civilization and Capitalism: 15th–18th Century*, vol. 2, *The Wheels of Commerce* (Berkeley: University of California Press, 1992), 458–514).

11. C. Marazzi, *Il comunismo del capitale: Finanziarizzazione, biopolitiche del lavoro e crisi globale* (Verona: Ombre Corte, 2010).

12. A. Fumagalli, *Bioeconomia e capitalismo cognitivo: Verso un nuovo paradigma d'accumulazione* (Rome: Carocci, 2007).

13. See, for example, the statement on the Committee on Transforming Finance of the think tank "ethical markets," http://www.ethicalmarkets.com/2010/09/12/transformin finance-groups-call-recognizes-finance-as-a-global-commons/ (accessed September 20, 2010).

14. R. Schiller, *Finance and the Good Society* (Princeton, NJ: Princeton Univerity Press, 2012).

15. T. Manwring and M. Goyder, *Tomorrow's Stewardship: Why Stewardship Matters* (London: Tomorow's Company, 2011), 2. See also P. Block, *Stewardship: Choosing Service Over Self-Interest* (San Francisco: Koehler, 1993).

16. E. Ostrom, *Governing the Commons: The Evolution of Institutions for Collective Action* (Cambridge: Cambridge University Press, 1990, 184.

17. N. Marres, "The Costs of Public Involvement: Everyday Devices of Carbon Accounting and the Materialization of Participation," *Economy and Society* 40, no. 4 (2011): 510–533. On the gap between ideals and action in ethical consumer practices, see T. Devinney, P. Auger, and G. Eckhardt, eds., *The Myth of the Ethical Consumer* (Cambridge: Cambridge University Press, 2010). On mobile devices for malaria drugs, see D. Zurovac, A. Talisuna, and R. Snow, "Mobile Phone Text Messaging: Tool for Malaria Control in Africa," *PLoS Med* 9, no. 2 (2012), http://dx.doi.org/10.1371%2Fjournal.pmed.1001176 (accessed April 5, 2012).

18. See, for example, A. E. Marwick, "Status Update: Celebrity, Publicity, and Self-Branding in Web 2.0" (Ph.D. diss., Department of Media, Culture, and Communication, New York University, 2010).

19. In a consultancy for the municipality of Malmö in Sweden, we suggested a similar system for determining the allocation of funds for non-institutionalized cultural activities. Let public ratings of the quality of rock bands and theater groups count in the determination of funding decisions; see A. Arvidsson and D. Tjader, *Laboratorum for Spontankultur: Slutrapport* (Malmö: Kulturforvaltningen, 2009).

20. See, respectively, P. Adler, "Market, Hierarchy, and Trust: The Knowledge Economy and the Future of Capitalism," *Organization Science* 12, no. 2 (2001): 215–234; P. Virno, *A Grammar of the Multitude* (London: Verso, 2004).

21. See J. Rifkin, *The Empathetic Civilization: The Race to Global Consciousness in a World in Crisis* (New York: HarperCollins, 2009).

22. This is similar to Habermas's argument in his *Between Facts and Norms*. There he suggested that since we no longer believe in the doctrine of natural law, or in legal positivism, jurisprudence could be opened up to processes of public deliberation. In analogue fashion, today we no longer believe in the labor theory of value and we no longer believe in the rational market hypothesis. Therefore the setting of economic value could be opened up to wider forms of deliberation. I suggest that publics and the reputation economies that they enact can constitute a possible way of doing this.

23. This is very close to George Simmel's theory of value. He proposed that economic value should be understood as an effect of the balancing of the affective attachments, the desire, that participants in exchange had in relation to the particular object exchanged. When Simmel wrote this, his theory was a bit naive, since he did not take the institutional structure—the furniture—of markets into account and did not consider how they distort and construct such affective balances. Our proposal is to construct new kinds of furniture that can minimize this distorting effect; see G. Simmel, *A Philosophy of Money* (1907; London: Routledge, 2011).

INDEX

BioBricks, 62
Biocurious, 62
biotechnology, 62
Bitcoin, 73, 124
Bloomberg (firm), 11, 123
Boltanski, Luc, 114
Bowyer, Adrian, 61
Brand, Stewart, 72
brand communities, 63, 68, 70, 81, 83, 91
brands: and affective proximity, 30,
    51, 78, 99, 147; and ethical capital,
    99, 102–5, 106, 108; and ethical
    economy, 147, 148; ethos of, 78, 147;
    and globalization, 52, 64; history of,
    45–46; as intangible assets, 8–10, 22,
    23, 31, 32, 37, 38, 45; management of,
    46, 52–54, 103, 147; and measures,
    112, 117, 119; personal, 98–99; and
    post-Fordism, 30, 33; and productive
    publics, 51–55, 58–59, 63, 65, 68; and
    socialization of production, 32, 51–55;
    and trust, 100–101; valuation of,
    8–9, 13, 46–47, 118, 119, 122, 127
Braudel, Fernand, 11, 140, 157n29
Braverman, Harry, 159n10
Brenner, Robert, 133
Bretton Woods system, 40
Buffett, Warren, 47
Bush administration, 39

CAD (computer-aided design), 29, 31
calculative frames, 43–44
Campetti, Loris, 1
Canada, 27
capital. See ethical capital; social capital
Capital Asset Pricing Models, 13
capitalism, industrial, viii, ix–x, xiv, 133,
    143, 144; vs. collaborative production,
    82, 84–85; vs. communism, 138;
    vs. consumer capitalism, 136; and
    cooperation, 36; vs. informational
    capitalism, 103; and intangibles, 9;
    legitimacy crisis of, 142; and markets,
    11, 157n29; and money, 140; Swedish
    model of, 21; time in, 138–39, 142;

wealth distribution in, 42. See also
    Fordism
CEO salaries, 1–2, 10
charisma, 93, 99, 102, 105–6
China, 27, 60, 79, 133–34
Chouliaraki, Lilie, 114
Christopherson, Susan, 95–96
Clinton administration, 39
CNC (computer numerically controlled)
    machinery, 29, 31
Coase, Ronald, 100
Coca-Cola, 103
cognitive surplus, 72, 78
Coleman, Gabriela, 88–89, 90
common resources, 82–85, 86; in
    ethical economy, 142, 146, 148;
    and excellence, 108, 109; and
    financialization, 137; and free labor,
    77; and manufacturing, 134; and new
    standards, 127, 131; and productive
    publics, 72–74, 78, 81; and public
    ethics, 151, 154; and reputation, 91,
    92; and value, 99, 143, 168n11
communism, 138; anarcho-, 83, 106,
    167n2; cyber, 82, 83
communities: brand, 63, 68, 70, 81,
    83, 91; collaborative, 18, 56–58,
    62–64, 97; definition of, 57; free-
    software, 88–90; online, 62–64; vs.
    productive publics, 58, 164n31; and
    social imaginaries, 67–68; and social
    production, 84
Community Supported Agriculture
    (CSA), 66
consumerism: and affect, 116; and
    brands, 46, 51–55; and decline in
    manufacturing, 133–34; ethical, 5,
    14, 17, 18, 152; and ethical capital,
    104–5; and Fordism, 25; global, 18,
    46, 113; and individualization, 16; and
    measurement of affect, 117–18; and
    New Deal, 135; and productive publics,
    59, 73, 83; and public sphere, 17, 112–13
consumption: vs. production, 23, 25;
    productive, 63–64

cooperation: and general intellect, 33–37; and post-Fordism, 30–32, 33; and value stream analysis, 38; weak, 17

Copenhagen (Denmark), 91, 95

corporate social responsibility, vii, xi; and brands, 58–59; and communication technologies, 147; and ethical capital, 99; and irrational valuation, 3–4; and market rationality, 12–13; and measurement of affect, 119, 122–23; as new value, 14, 17; and productive publics, xiii, 79; and public sphere, 114

corporations: and alternative value systems, 124–25; culture of, 56–59, 79; ethos of, 56, 99; and privacy, 67; and productive publics, xiii, 70, 74, 79, 99; in public sphere, 138; and time, 138–39

costs: labor, 26, 27, 30, 37; production, 30, 37; transaction, 100, 101

counterculture, xvi, 52, 59, 72, 83

Cova, Bernard, 54

Covalence (brand valuation firm), 119, 123

crowdsourcing, 57–58, 61, 98

culture: and collaborative production, 82–83; corporate, 56–59, 79; participatory, 50, 59–66, 78, 81, 86; and productive publics, 50, 62–66, 79. See also consumerism

currencies, alternative, 73, 110, 111, 123, 124

Customer Relations Management, 147

Danielsson, Albert, 21

Danone brand, 99

data mining, xvi, 50, 64, 121; and measurement of affect, 118, 119, 122

Debian, 73, 88–89

democratization, 78, 124, 131, 136, 142–43, 145

deregulation, x, 11, 39–40, 52, 134

Derwent Capital Markets, 119

digital media, 58, 64, 83, 110; and measurement of affect, 118–19; and

productive publics, 50, 72, 78. See also information and communication technologies; social media

Dingpolitik (politics of things), 137–41

"Does Ethics Have a Chance in a World of Consumers?" (Bauman), 16

dot-com boom (1990s), 3, 44, 82, 98, 133, 135–36

Drucker, Peter, 33

Durkheim, Emile, 101

eBay, 100, 101

electronics industry, 29, 30, 31

emotional intelligence, 105

ethical capital, xi, xvi, 88, 92–106; conventions in, 102–5; in ethical economy, 142; and new standards, 127, 130; and reputation, 92–93, 105, 106–8, 109; vs. social capital, 92–93, 99, 100, 102, 107; and value, 106–8

ethical economy, viii; description of, 141–50; and measures, 110–11; and new standards, 130–31

ethics: communitarian, 150, 152; of modernity, 15; vs. morality, 14–18; and new value regime, 47, 129–30; public, 150–55; vs. shared values, 14–18

ethos: and brands, 78, 147; and corporations, 56, 99; and ethical capital, 92, 93, 105; and excellence, 108; of guilds, 71; and productive publics, 68–69, 79; and reputation, 88, 90–91; and trust, 101, 102

Europe, 27, 40, 42, 76, 98, 133

excellence, 82, 127; and common resources, 108, 109; and public ethics, 152–53; and reputation, 87–92

fab labs, 61

Facebook, 60, 62, 64, 76, 116; and labor, 86, 168n11; and measurement of affect, 118, 119, 120; and Net neutrality, 125–26; and standards, 128, 141; valuation of, 7, 102–3

122, 124, 128, 129–30, 141; valuations
of, 7, 102–3
socialization: of brand, 32, 51–55;
and financialization, 40, 43, 46;
of knowledge production, 36; and
labor theory of value, 168n11; and
new standards, 131; and online
communities, 62–64; of production,
29, 34–37, 46, 49–50, 72, 78, 107;
and reputation, 150; of value creation,
49–50, 143
Stallman, Richard, 86
standardization, 24, 29, 36
standards, common, xii, xvi–xvii; and
Dingpolitik, 139–41; and general
sentiment, 121, 122, 125, 127–31;
network power of, 140–41; and
politics, xvii, 121–26, 127, 141; and
productive publics, 127–28, 131. *See
also* measures
Stark, David, 5, 45
stewardship, 146–48, 151, 153
Stewart, Daniel, 87–88
StreamBase (firm), 119, 122
Structural Transformation of the Public Sphere
(Habermas), 112
Success of Open Source, The (Weber), 94
sustainability, 5, 14, 17, 18, 101, 104;
and ethical economy, 134, 138, 141;
measurement of, 125, 127, 129, 131
Sysomos (firm), 119

Taiwan, 28
tangible assets, 26, 33, 46. *See also*
intangible assets
Tapscott, Don, 83
Tarde, Gabriel, 66, 69, 116, 121
Taylor, Charles, 67
Taylor, Frederick W., 24
Taylorism, 24, 26, 28, 139, 168n11
TCP/IP protocol, 139
technology: and cooperation, 37; and
decline in manufacturing, 134, 135;
in ethical economy, 147; in film
industry, 95; and financial markets,

39; and Fordism, 23, 26; and free
labor, 75–77; mass-production, 24;
networked digital, xv, 72, 110, 134–35,
137; and organization, 73–74; and
participatory culture, 60–62; phases
of, 134–35; and productive publics,
xiv, 70, 72–74; protocols in, 139–41;
and social production, 83–84. *See
also* digital media; information and
communication technologies
television, 114, 117
Terranova, Tiziana, 74, 86, 168n11
Thatcher, Margaret, ix, 39
Tomorrow's Company, 146
Total Quality Management (TQM), 38,
168n11
Toyotist model of production, 28, 29,
31–32, 56
tragedy of the commons, 146
trust, 85, 100–102
Turkle, Sherry, xii
Twitter, 103, 116, 118, 119–20, 124, 126,
141

Ugarte, David de, 79
United States (U.S.), 1, 21, 25, 27, 29, 133;
education in, 76, 95; financialization
in, 7, 39–40, 41
UNIX, 90
urban underground, 77, 88, 91, 93, 94,
95

value, 81–108; and action, 82, 87–88;
book *vs.* market, 7–8, 22, 26, 39, 45,
46, 102–3; and brand, 8–9, 13, 46–47,
118, 119, 122, 127, 147; and charisma,
105–6; and common resources, 82–
85, 86, 99, 143, 168n11; conventions
for, 102–5; criteria for, 4–5, 17, 45;
and ethical capital, 92–108; in ethical
economy, 141, 142; and excellence,
82, 87–92; financialization of, 137,
143–46; and gift economies, 166n2;
and knowledge workers, 94–99; of
labor, 87–88; labor theory of, 18–19,